MORE PRAISE FOR

The *Opposite* Field

"Katz is a gifted and honest writer . . . [*The Opposite Field* is] about fatherhood, growing up, and the success and failure of people trying to establish and maintain a community. It is also a fine and worthy self-examination of a fellow determined to do the best he can."

—BILL LITTLEFIELD, *Boston Globe*

"A grand slam . . . a moving and humorous story."   —*The Oregonian*

"A startling poetic chronicle of personal relationships, race issues, and father-and-son concerns . . . this is great writing."   —*The Progressive*

"Engaging . . . the book's candor, generosity, and tolerance should be a lesson for any parent coaching any sport."   —*Seattle Weekly*

"A moving meditation about baseball, politics, and the unease of negotiating a new kind of American place . . . Jesse Katz has sailed a fly ball deep into what it means to be an Angeleño. It will be fielded and remembered, I hope, by readers who love the game, love the possibilities of redemptive Los Angeles, as much as Jesse Katz does."

—D. J. WALDIE, Truthdig.com

"Warm but admirably unsentimental . . . the real story is the community as a whole, and how, as an outsider, Katz came to have such a very natural role in it. A surprisingly complex, well-crafted story."

—*Kirkus Reviews*

"Transcends the simple stories of a father and son and a baseball league to create a compelling story about what it means to live and love in Los Angeles today."   —*Orange County Register*

"[Katz weaves] a **disarmingly affecting** narrative of a failed marriage, a stepson gone wrong, a sad affair with a married woman, his mother's battle with cancer, and his imperfect efforts to raise a son as a single dad—all as he tries to keep the Monterey Park Little League from crashing down around the community . . . **like baseball fans everywhere, he holds out for transcendence. And baseball, true to form, gives it to him."** —*Booklist*

"**Cast through the prism of one of America's oldest pastimes, Jesse Katz's memoir illuminates contemporary American life with wonderful detail and honesty.** *The Opposite Field* brings to life the eastern suburbs of Los Angeles, drawing them out of the shadows of Hollywood glitz and gangland portraits we typically read about, evoking the struggles and dreams of the children and parents in and around the hidden-away baseball field of La Loma. **It's a heartfelt story, well told."** —NORMAN OLLESTAD, author of the *New York Times* bestseller *Crazy for the Storm*

"Jesse Katz has captured the hybrid soul of California's Monterey Park, a community that is unique in ways that Katz deeply understands and eloquently evokes. **And the poetry of his prose—Katz may be the next big writer dude of the L.A. style."** —LUIS J. RODRIGUEZ, author of *Always Running*

"**A 'Little League Dad' book like no other.** Jesse Katz's *The Opposite Field* is set not in the usual WASPy suburb but in a community on the edge of Los Angeles with a majority Asian and Hispanic population. In addition to evoking **surprising cross-cultural discoveries and conflicts,** Katz portrays everything from his legendary mother's flight from the Nazis to the shooting of his stepson—and critiques not only his failings as a baseball manager but as a parent." —GREG MITCHELL, author of *Joy in Mudville*

The *Opposite* Field

A MEMOIR

Jesse Katz

THREE RIVERS PRESS • NEW YORK

Originally published in hardcover in the United States by
Crown Publishers, an imprint of the Crown Publishing Group,
a division of Random House, Inc., New York, in 2009.

Library of Congress Cataloging-in-Publication Data
Katz, Jesse.
    The opposite field : a memoir of love and little league /
by Jesse Katz.—1st paperback ed.
        p. cm.
    1. Little League baseball. 2. Katz, Jesse. 3. Fatherhood.
4. East Los Angeles (Calif.)—Social life and customs.
I. Title.
    GV880.5.K38   1986
    796.357'62—dc22   2010011536

ISBN 978-0-307-40712-2

Printed in the United States of America

Design by Barbara Sturman

10 9 8 7 6 5 4 3 2 1

First Paperback Edition

To Vera, Mel, Dianne, and Thelma,

Max's grandparents

The man who finds his homeland sweet is still a tender beginner; he to whom every soil is as his native one is already strong; but he is perfect to whom the entire world is as a foreign land.

—*Hugh of Saint Victor*

The

Opposite

Field

Prologue

MY PARK IS CALLED LA LOMA. I HAVE ALWAYS LIKED THE
sound of that, the symmetry of those double-barrel *L*s, the femi-
ninity of the final Spanish vowels, the spacey La-La Land echo, all
an improvement on its stiff translation: the Hill. La Loma is pret-
tier, softer and rounder, earthier—*loam*ier. A park for losing yourself in. The park I went looking for myself in.

Max and I have spent nine springs and summers there, through
squalls and droughts, heat waves and cold snaps, from his pre-
school years to the onslaught of adolescence. We have celebrated
there and we have sulked there, twirling like fools across the dirt
and chalk, drowning our broken hearts with fusillades of water balloons. We have made friends for life at La Loma and, I suspect, ene-
mies for just as long. We have gone there to forget and to remember,
to stop time and to grow up. The park is under our skin: season after
season of bites, burns, stings, cuts, sprains, scars. Max has bled at La

Loma. He has barfed there. He has wet himself. I have rinsed his wounds at La Loma, iced him, kneaded him, bandaged him, scooped him off the ground, his face streaked with sweat and clay and eye-black grease, and held him in my arms. Max has stood there, in jersey and cap, and hacked out "The Star-Spangled Banner" in front of a thousand people on his electric guitar. I have given myself to those same people, cheered and groaned alongside them, accepted their prayers and shared their beers, slipped to me in Styrofoam coffee cups. Whenever we have needed it, whenever I have felt burdened or alone, La Loma has been there. The park is always the park. Our refuge. My excuse.

It rises from the haze and glare of inland Los Angeles, far from Hollywood, beyond the margins of the tourist maps. In a city that skews west, toward the surf, La Loma is on the wrong side, east of the skyline, east of skid row, east of the rail yards, the slaughter-houses, the riverbed. By a shade, it is east of East Los Angeles, the original gangland, the cultural heartland of Mexican America. La Loma marks the spot roughly at which the barrio ends and the burbs begin, where inner-city Los Angeles meets bedroom-community Los Angeles. Knots of prickly pear give way to tidy rows of jacaranda, with flurries that dust the sidewalk purple, and Depression-era adobes fade into 1950s subdivisions of a style known as California ranch, with gas fireplaces and attached garages and faux clapboard shutters.

La Loma falls within Monterey Park, one of those invisible municipalities you could spend a lifetime in L.A. and never visit, maybe even never hear of. The town is blandly provincial and yet stunningly foreign: Forty thousand of its sixty-three thousand residents are of Asian descent, the highest concentration in any city in the continental United States. It was this fact that first drew me here, as a novice journalist, almost twenty-five years ago. I was new to L.A., new to adulthood, and the battles then raging between Chinese émigrés and Anglo nativists—over language, over customs, over the right to belong—were redefining what it means to be middle class and American. From the polite liberalism of Oregon,

via a fancy college in Vermont, I had been transported to a furious
social laboratory on the haunches of Los Angeles. A new form of
white flight was under way, not from a decaying urban core but from
an ethnically convulsing suburb: Rather than embrace the new
Monterey Park, twenty thousand white folks up and split. At the
time, I could never have foreseen that this curious place would one
day lure me back, not as a writer but as a father, that I would be returning, against the tide, to make Monterey Park my own. But that
was long ago, before I married a barmaid from Nicaragua, before I
inherited an extended family of aliens and castaways, before we had
Max, our maple-skinned, almond-eyed chameleon of a son, whose
childhood I was determined to mold and preserve.

Through eucalyptus, past weeping red bottlebrush, over bark
mulch, La Loma hugs the hill, pausing and ascending and pausing
again—a vertical park, winding to some unseen pinnacle, rather
than the naked grid of a playground. Each level of La Loma is
distinct, concealed by shrubs and connected by stairs, exactly forty
of them from bottom to top. Climbing them all is like scaling a
labyrinthine tree fort, part Dr. Seuss and part Swiss Family Robinson. La Loma twists and strays, a dense wall of ice plants here, a secluded meadow there, a nest of hornets, a shock of wildflowers, a
connect-the-dots of gopher holes, another rise and a thicket and a
clearing, the park revealing itself with each turn. For as long as we
have been going to La Loma, Max has been carving his own path,
as all the kids do, finding freedom in the bramble. He squeezes between the narrowest gaps, scampers up the trickiest banks, and
slides down the steepest chutes on rafts made of twigs and cardboard. Their name for this caper is Mission Impossible, and I can
almost hear them *dun-dun-dern-dern-dun-dun*-ing the theme as they
traverse the slopes, imbuing the topography of La Loma with
drama.

Up the steps, on the highest levels, La Loma grows flat. The
terraces unfurl into broad fields, like the mesas of a Road Runner
cartoon. It is there, between March and July, that we play
baseball—hundreds of boys and girls, hundreds of games a year.

Because of the grade and the foliage, it is difficult to see from the street that any of this is happening, difficult to imagine that the fortunes of an entire Little League could be contained within the undulations of this one hill. To discover La Loma, to cross its threshold, to rove its crooks, to emerge, breathless, at its summit, is to view Los Angeles from the inside out. Downtown is just seven miles away—the basin sprawls below us, the skies above sparkle with LAX-bound jets—yet from this perch, it is quite possible to think of La Loma as its own universe, a secret park, into which nobody ventures without meaning to be there.

At night, when the last games are over and the lights shut off, I often take a moment on the bleachers, to watch the moon and listen to the crickets, just me and Max. I have been coaching his teams at La Loma since he was in T-Ball. He was six then, a guileless kindergartner, with no choice but to trust the decrees of his dad. Max is fourteen now and more complicated, a rocker and a skater, with a MySpace page and a life I will never again know everything about. On these diamonds I have witnessed him fail and triumph and fail again, his baby fat replaced by sinew and poise. Over the course of perhaps a thousand innings, he has known every possible outcome: the game-winning hit, the game-losing pitch, the acrobatic catch, the booted grounder, the daring steal, the fumbled tag, the beanballs both dispensed and received. I believe he has loved it as much as I have. Nine years of jerseys hang in his closet, nine years of trophies line his bookshelf, nine years of team photos—Max growing taller and shaggier, me grayer and thicker—stick to our refrigerator door. But with high school about to start, I can see just as well that we are at the end of something, that this park that has framed our relationship for two-thirds of his life is no longer the place by which he measures himself. He has one more year left, but he is done with La Loma. He is gifted enough, I think, to go out for his freshman team, but he is done with baseball. Max, if I understand him these days, is done with organized sports, with the uniformity and the corniness and the genuflections to authority. "I don't know what happened, Dad," he tells me. "I'm just not feelin' it anymore." Soon enough, I fear, he will be done being the boy who feels the need to offer any explanations at all.

Some of these changes are surely inevitable, a child's natural course, but I am no less wistful about them. I did everything in my power to slow the process, to conserve La Loma for Max for as long as I could. When we started, it was all about the two of us, father and son tossing the ball, creating our own nostalgia in the grass. Four years later I was running the park. I had become the commissioner, Monterey Park's guardian of baseball. It is a position I assumed with equal measures of duty and dread, hoping to salvage a season on the verge of collapse. The league was imploding. Families were bailing. Nobody claimed to be in charge. When Max's team was my only concern, I had been able to tune out the warning signs, all the blustery dads who treated La Loma as turf, mining it for money and prestige. I was still Max's coach, but now I had volunteered to sweep up their wreckage—to preside over a community that had never quite invited me in. It was a decent thing to do. It was also mulish and self-destructive. You could say that about a lot of my choices.

The cliché of Little League, of youth sports in America, is one of lost perspective: By taking it too seriously, adults have ruined a children's game. I have begun to think that the opposite is true, that we do not take it seriously enough. Nothing in my forty-plus years has compared with the enormity, with the complexities or the sensitivities, of trying to keep La Loma afloat. Nothing has done as much to test my judgment. Nothing has made me feel so responsible for so much beyond my control. Being commissioner means being La Loma's publicist, accountant, emcee, detective, psychologist, chef, graphic designer, janitor, landscaper, paramedic, choreographer, and justice of the peace, one whose standing is based largely on the absence of anyone else willing to assume the office. No matter how many hours I put into it—and for someone who putatively holds a "real job," I have put in more than I should ever admit—there is always a parent to soothe or to scold, a protest to weigh, a schedule to juggle, a roster to scrutinize, a balance to collect. The league's operating budget eventually topped $50,000 a year, and with our various fund-raisers, I probably handled well over twice that amount, and I mean *handle*, my fingers growing sooty and metallic as I counted piles of cash atop my bed, like a dopeman, paranoid and exhilarated. I have disqualified players and expelled spectators, prosecuted thieves and mediated divorces, sopped up muddy fields and administered first aid with Mexican popsicles from our snack bar. I know which coaches have prison records. I know which coaches bounce checks. I know which coach is screwing around with his shortstop's mom and which coach has crippling headaches from a bullet lodged in her skull. Like natural disasters and family vacations, Little League brings out the best and the worst in people; it supplies the trials that reveal our inner workings. Because every fiasco ended up in my lap, because I wanted to be the kind of person who could be counted on to remedy each one, I probably have a more ambivalent view—maybe darker, maybe just more realistic—of what that portends.

My first season as commissioner, I lost a coach to a meth binge. Johnny was an electrician for the school district, a squat leather-clad pit bull of a dude with a bald head and a silver goatee. I knew little else about him except that he had three boys in the league, all from different combinations of moms and dads. We especially needed his two oldest, both teenagers. By the time kids got to middle school, they had a way of shrugging off parks like ours, and Johnny had done us a favor not just by enrolling his but by offering to manage their team. Then one morning Johnny's girlfriend, the mother of his youngest, called me, frantic and in tears. Johnny was missing. His van had been towed. She had not seen him since his last game, three days earlier, and nobody would give her a straight answer as to where he might be. "What am I going to do?" she sobbed. I offered my reassurances, promising to use all my journalistic tools to help her find Johnny. But I was already thinking ahead. He was my third coach to crash and burn in less than a month, so I was beyond any illusion that I might be a reasonable judge of character. I was looking at the schedule. His team had a game that night. "Do you happen to know where his equipment might be?" I asked. It had cost me $7,000 that year to replace the league's gear, all that had been thrashed or jacked. I was willing to write off Johnny but not his bag. She stopped crying. "He keeps it in the back of his van."

I called the cops. Johnny, I learned, had started tweaking after he left La Loma, wandering the streets, rambling about biker gangs. He was knocking on doors, pupils dilated, pulse racing, telling anyone who answered that the Mongols—the outlaw club that recently had brawled with the Hells Angels at the Laughlin Harrah's, leaving three dead on the casino floor—had a contract on his life. When sheriff's deputies tried to cuff him, Johnny pointed to his hands, to show that he was a marked man: They were tattooed, as the officers surely could see, with death threats. For all I know, the Mongols really did mean him harm, but as the police report would note, there was no evidence of that in ink. I asked about the van. I would have to come in and speak to the watch commander. Like I had time for that. I had work to do, a paycheck to earn. I was hopelessly behind on a profile of Magic Johnson, the retired Lakers icon who was flirting with a run for mayor, and my editor at *Los Angeles* magazine had every reason to assume I would be at the computer, in the throes of deadline. Eyeing the calendar, then the clock, I told myself that my professional doom was still a week off. If I could not salvage Johnny's equipment bag and recruit another parent to replace him as coach, I would be canceling a game in just a few hours. That would mean two dozen unhappy families, folks who would be wondering what sort of half-baked, slipshod, drug-addled organization I presumed to be running. Sometimes you just had to fix what you could.

I raced to the Temple City sheriff's station, a couple of miles east, out Interstate 10. I had been there years earlier, as a reporter, in the course of covering some atrocity or other, and I briefly considered introducing myself that way. I knew what information I was entitled to, what fell under the public domain, but I was not writing a story about Johnny, at least not yet. My credentials only would have interfered. This was a case for moral leverage: the plea of a Little League commissioner, on behalf of the poor children of Monterey Park, to be guided to the impound yard and granted permission to break in. I was asking for privacy laws to be fudged, evidence laws to be overlooked. I had no way of proving that I was the rightful owner of the property I was after, nothing to show that I had any ties even to the baseball program I claimed to be defending.

"It's kind of a long story," I told the sergeant at the desk. The sergeant grinned. As it happened, he had coached his own kids in Little League, in another San Gabriel Valley town, and now that they were grown he was still volunteering. We were on the same side. "My hat's off to you, guy," he said. "I know what you're up against."

He made a call to Freddie Mac's Towing, which was a couple more miles down the road, in the industrial hinterlands of South El Monte. I dropped his name when I got there and was led by an employee to Johnny's van. I felt like I was looting a corpse. Freddy Mac's was a graveyard of maimed and delinquent cars, their serial numbers written across the windows in grease pencil. Oil seeped into the gravel. Everywhere there were shreds of rubber and shards of glass, flies and gulls circling the debris. In the rear, I found Johnny's duffel bag, the *league's* duffel bag, and emptied it. I did not want to be accused of taking anything that truly was Johnny's, to have this unofficial sortie of mine backfire or to risk burning my benefactor. I was coming for what was mine, nothing more. I tossed back a few nice old mitts, no doubt belonging to his boys, extracted the bat, counted the helmets, inventoried the catcher's gear, then lugged it all to my car and headed for La Loma. I had blown a day, but I also had imposed some order on the peculiar little society that I had adopted, or that had adopted me. I liked the feeling. *Wishing you well, Johnny, wherever you are. But you fucked with the wrong motherfucker.* My league was not to be trifled with. At the park, I gave the bag to another parent, a Coast Guard officer, and begged him to fill in. He did fine, until the Fourth of July, when the Monterey

Park arson squad caught him blowing off skyrockets behind the league's "safe and sane" fireworks stand. That was pretty much the end of Johnny's team.

On those nights when Max and I linger, when the fog rolls in and the Pomona Freeway thrums like an ocean, La Loma is returned to us, cool and still and hushed. The crepe-paper Cinco de Mayo flowers that brightened our opening ceremony droop from the chain-link backstops. The fields I watered and raked that afternoon swirl again with lime and dust. Sunflower husks, peanut shells, popcorn kernels—the detritus of baseball—mix again with the soil. Up in the power lines an owl hoots and flaps, the same owl, I am guessing, that swooped into our backyard, a dozen blocks away, and absconded with Max's guinea pigs not long after his mother and I split up. I think of the chatter, the whoops and bellyaches, that moments earlier filled La Loma, the allegiances and grievances that percolate through every season, both inside and outside the baselines. All of it created by us, by parents and children inhabiting the same space, imagining the same future. La Loma is not a gymnasium. Nobody shows up just for a time slot. It is a village, our city upon the hill, tangled and mushy and occasionally petty but always stewing. People mill and wander, gossip and gripe, investing themselves in something larger than the score or the standings, something beyond a team or a league or a game.

Going to the opposite field takes patience. Perspective. Humility. If a batter is always trying to impose his will on the ball—a right-hander's tendency being to swing for the left field fences—he will never be able to handle the unexpected pitch, outside, breaking, off speed. By trying to pull it, he will more often than not be out ahead, waving at air, and even if he does get a piece, it is unlikely to result in anything but a feeble dribbler. His strength becomes his weakness. To go the other way, to slap a single through the infield or drive a double into the gap, is to choose contact over power. It means sacrificing ego. Holding back. Adjusting. The hitter takes what is given and goes with it, making the most of a pitch that was never

his to begin with. I have tried to teach this lesson to Max, with varying degrees of success. At the plate he still gets impatient, too eager
to pounce. I hope in the process that he figures it out off the field as
well, that he understands how this park, our town, the way we have
chosen to live, all follow the same contrary rule.

The more I have devoted myself to baseball, to La Loma, the
more I have come to realize that I have been cultivating something
else, something said not to exist in Los Angeles, something hard to
find anywhere in America: not a *sense* of community, not the pious
or politicized versions, but the real thing, tangible, human, imperfect, at once motley and utterly square. This is the L.A. I know and
believe in, an L.A. more satisfying than any of its myths generally
allow for. Or maybe it is because of those myths—because L.A. is
the capital of artifice and celebrity and unsteady earth—that an environment as unfashionable, as rooted, as La Loma is so hard for me
to resist.

Before we leave, I pull out the bases. I comb the dugouts for a
last fistful of trash. I peek under the bleachers and inside the bathrooms. I swing the parking gates shut, tugging the padlocks to
make sure they have latched. Some nights, as we head down the hill,
I wonder what it is about me, about my yearnings and voids, that
compels me to do this. Some nights I think, just maybe, I have found
the place I belong.

Chapter

One

I PLAYED MY LAST LITTLE LEAGUE GAME ON MAY 12, 1975,
a Monday. I know this because it is written on a scuffed and faded
Rawlings baseball, in Magic Marker letters that look to be in my
twelve-year-old hand. I know the score, too—"Cubs 17, Braves 15"
is printed where the seams curl into a horseshoe—and I remember
somewhat having been the winning pitcher, my team's only pitcher,
which explains how I ended up with the memento.

Prior to that day I had never been happier than I was in Wallace Park, the giant quad of grass and mud across the street from
my elementary school. I walked there alone, long before I would
have allowed Max to do the same, tramping across as many lawns
as I could to keep my Puma cleats from clacking on the pavement.
Our uniforms were stitched from the heaviest, nappiest flannel,
like Old West pajamas, and we wore genuine stirrups, not stripes
dyed onto socks, that rose all the way to our knees. I balanced a

flame-tempered Louisville Slugger upside down on my shoulder, with my glove dangling behind from the knob, like a Hobo Kelly knapsack. I fussed over that glove the way a 4-H kid might have fussed over the cow that it came from. I folded it and thumped it and massaged it feverishly with neat's-foot oil, whatever that was, then tucked it, with a ball in the webbing, under my mattress before bed. The leather grew supple and a little sticky, a deep, curvaceous, copper-colored canyon, and whenever I saw a boy with a vinyl supermarket mitt, I privately saluted my superior reverence for the game. I followed these rituals even when the season was over, when nothing was scheduled. "I'm going to the park," I would announce, hoping to find someone, anyone, willing to join me in a round of off the wall or strikeout or first bounce or fly. On muggy summer nights I would stay until the sky disappeared and the fruit bats swarmed, always wondering, as I trudged home, why nobody could invent a glow-in-the-dark ball that actually glowed enough to be seen.

That the zenith of my Wallace Park career was a fifteen-run hemorrhage suggests that my athletic gifts did not quite match my emotional attachments. I was a fanatic about form and technique—the stances, the grips, the motions, the deliberateness, the repetitiveness—but when it came to putting my diligence into practice, I proved to be slow and skittish. During my first couple of seasons, I was on the same team as Peter Norrie, an ox of a kid whose younger brother, David, would become a UCLA quarterback and lead the Pac 10 in passing. I thought of us as peers: My love of sports was no less than theirs, yet even then they were already beyond reach. Peter was our catcher, and as I fancied myself a shortstop, I would have to handle his throws down to second. A Peter Norrie ball sizzled—your ear picked it up before your eye could figure out where it was headed—and it was in those moments that I first came to understand that baseball, our serene, laconic national pastime, was also a game of implicit violence. Once, during the warm-up between innings, Peter hollered the standard "comin' down" and fired a bullet my way. I tried not to flinch. I wanted to be a worthy target. But in my zeal to do things right—to catch, as Little Leaguers are forever admonished, with two hands—I allowed my bare hand to get too close to the action. The ball cracked the bones in my right index finger, swelling it up like a plum. To this day, the tip veers off at a woeful angle. My lovingly tended glove remained empty.

Still I clung to the belief that devotion somehow translates into skill. I kept a manila Pee-Chee with notes inside on my methods and preferences. I anointed a twenty-eight-inch bat my "regular hitter." A twenty-nine-inch bat was my "slammer." A thirty-inch bat was my "slugger." A thirty-three-inch bat, which I would have needed a crane to swing, was, appropriately, the "bunter." About the same time, I wrote an ode to the baseball gods—"Baseball Everywhere"— in the tidiest schoolboy penmanship I could summon: "My best baseball stars are Jackie Robinson, Babe Ruth, Cy Young, Tony Oliva, Tom Seaver, Tommy Agee, Harmon Killebrew, and don't forget the GREAT Jesse Katz, and he wrote this story, too." At least my ego did not seem to be bruised.

The 1975 season was my opportunity to shine, the payoff after so many years of sharing the diamonds with older and bigger kids, and yet I hate to imagine how shaky our team must have been, how trusting or desperate or indifferent my coach had to be, for the finale to be riding on my arm. I had become a pitcher by attrition. When called upon, from what I can make of the evidence, I floundered spectacularly. I was both gutsy and lame, my inability to record outs exceeded only by that of the opposing staff. How I was allowed to remain on the mound for the entire game—how I allowed myself, inning after inglorious inning, to think that I could—is more mystifying to me now than it was then. I would never leave one of my own players, including, or especially, Max, so exposed to failure and not offer him a way out. All the same, I prevailed, with two runs to spare, and saved that gorgeous ball, stashed it in my old bedroom closet up in Portland, then forgot about it for twenty years. It is sealed today in an acrylic cube, between journalism awards and a wooden box holding Max's baby teeth—a reminder of what baseball meant to me, and what it would not mean again for a very long time.

We lived on the middle floor of the Bruce Apartments, a creaky three-story walk-up with a rope-and-pulley dumbwaiter for the garbage and a basement furnace that growled like a crematorium. None of my friends had to live in apartments. I envied the freedom of their big solid homes, the spare bathrooms and guest rooms, all the corners you could run off to and never be heard from. Our unit was directly above the manager. I was forbidden ever to run. The homes I envied were filled also with brothers and sisters, their screams and laughs and endless crises so much more lavish, more urgent, than anything I could muster. I was quiet because I had to be and because we were too few to be otherwise. Our bath towels were aligned in a neat row above the tub—mine always in the middle, between Mom's and Dad's—as if that one terrycloth rectangle were binding all three of us together. We had moved from Brooklyn to Portland in 1964, a few months shy of my second birthday. For my parents, it was like a voyage to the end of the universe, a journey not just across many miles and time zones but of such cultural distance that they might as well have made their way on the Oregon Trail. Portland had yet to become a boutique city, indie, handcrafted, pedestrian-friendly, the paragon of managed growth. Back then it was monochrome and proletarian, a dreary river town built on lumber mills and container ships. The joke has grown stale, but people really did drive around with bumper stickers that boasted: "Oregonians don't tan, they rust." Leaving the East Coast was an experiment for my folks, a gamble predicated on their hope that outside the New York orbit, away from the rhythms of Jewish life, beyond the cautiousness of their own parents, they might just discover something—about the world, about themselves. Who knew what could sprout in that Portland drizzle? There were only three or four other Katzes in the phone book, and I think they took that as a sign that they had come to the right place.

Even in our subdued apartment, the echoes of New York still resonated. I had no memory, naturally, of our earlier life there, but it seemed to be our touchstone, the clearest indicator of how we were not like everyone else. My dad had *The Village Voice* airmailed to him. My mom longed for an egg cream, a fizzy soda-fountain drink that, I strained to understand, apparently contained neither egg nor cream. I heard stories about Birdland and the Guggenheim and Coney Island and FAO Schwarz and a team called the Dodgers, who had broken their city's heart by heading west a few years before us. They were supposed to be bums but also lovable—and, what really captivated me, courageous. I knew nothing of race or prejudice. Wallace Park was white bread, just like its most famous alum, Mickey Lolich, who would pitch the Detroit Tigers to the 1968 world crown. But I knew that these Dodgers had toppled a barrier, defied the status quo, that they had changed the way America looked at itself. That was even better than winning.

Whenever my dad played catch with me, in the shadow of our apartment house, he would turn it into an elaborate fantasy game, with names culled from those Boys of Summer rosters. He would throw me a hard chopper—off the bat of Gil Hodges. A towering fly ball—smacked by Roy Campanella. I relished the wacky names—Duke, Cookie, Sandy, Preacher—and the rambunctious, savvy, ethnic spirit that they conjured. Baseball was colorful, from the logos to the skin tones to the big far-off cities in which it was played. The great injustice of my life, I had convinced myself, was that Portland did not have a Major League team to root for. I wanted to be connected to the headlines, the enthusiasms, that lurked somewhere beyond the melancholy Northwest.

The best we could do was the Beavers, of the Pacific Coast League, who had not won a title since the 1930s. I was five or six the first time my dad took me to see them, and if he had told me we were going to Disneyland, I could not have been more ecstatic. We were headed to a real game, populated by real players in real uniforms, even if I could not name a single one of them. I spent all day prepping, as if I were the one about to perform: I doused my glove in foam cleansers, I rehearsed my home run swing in front of the mirror, and I begged for us to leave early, to get an autograph, to snare a foul ball, to not miss one crucial moment of my Civic Stadium induction.

It was a soupy August afternoon, and our seats were in the sun. I was mesmerized by the greenness of the diamond and the precision of the chalk, the booziness of the men around us and the whimsy of the Jantzen Red Diving Girl, a swimsuit-clad mannequin, mounted on the outfield fence, who seemed to be daring every batter to wallop her. The players were stretching, jogging, loosening their bulging arms. We were roasting. I asked for a hot dog and then an orange soda. It seemed like the game would never start. I pounded my glove, ready for anything that might come my way. At last, the national anthem. I was finally going to see baseball. As I stood up, it all hit me, the heat, the nerves, the ballpark food, the vague sense that I was no longer just my parents' son but an heir to the triumphs and frustrations of a larger tribe, of a game that had preceded us and would surely continue after we were gone. My knees felt like Silly Putty. "Dad," I said. Then I threw up. We had not even reached "the dawn's early light." I tried to aim for my soda cup, to be discreet, but I was a supremely bad puker, and in my exaggerated retching I mostly splattered myself. "Oh, Jess," my dad said. He took me to the bathroom and wiped me down with damp paper towels. I grimaced and squirmed. "I'm okay, Dad." I wanted to get back to our seats, to prove I was ready to partake of this solemn new fellowship. But as with my Wallace Park travails, I was not quite as adept as I thought. I had embarrassed myself and failed the Beavers. When I was ten, the club left town for Spokane, citing dismal attendance, and did not return until I was in high school.

The one arena in which I found comfort, in which I felt I had some command over baseball's secrets, was in the statistical record of the game. There was an encyclopedia's worth of milestones and minutiae to pore over—Joe DiMaggio's fifty-six-game hitting streak, Johnny Vander Meer's consecutive no-hitters, Bobby Thomson's "shot heard 'round the world," Yaz's Triple Crown—and I could do most of it spread out on my bedroom floor. I had about a thousand baseball cards, a collection assembled almost entirely from individual ten-cent Topps packs, the kind that came with crumbly slabs of pink bubble gum, and I would spend hours on my hands and knees, sorting and sifting and stacking them—*organizing* was the word I used—in what must have looked like a deranged game of solitaire. I put them in alphabetical order. I ordered them by team. Long before sabermetrics or *Moneyball*, I made up my own esoteric formulas—lifetime batting average plus yearly RBI average plus best home run season—and ordered my collection accordingly. When I tried, as an adult, to take advantage of the overheated memorabilia market, I found that I had little to cash in: I had done so much "organizing" of my cards that I might as well have clothespinned them to the spokes of my bike.

During Hank Aaron's pursuit of Babe Ruth's home run mark, I wrote him a worshiping letter, care of the Atlanta Braves. He was about to break the most hallowed record in sports, yet he had somehow eluded superstardom. He was dignified and businesslike, a quiet giant, and by claiming him as my idol, by discovering him on my own, I was also looking to validate myself. I received a signed picture of him, which I held up to the light and rotated, intent on ascertaining that the autograph was done by hand, not stamped. There was no way of knowing if Hammerin' Hank himself was the one who signed it, but I chose to believe that he did and put it in a frame that still sits on my bathroom windowsill.

At one point I even took to clipping box scores from *The Oregonian,* just routine, everyday games—Cardinals 3, Reds 1; Pirates 5, Mets 4—and filing the tiny scraps in an envelope. Hunched on the floor, with scissors and mounds of shredded newsprint, I would lose myself in the names and tallies and abbreviations, in the way that nine raucous innings could be distilled into a perfect two-by-three-inch chart. Nothing could be more disposable than the sports agate of a daily paper, particularly during the slog of a season that can get under way when you are in third grade and still not have reached its climax when you start up again in the fourth, and yet to preserve those results was, in my mind, to hitch myself to something epic.

My parents, as I recall, briefly feared autism: My brain was that hypnotically wired. There is a fine line between the cuteness of a boy who knows that Harmon Killebrew of the Minnesota Twins led the majors with forty-nine home runs in 1969 and a boy who knows that "the Killer" lives in the eastern Oregon potato town of Ontario, about 375 miles from Portland, and who thinks this fact alone is reason to head there on vacation. My parents shot down that idea, but I do remember us spending a few days at the beach one of those summers, possibly our last trip as a family. We were walking, all of us, in the coastal gloom, Dad distracted by the heaps of driftwood and Mom and I chattering about what I wanted to be when I grew up, which was already a given, to play shortstop for the Dodgers. She liked to tell me, as parents are supposed to, that with hard work and sacrifice I could be anything, anything at all, even president of the United States, and that whatever I chose, I should be the best at it I possibly could. She also liked to use these moments to take a dig at my father, a painter and later a sculptor with a disdain for commercial tastes. He earned a modest salary teaching art twice a week at Portland State University, then spent the rest of the week giving it back—investing in the making of his own art, which was abstract and minimalist and inconveniently sized and for which, in those days, he received few accolades. To the extent that we qualified as middle class, his career ensured that we would just barely make the cut.

"Be anything you want to be," Mom told me as we sidestepped a chilly surge of foam and kelp, "just don't be an artist."

Maybe I sensed that their marriage was already in trouble. Maybe I was projecting my own fantasies onto their lives. I certainly was not trying to undercut my dad. If anything, I wanted to be understanding, to let my mom know that I had absorbed her lessons, that I got it—that our limits were of our own making.

"Why didn't you marry a baseball player?" I blurted. "Life would have been so much easier."

Nothing happened to make me quit. I suffered no trauma, no offense. After cataloging that last ball, I simply stopped going to the park, stopped archiving, stopped caring about all the trivialities that had defined my notion of boyhood. I suppose puberty was partly to blame or, as it may be, to thank. There was an electric guitar competing for my attention, and girls, and, soon enough, all the other intoxicants of the 1970s. Instead of learning to a hit a curve, I got on a train to Seattle and saw Led Zeppelin rock the Kingdome. I was becoming aware, too, of how institutions could be corrupted, and obedience to them exploited, in the world outside of Wallace Park. Raised in the era of Vietnam, under the cloud of Watergate, I had decided I no longer wanted to belong to a group, to wear a uniform, to submit to the edicts of a coach. I objected to the earnestness, the enforced optimism. I was feeling like I could never be rah-rah about anything again.

I sometimes wonder if it would have been different had my mom or dad been enmeshed in the league, had these two caring and creative people been more explicit about endorsing my involvement. I wonder what might have happened if I had grown up with siblings, to compete alongside of or against, to instruct or learn from or root for. I wonder how things might have turned out if my parents had found a way to be happy together, to discover themselves without losing each other. How would I have felt about baseball? About Portland? About my own notions of home and stability and acceptance? I have no memory of them even attending my games. It is not just that parents then were less insistent about orchestrating their children's time or that mine were too busy to fit Wallace Park into their schedule. Mom and Dad were engaged in something grander—societal, transcendent. When I stopped playing, Mom was in her second term in the state legislature. Dad had just helped found an avant-garde gallery and performance space, the Portland Center for the Visual Arts. They might not have said it this way, but Little League was the straight world, too narrow, too regimented, to be worthy of their focus.

They broke the news to me on a Saturday morning, when I was seventeen. I had taken a girlfriend to see B.B. King at the Paramount Theater the night before and, even in 1980, Portland was sleepy enough that I was able to score front-row tickets for $9 apiece. To sit at the feet of the greatest bluesman who ever lived, to bask in his joy and sorrow and dignity, was as close to religion as I had ever come. B.B.'s prescription was deceptively simple, twelve bars, three chords, one scale, and yet he was extracting from it something so heroic, so redemptive, that when he was done, I found myself leaping out of my seat, screaming and waving, begging for his acknowledgment. Why he responded, why he singled me out, I have no idea, except that maybe I was half the age of every other follower. His eye met mine, and his belly jiggled with laughter. He strutted toward me, wagging his guitar pick, then stopped at the edge of the stage and held it just beyond my reach. I strained. He toyed. The crowd yowled and egged us on. We stayed frozen like that, inches apart, for an eternity, a private communion in a three-thousand-seat auditorium. My arm was trembling. Finally, B.B. put the pick in my palm, and with an enormous hand, he folded my fingers around it. A secret grown-up world of temptation and experience, a bittersweet kingdom ruled by a large black man from a plantation in Itta Bena, Mississippi, had not just taken note of me but had issued a passport.

At the breakfast table, my brain still on blues time, Dad told me he was moving into his studio. We were living in our first real house, an eccentric gingerbread from the 1880s that my parents had bought a couple years earlier, even though they already had decided their marriage was done. They had been sticking it out for me. There were only eighteen months to go—eighteen months and I would be finished with high school, eighteen months and we could all go our separate ways—but they were too exhausted to continue the charade. I cried that day. I cried for our fractured little family, only three of us and yet we were such individuals, not even the sum of our parts. I knew then that I would leave as soon as I could, that I would not just go off to college but would seek my future somewhere else, on my own. I had probably decided this even before I was aware of making the choice. To stay was to settle. The story of the Katzes, what few of us there were, was the story of movement.

The place I ended up was not just a thousand miles from Port-

land: It was the anti-Portland, vast, restless, jumbled, ungovern-
able, a symbol of everything my parents, especially my mom, had
worked to immunize their home against. Just being in L.A. felt
illicit. I was twenty-two when I arrived, in 1985, having finagled
an internship at the *Los Angeles Times*. I found a rental in Echo Park,
in the bottom half of a two-story duplex that clung like an Anasazi
pueblo to the bluffs above Sunset Boulevard. This was the east end
of Sunset, not the Sunset of the Chateau Marmont or the Whisky a
Go Go but working-class, Latin American, hurly-burly Sunset,
close to its terminus at Olvera Street, the ersatz Mexican village
that honors the real Mexican village that is regarded as the birthplace, under the Spanish crown, of Nuestra Señora la Reina de Los
Angeles. If you had seen me then, you would have thought I was
some kind of New Wave lumberjack, the love child of L.L.Bean and
David Byrne. I had a crew cut and a green Mackinaw hunting
jacket and prescription sunglasses made from recycled safety gog-
gles. My face was lean and bony, monopolized by a wide, crooked
grin, and I had a way of sniffing sharply and cocking my head
whenever an occasion called for irony.

Needing a car for the first time in my life, I scraped together
$500 and sunk it into a 1964 Plymouth Valiant with no air-
conditioning, which soon proved irrelevant because of an exhaust
leak that was gassing me out; the only way to drive and remain conscious was with the windows rolled down. I armed myself with a
Thomas Guide, the L.A. highway bible, which partitioned the met-
ropolitan region into 190 pages of maps. For reasons that I was not
sure of—hipster kitsch, droll self-deprecation?—I adorned the
Valiant's dash with three rubber dinosaurs from the Natural History Museum gift shop.

As a journalist, I had a lot to learn about how to conduct myself,
but my true education, the training that would change my life, took
place on the streets, at the fringes. Up and down the boulevards,
Pico, Olympic, Beverly, and the avenues, Western, Vermont, Union,
I found an L.A. saturated with refugees and divvied up by gangs,
neglected by city hall and protected by saints, nourished by taco

trucks and nursed by cantinas—a mad neon-lit stew of tongues and pigments and counterfeit IDs. Somewhere out there was Rodeo Drive and Zuma Beach, the L.A. of plastic surgeons and paparazzi, but I was too transfixed by the other L.A., too consumed with cracking its codes, to care. I took the Valiant out on reconnaissance missions, to the Central American crossroads of MacArthur Park, the Armenian hub of East Hollywood, the Afrocentric oasis of Leimert Park, the enclaves of Koreatown, Thai Town, Filipinotown, the archipelago of Little Tokyo, Little India, and Little Ethiopia, daring myself to open up, to drink it in. It was silly to think that I was going to get very far—I had one year of college Spanish, a senior thesis about the Sandinista revolution under my belt—but I was turned on by the adventure of it all, by the uncertainties and the discoveries, by the way I could pretend to be a foreign correspondent just by stepping out my door.

I suppose it was a bit of a cliché, to come to L.A. and turn all multiculti. I was exoticizing what for millions of immigrants was the stuff of survival. For the first time in my life, though, I had become mindful of how different I looked—what a white boy I was. Until then I had always thought of myself as being sort of racially neutral, invisible. That is what happens when you grow up sheltered, in the homogeneity of Wallace Park, even if you take pride in your openness. Our jargon contributes to that perception; if you have people of color, you must also have people absent of color. White was the norm in Portland, the starting point. Everyone else was, well, nonwhite. Overnight all those assumptions were reshuffled for me, my skin suddenly setting me apart. I had entered a world that was fast turning brown, a world that was looking a lot more like the world really is. The way the rest of America was destined to be. I had become a minority, the exception. If I wandered far enough afield, I was a curiosity even. God, how I loved it! Los Angeles, my mysterious cinnamon princess, where had you been my whole life?

Down the hill from the Echo Park house, on Sunset, there was a dive called The Sunset. It is gone now, reduced to a parking lot. But

I can still see its glowing sign, in cherry-tinted script—immortalized for a split second in the opening credits of Bukowski's *Barfly*—the dank, murky cavern of its insides, the saggy leatherette booths, the jukebox permanently tuned to "Me and Mrs. Jones," and the hellcat bartender, with her silver tooth, who always wrapped my Corona in a napkin and doused the lip in salt. Her name was Raynelda Pastora Gutiérrez, although she told everyone it was Patti. She had Asian eyes and Mayan cheekbones and the complexion of a burnished penny. She wore spandex tube skirts that rode up smooth, sturdy thighs and that required constant tugging, and she was forever swinging her ornery black mane away from her face, heedless of who might get swatted. The Sunset was not a hustle. Nobody was cadging or soliciting. Raynelda merely smiled and poured and hinted just enough to make anybody, even a stranger like me, feel special. The first time I shook her hand, she slid it into a homeboy grip, then butted knuckles with me. "You know what this means?" she asked. "Friends. *Tú y yo.* You and me." She was three years younger than me, a product of Managua's shantytowns, without papers. I noticed that she smelled like cloves.

More and more, I began making the two-block descent to see her, to drink and flirt and ease my loneliness. Whatever I was up to, it was complicated—risky, humbling, generous, conniving—a paradoxical, politically incorrect hunt for affection. I was trying to insinuate myself into an immigrant bar, to gauge the availability of an immigrant bar girl, as if she was not just doing her job but auditioning for suitors, looking for a way out. A moralist could have accused me of slumming, a feminist of worse. As a college-educated, American-born novitiate to the MSM, I was a symbol of status and privilege, my access to opportunity beyond the hopes of anyone in The Sunset. It gave me an edge, maybe an unfair advantage: I had more to offer Raynelda than my competition. If it appeared that way, like I was a poacher, I never thought of it in those terms. To the contrary, I felt like I was shedding my pedigree, putting myself at Raynelda's mercy, teaching myself to adapt to The Sunset's rules and lexicon. No matter what I looked to be, I wanted to prove that I was not like that, not like the rest of them, not too good or too squeamish to get down in the beer-soaked trenches. I found myself saying things in Spanish, repeating phrases gleaned from songs and soap operas, that I would never have dreamed of uttering in English, a language that was suddenly flavorless, antiseptic. By my sixth or seventh beer, I was almost fluent. "Your eyes are my heaven," I told Raynelda. "You have the keys to my soul. What would I not give for one of your kisses?"

To the west, where the city was richer and thinner, there was no shortage of illustrious nightspots, places where my résumé might actually have been an asset. Hair metal was being born at the Troubadour and the Roxy, California cuisine was reaching its apex at Spago and Michael's, my bestselling classmate Bret Easton Ellis was swilling vodka at Trumps and the Polo Lounge, and yet that world felt even more foreign to me, all wrapped up in fame and glitz and image. I suppose I was channeling a bit of Groucho Marx, not wanting to belong to any club that would have me as a member. Because I did not belong in The Sunset, I was at home in The Sunset, in its wornness, its baseness. Men drank there to disappear, not to be seen. Their drunkenness was ritualized, medicinal. It was about salving wounds and inflicting new ones, about bleeding and purging and absolving. I did not exactly think of myself as someone in need of that catharsis—the word in Spanish was *desahogarse,* which meant, literally, to *un*drown oneself—but I was enticed by the directness of it, the willingness of my hosts to be laid bare, and I tried to follow their protocol. You addressed everyone in formal verbs. You bought a round for anyone who listened to your story. You bought a round for anyone who bought you a round. You left your money on the countertop and let Raynelda thumb through it for whatever you owed. When the mariachis, in their spangled cowboy suits, wandered in off the street, you were expected to request *"El Niño Perdido,"* and the trumpeter, to mimic the lost boy's cries, would ensconce himself in the bathroom and, from the ice-filled urinal, blow his plaintive horn. I sometimes ended up with so many courtesy beers that I had to duck in there myself and, while pretending to take a leak, spill one of my bottles.

Maybe I am romanticizing a shitty little bar, a slippery, tragic sump, but it was still a community and the door was open and even a nerd from virtuous Portland, if he exhibited the right combination of desire and humility, had a chance of being welcomed. I told myself I was at the vanguard of something, of L.A.'s ethnographic makeover, of my own L.A. transformation.

Our first date was a concert, Celia Cruz at the Hollywood Palladium, March 5, 1988. Raynelda wore a slinky, sleeveless blue-and-white striped dress, which might have been the most conservative item in her wardrobe and still hugged every curve and cleft. Her jewelry was all fantasy, her cosmetics mostly bootleg. She lived off her sensuality—on tips and trinkets, the offerings of admirers like me. We drank cocktails and held hands and, wherever we turned, felt the gapes. I am sure I did not look up to the task of managing such an immodest date, but instead of shrinking, I relished the scrutiny. I liked what *I* thought our pairing implied: that I was cosmopolitan and unprejudiced, that I had been liberated from the world of convention and admitted to the other side. Perhaps it is crude to put so much emphasis on Raynelda's allure, reductive to portray her as such a voluptuous prize, but she knew that it gave her what power she had, and she seized any chance to flaunt it. She had a knack for curling her upper lip and clicking her tongue—I had friends, concerned about what I was getting myself into, on the receiving end—to signal contempt for anyone who questioned her appropriateness. In Raynelda's mind, humanity was divided into two camps: *la gente sencilla,* who were simple and unaffected, and *los hipócritas,* who were too repressed, too urbane, to reveal their true nature. If she happened to be *muy sexi,* she was not about to disguise it, especially to placate someone who was prudish or, more likely, jealous. "I am who I am," Raynelda was fond of saying, "and whoever doesn't like it can suck my dick."

When the band started up and the Queen of Salsa greeted us

with a thundering *¡azúcar!,* I got to see Raynelda dance. Her gyrations were pure and raw, more African than Latin. She could make her entire body quiver at once, then she could freeze everything but her hips, which continued to pulse and quake like a paint-mixing machine. Sorry, but no white girl could shake it like that: Raynelda said so herself. I tried to give myself to the delirium, but I was both hasty and sluggish. I soaked through my shirt. Raynelda laughed and threw her arms around my damp neck, pressing her pelvis against mine and nudging me to match her rhythm. We were at the foot of the stage, on a crowded floor, with hundreds of other couples. I expected to feel chagrined. In another time or place I might have, but not here, not tonight, not under the spell of this audacious Third World hoochie mama. I was grateful to be getting schooled. She was my L.A., my frontier. I grabbed Raynelda's waist and I pulled her even closer.

We became the royal couple of Echo Park's cantina row. In those days you could walk to a dozen raffish saloons in the span of a half mile—gentrification has since shuttered or spoiled nearly all of them—and whenever Raynelda's shift ended at The Sunset, we would parade through the others, The Gold Room, The Hollyway, El Prado, Los Pinos, The Suku Suku, Little Joy. Someone always wanted to buy us a round, if not gentlemanly runners-up who wished to pay their respects, then sad-faced bar girls who dreamed of themselves being spirited away. Raynelda and I were cheered as proof that in the den of sin, there were still fairy-tale endings. She was bewitching, ambitious, uninhibited, hardly the stereotype of an *indocumentada* cowering in the shadows, and unlike most white guys, whom Raynelda thought of as uptight and arrogant, I seemed to derive pleasure from being a fish out of water. She was my entry into what I had come to think of as the real L.A., my escort through the kaleidoscopic, dystopian *Blade Runner* city I was just learning to navigate, and I was her bridge out of that, to security and legitimacy, to the L.A. of the haves. It was a pretty good deal, all around. We were both on our own, without family to impede us, free to feed our cravings and curiosities. We observed the Day of the Dead in

East L.A., and we skinny-dipped under the stars at the Bonaventure
Hotel; we cured ourselves with intestinal soups at Roy's Carniceria,
and we juiced up again while playing the ponies at Santa Anita
Park. I was blathering in Nicaraguan idioms, spending more money
than I had, savoring my new home through the eyes of someone who
had risked her life to get there. It was all so visceral, so freakin' seductive. We would race back to my place, blood full of tequila and
fire, and gorge on the unlikelihood of our liaison, on our exquisite
contrasts.

After a few months of euphoria, Raynelda raised the stakes. She
had a son. His name was Freddy. That was exactly how it appeared
on his birth certificate, not Federico or Alfredo, but the American
shorthand, glib and colloquial. She showed me a picture. It was
black and white, like a Walker Evans portrait from the Dust Bowl.
The child was invisible under his swaddling. Raynelda, who wore
a peasant frock and rubber sandals, was seventeen, gaunt and severe.
The father was nobody, just another Managua boy. It was unclear to
me if he even knew he had a son. Raynelda had waited two or three
years and then come north, sneaking into California just as I was
pulling up in my Valiant. She had left Freddy with her mother. He
was six now. *"Pobrecito,"* she kept saying. "My poor little boy."

The seventh of nine children, Raynelda had grown up in a
cement-floor shack without utilities, no refrigerator, no stove, no
washing machine or hot water. They subsisted on rice and beans and
little else, slept two and three to a mattress, suffered the scourges of
poverty, bedbugs, tapeworms, lice. Her mother worked the machines at a textile mill. Her father, an electrician, beat the kids until,
eventually, he found a new wife. The earthquake struck a day before
Christmas, when Raynelda was seven. It flattened downtown Managua, burying five thousand, maybe ten thousand people in the
rubble—mass graves, to ward off disease, made the final toll un-
knowable. With more than half the city displaced, looters prowled
the streets. Raynelda joined the throng, door to door, looking for
signs of prosperity. Appliances were carted off. TVs and stereos disappeared. She was scared and thrilled. If you have nothing and all of

a sudden the rules are suspended, what is it that you are supposed to take? Raynelda peeked through a window and saw, on a hutch, the one thing she imagined every girl should have. It was something she had never held in her life, the present she would not be getting, once more, that year. She summoned all her courage and burst into this strange rich person's house. When she came rushing out, heart ablaze, Raynelda was clutching a doll.

Under the virulent regime of Anastasio Somoza Debayle, her oldest brother had joined the Sandinistas, a teenage guerrilla fighter. There was combat on their street—Villa Revolución, the neighborhood was later renamed—and even now, an unmarked tomb, right where a young rebel fell, rests outside their front door. Instead of high school, Raynelda joined the army. Then she got herself pregnant. Her life had been a trial of war, hunger, disaster, abuse, and yet she had extracted herself, found enough sugar daddies to pay for a smuggler, and gotten herself to America, to L.A., to The Sunset, and was now in the process of improving her station again. Wherever you came down on immigration—and I would not expect everyone to share my sympathies—you had to admire the tenacity, the absolute refusal to be crushed, that propelled the Raynelda Pastora Gutiérrezes of this world across the border. I was neither equipped nor inclined to raise a child at that point, but it was hard to argue that Freddy did not deserve to be with his mom or that I should get to enjoy her and not have to contribute to his passage.

The details elude me now. I am not even sure how many hundreds I chipped in. There would be so many more payments in the years to come, so many more Gutiérrezes making the trek. In addition to Freddy, I can think of twenty-one in-laws who slipped past *la migra:* five of Raynelda's brothers and sisters, fifteen of her nieces and nephews, plus Doña Thelma, her mom. None of them ever saved enough, either, or sought the blessing of those already here. They would simply take off, get as far as they could, then call us collect, from Guatemala or Chihuahua or Nogales, after it was too late to turn back. That is what I remember about Freddy's journey, that by the time I understood what was happening, he was already

in transit. The phone would ring in the middle of the night—
Raynelda was more or less sharing my bed—and there would be
sobs on the other end. The *coyote* was demanding cash. Freddy was
starving. He was under the watch of Thelma, who was also chaperoning her youngest son, Nestor, who was thirteen, but most of the
time they were not even sure where they were.

"*Mija,* help us," Thelma pleaded. "For the love of God. *Por
favor.* Help."

I would try to console Raynelda, vowing that we would find the
money, even if I had to take cash advances from a credit card, but she
was plunging into darkness. Our drinking sessions no longer
ended in a frenetic tumble but with Raynelda whimpering, eyes
peeled wide, lost in traumas I could not possibly understand. "*Me
quiero morir,*" she would say, night after night. I would try to snap her
out of it, tapping her cheeks with my fingertips. "*Amor,*" I would say.
"Please." But she kept repeating it: "I want to die. I want to die." It
went on like that for at least a month, Raynelda paralyzed and me—
me?—what the hell was I thinking? I had been a naïf and a tourist
and a sex zombie. Now Raynelda needed me. For the first time in
my life, I was trying to be grown-up.

We finally got a call from Brownsville. They had waded the Rio
Grande and were about to board a Greyhound. Two days later the
bus lumbered off I-10, into downtown L.A. We paced the terminal,
neither of us wanting to admit that we were unsure what to look for.
Raynelda had been gone maybe three years. Freddy was a stranger to
her, too. He was already sprinting by the time we spotted him—
lean and anxious, with a ruffian's mullet and bangs that could have
been cut with a bowl. He dived into Raynelda's arms. She dropped
to the ground and squeezed him, whirling him, smothering him
with kisses. "Baby, baby," she gasped. "My beautiful little sweetheart." Freddy pushed her away for a moment and looked up at me.
He scrunched his nose, then looked back at her. "*¿Él es mi papá?*" he
asked. No, son, I am just the Americano doing your mom. Dammit!
What was the right answer? We had never even discussed what we
might tell him. I had no idea what he had already been told.

Raynelda and I were still figuring each other out. I was not a husband, much less a dad. "We'll, uh . . . just, uh . . ." I stammered. But Raynelda's mom had caught up, along with Nestor, and the reunion was in full swing again. I pursed my lips and let out a sigh. I would try, somehow, to learn.

When I was Freddy's age, maybe six or seven, I witnessed my first piñata. That sounds funny today—what kid does not know the drill?—but in Oregon of the late 1960s, I had managed to make it to elementary school without any inkling of the unruly passions that a papier-mâché donkey could unleash. Mom was just beginning her political life and had dragged me to a labor camp in the Willamette Valley, where, on behalf of the Kennedy Action Corps, she was documenting the feudal conditions under which tens of thousands of Mexican farm workers toiled. (I still have a copy of her spiral-bound study, its title a Great Society classic: "The Green Ghetto.") It was there, in the silt of the floodplain, between rows of lettuce and onions and grapes, that our hosts strung a piñata over a tree and invited the children to take a whack. The spectacle was liberating and subversive, a rebuke to every rule about playing nice. I was afraid to actually do any damage myself, but when the piñata erupted, my reserve vanished and I broke free, hurling myself into the scrum. The earth was blanketed in candy, and we were all jostling for it, greedily and gleefully, the way kids are supposed to. I scooped up everything in sight—chocolates, suckers, gum balls, jellybeans—my hands swelling into fists. Then I felt a tug. Mom was behind me, clasping my elbow, pulling me out.

"You can have sweets any time you want," she told me. I was confused. I thought I had done the right thing, mimicking the Mexican boys and girls. With an open palm, she gestured toward the ground. "These are poor children," she said. "Put the candy back."

My life, to a ludicrous degree, has been defined by that moment, but not in terms that I entirely understand. I can think of a million things I have done to internalize her instructions and I can think of a million things I have done to reject them. It seems safe to say that I have an overdeveloped sense of social responsibility, maybe even a reckless disregard for my own comfort and care. I had ventured to the big city to start a career in journalism, not to administer an underground railroad. My mom was a public figure, speaker of the Oregon house when I got hired at the *L.A. Times,* and if someone (a political rival? a disgruntled reader?) were to have taken note of my entanglements, I might well have left her or the paper in an awkward spot. I will cop to liberal guilt. I seem determined to be a rescuer, to cash out my security, to take all the advantages I have inherited and offer them, freely, rashly, to people with needs greater than mine. I have, at the same time, also indulged myself, returned to the giddiness of the piñata—all that candy, all those limbs—and tried with everything I had to blur the lines that once kept me separate. I have reinvented myself, adopted an identity, a culture, that I did not have access to as a kid. I have taught myself to think in Spanish, to love in Spanish, to dream in Spanish. I have traveled in almost every Spanish-speaking country on the planet, mostly for fun, and in my life as a writer, I have used my affinities to plumb the arts and politics and vices of Spanish-speaking communities across the Southwest. No matter where I have roamed or whose confidence I have sought, there is nothing like that moment of validation, that handshake or toast or caress, when the divide between "us" and "them" evaporates and my barrio pass is renewed. If assimilated Latinos can be disparaged as coconuts, a term I hesitate to introduce, I have come to think of myself as the opposite: white on the outside, brown underneath.

When I was twenty-six, which sounds so young now, which truthfully sounded young to me even then, Raynelda once more upped the ante. It was 1989, a year and a half after we had danced to Celia Cruz, and she thought it was about time I married her. "You mean, like, a real marriage?" I asked. "Or just for a green card?"

"It doesn't matter," she said. "We can figure that out later."

"That's just—wow," I said. "Such a big step. I'm, uh, not sure, you know, if I'm completely ready."

" 'Oh, I'm not *sure,* ' " she mocked me. " 'I don't know if I'm *ready.*' Well, listen, I don't have that kind of time."

"I mean, I do love you. I feel like that's for sure."

"And what good is that going to do me? This is a crisis! I need papers, for me and for my son, someone who is going to help me raise this boy, and if you can't help me, I'll find a man who will."

It was an ultimatum: Make her and Freddy legal or we were done. I wish I could say that I was dumbfounded, that I never saw it coming, but something almost identical had happened a couple years earlier. Before I knew of The Sunset, I had begun frequenting a hole in the wall called The Lotus Room, which was off the Hollywood Freeway and staffed entirely by Thai girls. It had a curtain over the doorway, which opened into a narrow lounge that was decorated with Christmas lights and soft-core velvet paintings. A hostess named Lee took an interest in me. She was not a girl, actually, but a thirty-year-old woman, afraid that her prospects were running out. I learned my first Thai sweet nothing, *khun suay mak*. She said I was a nice boy. Part of me wished I was not. After a month or two, Lee asked me to marry her. She was going to pay me $3,000. While I had been dabbling at The Lotus Room, she had been hatching her escape. "Please," she said. "I need." My brain was in meltdown, every synapse trying to calculate the implications: cowardice versus providence versus self-preservation versus shame. If Lee was hurt by my answer, she did not show it. Maybe life had accustomed her to disappointment. I hated what it said about me, though, about my capacities and motives.

My relationship with Raynelda was more advanced—we at least had a life outside The Sunset—but she was still putting me on the spot, calling my bluff. Was I a poseur? A romantic? A colonialist? A martyr? I resented having to choose. I knew this was no way to get married, to become a family on command. I was broke and imprudent, established in nothing, paying off student loans and sleeping on a futon. I had grown a feeble mustache and, at the back of my neck, a slender braid, the kind that used to be called a rat tail. Of course, I could have shined Raynelda on, called *her* bluff, but I knew that her desperation was genuine. She had no other hope, no other path to citizenship but marriage. If I let her down, I was

afraid I would lose her. If I chickened out, again, I was afraid of
becoming something I did not want to be.

I got on the phone and dialed Portland, first my mom, then my
dad, and told them that in a month Raynelda and I were going to
marry. It would be no frills—a courthouse wedding—and since I
could not say for certain that I was doing it for the right reasons, I
saw no need for them to come. To their credit, my parents did their
wigging out after we hung up. As best as I recall, they had not even
met Raynelda, much less Freddy, and if they had, the conversation
would have stalled after "nice to meet you." They each congratu-
lated me, without sarcasm, and said they looked forward to the ex-
pansion of our family, but on one point they were adamant. "It's
still a wedding and you're still my only child," Mom snapped,
"and I'll be damned if I'm going to miss it."

On a warm fall morning, we all headed downtown to Hill
Street, a block and a half from Times Mirror Square. Mom had flown
in from Portland. So had Dad. I introduced them to the bride, translated their greetings to Thelma. Freddy was at school. We waited in
line to see the judge, Raynelda and I both in white, jeans and embroidered shirt for me, miniskirt and cropped jacket for her. Our
rings came from a Native American jewelry store in Burbank,
black onyx set on sterling bands. Hers cost $15. Mine was $10.

Chapter

Two

I WANTED TO CALL HIM MAX. NOT MAXIMILIAN OR MAXIMO
or Maxwell. *Max.* It was rustic and durable, free of singsongy sylla-
bles. *Max Katz.* Even better: old country, symmetrical, high Scrabble count. Although I got no objections from Raynelda, she feared it
might circumscribe his identity, cheat his Latino half. I suggested
we add a middle name, something grandly diametrical, to confound
whatever perceptions the world, or a scholarship committee, might
have of him. None of the Katzes in my life have middle names—
historically, I guess, my people have done without them—although
when I was a kid, I did privately adopt an *F* so that my initials could
be JFK. We pored over Nicaraguan mythology and Nicaraguan folk
hymns, drawn to indigenous figures and proverbs. On the outskirts
of Managua, there is a granite statue of Nicarao, the tribal cacique
who ruled at the time of the conquest. That had just the right flavor.
By combining his name with their word for water, the Spaniards had

come up with *Nicaragua*. So it was that our son's birth certificate came to say Max Nicarao Katz, the quixotic union that produced him forever logged in the archives of the Los Angeles County Registrar-Recorder. A colleague of mine, who has been a frequent dinner guest of late, always greets him with the same salute: "Max Katz, the world's only Nicaraguan Jew."

Max was conceived shortly after the Rodney King riots, in 1992, not exactly planned but neither entirely an accident. While Los Angeles was still burning, Raynelda and I were flying to the Caribbean, a trip that we had been looking forward to as a belated honeymoon. This was bad form as a journalist: I was by then the *L.A. Times* gang reporter, as high-profile a job as there was in the newsroom, and I was abandoning my post in the middle of a catastrophic uprising. We were being just as derelict, I hate to admit, as parents: The city was under curfew, the streets jammed with soldiers, and we were leaving Freddy behind with my mother-in-law for an entire month, our only worries being sunburns and hangovers. Even though Raynelda had been frantic about getting Freddy out of Nicaragua, she was slow to find her maternal bearings once he was here, to put the brakes on our self-involved escapades. She continued to moonlight on the cantina circuit, to revel and rant and disappear with me on weekends, while Thelma continued to do the raising of her son. I am not laying blame. That suited me fine, delayed my own coming out as a father. As long as I was following Raynelda's example, I had nothing to apologize for. We did not move Freddy in with us until after the wedding, and even then, it seemed like we were forever dropping him off on our way to somewhere else. We had found a one-bedroom bungalow in Silver Lake, not quite big enough for the three of us, but it had a utility room below, which was reached by stairs inside the hall closet, like a storm cellar, and that is where Freddy slept, somewhere between privacy and exile.

At least our marriage was proving to be more than an arrangement. As much as I brayed about being roped in, I already had concluded that it was not in my nature to do anything halfway, to be party to a sham. If there was going to be a Mrs. Katz, I was going to treat her as one, a full-fledged partner, my wife. Before the wedding, as a precaution, I had drafted a prenup. It was absurd—the $300 I spent on the lawyer was more than my net worth—but I was scared and shortsighted. Raynelda signed it, with a hiss. Every disagreement we had, that damn contract came up. "Say whatever you want," Raynelda would tell me. "You already showed your true colors." Once we got settled, falling into what passed for our domestic routine, I announced that I wanted to start fresh. I pulled out the papers and, making a show for Raynelda, began to rip, once, twice, three times, until the pieces were too thick to split. Making her own show, Raynelda found a cigarette lighter and burned what was left. The lawyer had said he would keep a spare copy, in case something like this happened—Raynelda suspected as much—but I never intended to ask for it, and anyway, I later forgot the name of the firm. "You are the owner," I told Raynelda that night, "of my heart."

In time, Raynelda enrolled in English classes. I used my insurance to replace the grillwork on her front tooth with a porcelain cap. We watched *Sábado Gigante* on Saturday nights and *The Simpsons* on Sundays. On Thanksgiving I invited all my in-laws over for turkey—one cooked the night before, a second the morning of—which we had to serve in shifts, on paper plates. Alone on the beaches of Cartagena, far from the unrest of L.A., we felt so at ease with each other, so connected, that we upgraded our wedding rings, to gold bands with Colombian emeralds. The way I remembered it, Raynelda got pregnant before we returned, but as I check the math now, it had to be a month or so later, albeit still in the warm afterglow. I was about to turn thirty. Raynelda was looking for an excuse to quit the bars, to devote herself to being a full-time mom. A baby would be the final component of our relationship, the creation that made clear we were in it for the long run. "This time," I told Raynelda, "I'm ready." That fall my mom was elected mayor of Portland. We all flew up for the inauguration, me, Freddy, and a very large Raynelda, whose swollen profile even made the pages of *The Oregonian.*

There must be something about fatherhood that awakens the baseball gene. After so many years of dismissing the sport, the whole notion of competitive play, as the domain of frat boys and hard-asses, I found myself captivated by it again, the structure, the senses, the soothing drumbeat of a season in which 162 games are played in 182 days. I would look at Max, a pudgy bundle in the same red leather carriage that my parents had wheeled me around Brooklyn in, and I would want to tell him all about it: the cowhide, the wood, the dirt, the grass, the twilight. I was the one who would go shopping for his baby clothes, the onesies and the footies, to make sure they had pinstripes or "Little Slugger" stitched on the chest. I took Max to his first Dodger game while he was still in diapers, outfitted him in a kiddie cap with that splendid logo, the brilliant white on blue, the genius of the *L* overlapping the *A*. When he was two, I bought him his first mitt, the priciest model I could find for such a tiny hand. I showed him how to condition it with oil, just as I had done with mine, and when I would come home from work, he would race to the door and gush, "Daddy, Daddy, can we *soil* our gloves today?" I taught him to play catch, with what he thought was a "waffle" ball. That October, at his prodding, we curled up in front of the TV and, for the first of many times, watched the "World Serious" together. For his third birthday, Max wanted to be a baseball player, as if the occasion called for a costume, not a party. I got him his first bat, the lightest Louisville Slugger in production, which he still had to grip halfway up the handle to have a chance of lifting it off his shoulder.

My good friend Abel came over one day and offered to throw Max a few pitches on the front lawn. They were gentle underhand tosses, with a tennis ball, served up from close range. "Here you go, *mijo,*" Abel said, encouragingly. "You can do it." Max squinted. He cocked and stepped. He twisted his hips and threw his hands and drilled a perfect line drive right back into Abel's larynx.

"Aaarrrghk," Abel gasped, dropping to his knees. I rushed in from my outfielder's position, not sure whether to laugh or dial 911. "Dude, are you all right?" I asked. Abel was huddled, clutching his throat, trying to nod. I turned to Max. He had never been bratty, much less cruel, but I could have sworn he looked more than a little pleased with himself.

Everything, not just baseball, came easy for Max. From the day I snipped his umbilical cord—and got a quizzical stare right back—he has been focused and composed, bringing a preternatural calmness to whatever he does. In the bathtub, over dinner, at the movies, with a doctor, all the situations in which kids tend to fuss and act out, he never once shed a tear. When he was five, I asked him to recite the most grown-up words he could think of. At the top of his list were *actually, perhaps,* and *man overboard.* I had to write that down. When he was six, we put him on a plane up to Portland—a kindergartner, flying solo—so that he could ride with my mom in the Rose Festival parade. "Why is everyone waving at you, Grandma," he asked as they crept through downtown on the back of a convertible, "and nobody's waving at me?" When he was nine, visiting his grandparents again, he accompanied my mom to the tarmac of Portland International Airport to bid an official bon voyage to George W. Bush. The president, who had been in town for a fund-raiser that drew rowdy protests (and a hail of rubber bullets from the police), tussled Max's hair and patted his cheek, then presented him with a box of commander-in-chief M&Ms. A TV reporter was standing by, waiting for Max to provide a recap. "He said, um, 'How ya doin', sport?' And I said, uh, 'I'm doing fine.' And then, that's all I said," Max told viewers of Portland's five o'clock news.

Max's precociousness—and the joy that I derived from it—made Freddy's shortcomings all the more agonizing. I had convinced myself that once Freddy and I got acclimated, I could be a stable and benevolent presence in his life. I did not want to be the kind of man who thought of a stepson as a drag, and I had assumed that since he did not even know his real father, whatever I could

offer him would be better than what he had. How hard could it be
to be an improvement? Even before I got diverted by Max, though,
I could already sense the distance between Freddy's capabilities and
my expectations. I had zero experience around kids, no brothers or
sisters, nieces or nephews, no reservoir of jokes or tricks or games to
draw on, and I suspect that Freddy found me even more of an
enigma: his introduction to male authority, to a male breadwinner,
to a male body in the same bed as his mom. He had waited all this
time to be reunited with her, only to have to compete with me. I
knew I should be treating him as if he were my own, calling him
my son, not my stepson or Raynelda's son, but having never fa-
thered a child, I struggled with the terminology. It felt more like I
was picking up a son, the player to be named later in a blockbuster
trade. Even so, I trained myself to do it, to not engage in some petty
semantic game: *Freddy is my son.* But he was not, and he seemed to
know better than I did that he never would be. As a show of respect, he addressed Raynelda in formal Spanish, as *usted.* I was simply Jess.

From the day he started school, Freddy was behind, unfamiliar
with books, with the alphabet, with writing his own name. Once we
were all together, I introduced him to bedtime stories, always in English, but in the morning he would be back in his ESL classes, learning the rudiments of Spanish. I went to see an administrator about
transferring him out—Freddy could not read or write in either language, so why not just suffer through the one that he was ultimately
going to need?—but the school rebuffed me: Hispanic kids failed at
such high rates, I was told, it was essential to hold Freddy back, to
let him succeed first in his native tongue. "This can't be a typical situation," I protested. "He's got a parent—well, a stepparent, but
still, *me*—who speaks English, who writes in English. I mean, this is
what I do for a living." The bilingual coordinator at Micheltorena
Street Elementary frowned. "I don't think you understand," she said.
"The odds are really stacked against him."

I looked for other ways to reach out to Freddy, to impart my
standards and aspirations. I took him to museums, signed him up

for piano lessons, bought him the sorts of toys my parents had bought me—LEGO sets, an Etch A Sketch, a Hocus-Pocus magic kit—but Freddy seemed to be everything that Max would prove not to be, antsy, undisciplined, petulant, prone to tantrums, and full of hurt. We had begun celebrating Christmas with the rest of the Gutiérrezes, Nicaraguan-style, on the twenty-fourth, at midnight, by which time the adults were sloshed and the kids cranky and dazed. Everything under the tree got ripped open in one tempestuous flurry, and Freddy, year after year, ended up in tears, from anticipation and disappointment and exhaustion, nothing ever all that he needed it to be.

We took him to Magic Mountain for his birthday, not what I would have chosen, but he was enthralled by the nonstop commercials, with their mechanized thrills and tributes to Americana. The day was blazing, and the lines snaked forever. We waited for an hour, only to discover that Freddy was too short for the Viper, the nineteen-story, seventy-mile-per-hour looping roller coaster that I had never intended to board myself, and that we needed to start over, in another interminable line. Freddy was pouting, Raynelda itching for a drink. I was footing the bill. "Nobody's fucking happy," I snapped, finally, herding them both to the car. We got vouchers to return, but I knew, for me, that was it.

While we were in Portland for my mom's swearing in, Freddy did a thousand dollars in water damage to her dainty old Victorian—taking a shower in a claw-foot tub, on the second floor, without closing the curtain. Over breakfast at a diner back in L.A., he pushed open an emergency exit and set off the alarm—and when I overheard a gay couple in the next booth muttering about children who could not heed clearly marked warnings, I was not sure whether to feel indignant or humiliated. Whatever deprivation he had been exposed to in Nicaragua or on his journey north, whatever wounds were still festering, Freddy reminded me of some untamed wolf-boy, plucked from the wilds and forced to adapt to practices he could never hope to master. He was pacified by cartoons

and candy, but whenever I tried to limit his intake, I was met with
yet more wails of misfortune.

As powerless as I sometimes felt at home, I seemed at last to be
finding my voice at work. After years of apprenticing in the *L.A.
Times* suburban zones, I was promoted to the metro staff, which put
me, at the age of twenty-eight, in the heart of the city just as urban
violence was reaching a historic peak. Homicides were annually top-
ping two thousand in those days, seven hundred or eight hundred of
them committed by gang members, and because I was young and
still trying to prove how simpatico I was, I kept volunteering for
stories that thrust me closer and closer to the front lines.

A few months before the riots, the paper sent me to Watts, my
first visit to that patch of despair and neglect. The assignment was
daunting: to cover an arson fire in Jordan Downs, the hermetic,
seven-hundred-unit housing project that serves as home turf for the
Grape Street Crips. Two days before my arrival a couple of crack
fiends had made a funnel out of cardboard and, in the wee hours of
the morning, wedged it into a neighbor's mail chute. Their intent
was to silence a large, extended Mexican family, seventeen of them
packed into a three-bedroom town house, that had dared to complain about Grape Street's drug trade. They flooded the apartment
with gasoline and, while the occupants slept, put a flame to the
opening. Five bodies, spanning four generations, were found in the
embers.

When I pulled up to 102nd Street—I had by then invested in a
Toyota Celica, which was feeling prim and trite all of a sudden—I
found a community in such anguish, I scarcely knew what to ask.
Latinos, the new majority in Watts but still a minority within the
confines of Jordan Downs, were approaching me in tears, pleading
for help, even demanding a segregated wing for their protection.
They were being cut short by the complex's African-American
managers, who took exception to my meddling, my shock, another
parachuting journalist who was going to remind the outside world
what animals they were in the ghetto. A chiseled young tough, in

wooden beads and a wifebeater, intervened. His name was Chopper. "There's nothing you're going to learn down here today," Chopper told me. "This is just the eruption." If I really wanted answers, he said, I would have to understand the conditions that kept Watts at a simmer all the time. I liked the way Chopper spoke, a voice of discontent but also hope, as if the horror of the moment could be transcended just by perspective. He probably thought he was scaring me off—he wanted no part of the story I had to file that afternoon—but I wanted to believe, perhaps, he had seen something in me, a hint that I was willing to listen. If he was for real, so was I. "Teach me, then," I said.

Chopper suggested I get my first lesson from, of all people, Jim Brown, the Hall of Fame fullback/actor/*Playgirl* centerfold, who had developed a recovery program for Bloods and Crips, a fifteen-step plan that was part Malcolm X, part Alcoholics Anonymous. Jim lived high in the Hollywood Hills, in a major shag pad, with a mirrored living room and a steam-veiled swimming pool and a view that twinkled across the horizon. Every Wednesday night, he opened his doors to gang leaders from the basin below, guys like Chopper and Jawbone and Wig Out and Twilight, who had wreaked so much havoc and, having made their names, were proposing to be part of the solution. He greeted them all with the smooth, grip-shifting salutation of the hood, just as Raynelda had welcomed me to The Sunset. They addressed him as "Mister Brown." He was fifty-five, creaky but still cut, with a dense mustache and an African skullcap. It was at the minimum great theater: the gridiron legend and the antiheroes of South Central, all of them in their own way warriors, old before their time. In that sea of gold chains and teardrop tattoos, I felt like an innocent again, the kid from the land of GORE-TEX and Birkenstocks. Despite our gulfs, or maybe because of them, I found myself drawn to all that underworld energy, to the sensation of rubbing shoulders with certifiable thugs: *See, I'm not intimidated, I don't flinch. I might be white on the outside, my bruthas, but don't be making assumptions about me any more than you'd have me make assumptions about you.*

The story I wrote ("Jim Brown Taps Potential of 'Baddest Cats' in City") landed on the front page and earned me the kudos of my editors, who had been looking for someone on staff to cover gangs as more than just a criminal problem. I was asked to invent a new beat—the culture of gangs—making me, to the best of my knowledge, the only daily newspaper reporter in the country with such an assignment. As with so many of my leaps, the whole idea was almost comical, folly bordering on arrogance. Who was I to think I could pull this off, to grasp the racial inequities, the social and economic breakdowns, that had put 150,000 gang members on the streets of L.A.? Was there not a single Latino or African-American reporter available, nobody with connections or insight or, if nothing else, the ability to blend in? I decided I would have to be that much more empathetic, that much more obstinate, to make up for all the ways in which I was unsuited for the job.

Up to that point most gang reporting had been done largely through the window of a squad car, the obligatory ride-along with the world-weary detective, but I was determined to make my subjects the stars of their own stories, to name names, to see humans where the cops saw only invading armies. I no longer would have to pretend to be a foreign correspondent: I was going places no outsider dared. Oddly, as I threw myself into it, I found that being out of my element, having no authority or allegiances, granted me a certain freedom. I was from nowhere—and so I could go anywhere, crossing borders, changing stripes. I interviewed gangbangers at schools, in jails, at parties, in crack houses, trusting in the right mix of tenacity and deference to cover my ass. Sometimes I had the benefit of an introduction or an escort. Other times I just wandered on my own, taking chances, pushing my luck.

Once I spent an afternoon exploring an unfamiliar neighborhood, driving up and down Hooper and Avalon and Central, scanning the parks and alleyways, hoping to stumble upon the representatives of a gang, any gang, to hang with for a few hours. I worried that I might choose poorly: I did not know what was worse, introducing myself to a band of murderous sociopaths or presuming I had found some gang members and discovering that, in fact, they were not gang members at all. Finally I spotted a group in cornrows and starched T-shirts, passing around forty-ouncers in front of a squalid apartment complex on 68th Street. I parked right in front of them. "Hey, guys," I said, stepping up to the curb. For a moment they stared in disbelief, not sure if I was a cop or merely nuts. "I'm just a reporter," I added, trying to strike a reassuring note, for their benefit and for mine. One of them took off running, a full sprint, saggy jeans slipping toward his knees. Another hiked the neck of his shirt over his nose, bandito-style. "What the fuck do you know about the ghetto?" he snarled through his cotton mask. I felt a chill. This was not going well. I figured the odds still favored survival—journalists did not just get gunned down for sport on the streets of L.A.—but all that could change in a heartbeat. If one of these fools wanted a notch in his belt, would I even see it coming? "Well," I said, "maybe not too much, but I'm here. If you want me to leave, I will. But I hope you'll give me credit for wanting to learn." It was then that a third guy—I still remember his name, Lep Loc— intervened. "Where's the rest of yo' people?" he asked. I was not following. "You know, man, yo' security," he said. "Who's watching yo' back?" I started to laugh. "It's just me," I said. "At your mercy." Lep Loc shook his head, laughing now along with me, maybe at me. I could tell that he was flattered. By coming alone, unprotected, I was not simply putting myself at his mercy but depending on him for my safety.

"Somebody could drive by and just start blastin' on us," he said.

"When you duck, I'll duck," I said.

I offered to spring for another round of malt liquor, but Lep Loc insisted on bringing me Budweiser, the whitest beer he could probably think of, which we sipped together on the sidewalk out of plastic cups. I did know how to do this. I had been training all along. Despite my ill-timed vacation, I was a runner-up that year for a Pulitzer Prize, one of three finalists in the beat reporting category. The assistant city editor, my immediate boss, thought I needed a moniker. To this day, he calls me K-Bone.

As the gang expert, in the gang capital, I was gaining a fair amount of notice, invitations to speak at law enforcement conferences and juvenile justice seminars, $2,500 just to bat around ideas with HBO. I appeared to be so perceptive, to have such access, and yet the very thing I was being praised for had begun to torment me under my own roof. It was one thing to have a sullen, vulnerable child moping around, quite another to see Freddy take on the affectations of a *cholo,* the defiance, the posturing, the "smile now, cry later" fatalism. When he was in fourth grade, about the time we learned Raynelda was pregnant, Freddy started drenching his hair in Dippity-do and slicking it back, tight and hard, even wearing a stocking cap to bed. He got a hold of *2Pacalypse Now* and soon the thudding bass, the "nigga" this, the "muthafucka" that, was reverberating through the floorboards. On shopping trips to the mall, we battled over baggy pants, Raiders gear, the connotations of black nylon, white swoosh Nike Cortezes. "It's cool," Freddy would say. No, I would tell him, it was an invitation to getting shot. He would start to sniffle. "You don't let me do anything. You think everything's bad."

He once spent his allowance on a toy gun. I suppose that was better than a real one, but there was no way I could let it slide. As a legislator, my mom had authored some of the strictest gun-control laws in America. "Never point *anything,*" she would tell me, even if I was just pretending with my index finger and thumb. When I found the toy, a cap pistol, I threw it in the trash. I vowed not to be a grump. I was going to explain myself to Freddy, to convey the sensibilities that I had inherited, not punish him. I put an arm around him. I would reimburse him for what he had lost, our own version of a money-for-guns program. He was inconsolable. "That was mine," he cried. I tried to tell him about the risks, the wrong messages, the potential for someone—cop or criminal—to think his fake revolver could really shoot. "This isn't a joke, Freddy," I told him. "I've had to write stories about kids like you." Freddy was having none of it. Life, he made clear, had dealt him a bad hand. He was not about to be held accountable to some fancy-pants reporter—a Jew, no less—

who had been lured into being his dad. "I can't be perfect," Freddy fired back. "Like you."

It got worse after we had Max, a living, breathing testament to all that Freddy had been denied. There were two males now between him and his mom, both of them in her bed, both of them named Katz. I appreciated the psychology of it, recognized that I would have to work harder if I hoped to hold my family together. Because Thelma had done most of his raising, Freddy was using the last name of her longtime companion, Nestor's father, who had stayed behind in Nicaragua. I talked to Raynelda about adopting him—uniting the four of us under a single name would go a long way, symbolically—but I kept wishing, or waiting, for the rapport between me and Freddy to evolve. I visited his fifth-grade teacher, to see if I could persuade her to call him Freddy Katz. "I haven't officially adopted him," I explained. "That's still in the works. But we're starting to have some trouble at home, and I just, you know, don't want him to feel like the odd man out." She agreed to note the change, to acknowledge him as my son for classroom purposes, but to record it on his transcripts, I would need to show adoption papers. In the meantime, I cast about for more help: reading tutors, diagnostic tests, summer camps, memberships at the Y. I even enrolled Freddy in Little League—baseball, surely, was the right thing to do—but I was looking to the outside, to someone else, to make up for what I was unable to remedy on my own. I have no memory of Freddy's games, no recollection of him actually playing. I must have bought him a glove, but I cannot say for sure that I taught him how to use it.

When Max was a year and a half, which would have made Freddy twelve, I applied for a job on the paper's national staff and was sent to Houston, as bureau chief. I was exhausted from the gang beat, eager to explore the world beyond L.A., but I was also hopeful that getting Freddy out of town would shape him up, or at least decelerate his spiral. As could have been predicted, Freddy hated the move, hated me for making us move. His closest friends were all cousins, my mother-in-law's apartment in Echo Park his one island of familiarity and freedom, and I was dragging him to some insufferable cowboy town halfway across the country, to start over, once again. Freddy slipped into a depression, sulked, lied, stole, numbed his mind all night with torpid, trippy hip-hop—Houston was ground zero for the cough-syrup sound—then refused to get up in the morning for school. Raynelda had nowhere to be, either—she was supportive of my career but disillusioned about her own penchants and abilities—and so Max and I would get dressed and have breakfast and head out together, me to the office, him to pre-K, while his mother and brother slept, avoiding another day.

In those years, Raynelda could still summon the enthusiasm for doting on Max, for praising his handsomeness and cultivating his athleticism. They invented games of patty-cake, serenaded each other with the "I love you, you love me" theme from *Barney*. Sometimes I would come home from work to find them balancing on the bed, Raynelda on her back, knees bent, feet upturned, and Max climbing her like a tree. At the top he would teeter, steadying himself with his mother's hands, until at last he could stand up and let go, nothing but his soles on hers. "Look at you," she would coo. "Superman!" With Freddy she was crippled. She had abandoned him once, and she feared doing anything that might ever again damage that bond. Freddy understood this, probably better than she did, and was only too happy to use her guilt to his advantage. With every outrageous stunt—and there was more to come, an unthinkable accident that rightfully should have killed him—he ensured that his mom and I would turn on each other, arguing about his influence on Max, the perils he posed to us all.

"We can't go on living like this," I would say. "There has to be a line." Raynelda would agree to setting rules but could never bring herself to enforce them. "If he were your own son," she would tell me, "you would be more understanding."

I wished I could have been less of a curmudgeon. In my writing I had shown myself capable of demystifying the scariest dudes, of rationalizing ("glorifying," the cops often complained) the most atrocious conduct. As a father I demonized it. It should have been

the other way around—my capacity to accept and forgive Freddy enhanced by my own initiation—but I refused to believe that his life
had anything in common with the characters I had tried to make sense
of. He had advantages now, options that he never could have hoped
for, and frankly, I thought he should have been a little more grateful.
To him, it must have seemed like an awful double standard, both of
us looking to the streets for our identity yet my quest the only one
considered meaningful and adventurous. Freddy had heard me re-
galing his mom with tales from the hood. He saw me winning plau-
dits at the paper. There were surely other reasons why he was drawn to
that world, but I have since wondered how much of Freddy's stray-
ing was designed to get my attention, to earn him the same compassion I was affording the subjects of my stories.

Max was too young to know about the circumstances under
which our family was formed, but he was already aware of the contradictions: profound distrust living side by side with unwavering
love. Freddy, thank goodness, was remarkably gentle with him, to
the extent that Freddy was home and awake, so Max's perceptions
were based mainly on the misgivings he saw in me. He would
never have done anything to risk my disapproval, and he could not
fathom how Freddy always seemed to invite it. "Dad," he asked me
more than once, "why is Freddy so bad?"

From the moment we selected his name, I imagined Max to be
everything I was not as a kid. I cherished his duality, coaxed him to
be more fluent, more unflappable. He was too brown to be white
and too white to be presumed Latino. His eyes had a hint of
islander—Polynesian? Aleutian?—with lashes so extravagant that
they tangled. He had his mom's physicality: big hands, strong
calves, buttocks as high and spherical as a Jamaican sprinter's. He
had my facial repertoire: the nostril flare, the eyebrow furl, the
tongue stuck at the left crease of his mouth in moments of concentration. At Christmas he danced *palo de mayo,* the rapturous, hip-
shimmying step of Nicaragua's Atlantic coast. (I insisted that he
wait until the morning of the twenty-fifth to open his presents, to
encourage a more reflective experience.) On Passover he snatched the

afikomen while I translated the story of the plagues into Spanish for
my Pentecostal mother-in-law. Really, he could have passed for almost anything—his mix was Western and Eastern, privileged and
subaltern, Ashkenazi, pre-Columbian, European, Iberian, American.
I wanted it that way, and I still do; he is international, universal, the
perfect L.A. archetype. As our home turned more chaotic, though, as
I saw more clearly the patterns and limits of my blended family, I
became obsessed with safeguarding Max. All that Nicarao stuff
was fine, but he was still my son, my parents' only bona fide grandchild, and I could not allow him to assume Raynelda's misery or absorb Freddy's alienation, to inherit the psychic scars of Nicaragua's
calamitous history. I would become the buffer, insulating Max
from all the craziness, maybe from his own half-Nicaraguan self. If I
was betraying a certain arrogance, so be it: I was a father now. For
the sake of my son, I had to ensure that nothing compromised the
part of him that was me.

Baseball was suddenly more than warm, fuzzy memory making.
It became a tool, for instilling my values, for inoculating Max.
Every time I suggested we "throw the ball around," it was really
code for getting us out of the house. In the name of catch we were
constructing a relationship that was separate and proprietary, a relationship designed to survive whatever tumult lay ahead. It was a relationship that threatened Raynelda and that, to be blunt, she was
unable to compete with. I had a century of tradition on my side, of
metaphor and pageantry, sentiment and rationality, and Max was
lapping it up, seeing his own image reflected in the grandeur of the
game. Raynelda could not exactly object—it was just baseball,
after all—but she let me know that she was on to me, that she considered my reborn fascination little more than a scheme for hoarding
Max to myself. In her exasperation, she reached for the same phrase
that Freddy had employed, the commendation that doubled as a
taunt. To Raynelda, I was *el perfecto*. "We're always the ones with the
problems," she told me, "but you? Oh, no, never. Mister Perfect.
You've got it all figured out."

The danger, in hindsight, was not that I was driving a wedge into our household. Those fissures predated Max. I was saddling him with the presumption of success, with the weight of being my golden child. I suppose there are worse things to do to a kid. Given the choice, I would rather err on the side of high expectations. Still, by staking so much of myself on him, by insisting that Max be nothing like Freddy, I was pressuring, plotting for the day he would give me something to cheer about. Unlike my parents, who had thought of Little League as more my thing than theirs, I never considered letting Max go it alone. Baseball was too precious, too useful. By the time he reached T-Ball age, I had made a decision that would alter both of our lives. I would be my son's coach.

Chapter

Three

SIGN-UPS WERE ON SATURDAY, OUTSIDE THE CIVIC CENTER
gym. I expected to see banners, maybe uniforms, a logo, some evidence of what league we were joining and how official it was, but there was nothing, just a folding table and a carton of doughnuts. "I hope we're in the right place," I told Max. He was halfway through kindergarten, at the cusp of a life beyond his parents, our home. He still clutched my hand when we crossed the street, still expected me to fill his bath with bubbles and roll him up in a towel afterward like a burrito, but he was being introduced to the world now, saying his name, writing it, discovering the need to spell parts of it out, *K-a-t-z,* for adults perplexed by the sound. We were back in L.A.— it was 1999, my Houston tour complete—or, to be more precise, we had returned to Monterey Park, the bewildering slice of immigrant suburbia I had covered in my earliest days at the paper. Our time away had been good for me professionally, but as a family, in

the isolation of Texas, we were barely holding on. Raynelda wanted to be closer to her mom. Freddy needed a change of scenery, again. Max was ready for baseball. Funny little Monterey Park, incongruous, anomalous, more Asian than ever, turned out to be the solution.

"This is my son," I announced, prodding him to the front of the line. I was surprised by how nervous I felt, eager, unsteady. Not on Max's behalf—every child, from what I gathered, was guaranteed a spot in the league—but for myself. I was banking on being his coach. What if *I* failed to qualify? I started to recount my Little League experience, not that it was so distinguished, to tabulate all the years I had spent nurturing Max's baseball IQ, not that it mattered how skilled he was, but it was clear from the bored expressions across the table that I was selling myself to people whose hearts were not in the same place. *Thanks for sharing, guy,* they seemed to be saying, *but it's just fucking T-Ball.* Looking closer, I realized that nearly everyone in charge was Latino, mostly blue-collar, Mexican-American dads in their thirties and forties with double chins and hungover eyes. They were not jocks and they were not do-gooders. They reminded me more of bouncers at a nightclub, gatekeepers to an insular and jealous society. Their organization, I came to find, was called the Monterey Park Sports Club, a private, nonprofit corporation that had been around at least since the 1960s. It was homegrown and independent, unaffiliated with any sanctioning body—a Little League only in the generic sense—but it seemed to have the city's blessing. Or at least the Monterey Park Sports Club was doing a job the city preferred not to do itself. They thought the club could probably use me—what harm was another coach?—but they would have to get back to me on that. There was nothing else they wanted to know, nothing for me to fill out, no references, no certification, no background check that might tilt the odds in my favor. I had so much invested in this moment, in the prospect of being linked to Max's athletic development for years to come, and instead of being anointed, I had drawn a collective shrug.

In time, I would learn all about the clannishness of the Monterey Park Sports Club, its inner circle born and raised within a five-mile radius, many related by marriage, some still living in the homes they grew up in. They knew one another from church, from parochial school. As kids, a few had even played in the Monterey Park Sports Club themselves. They were, in the vernacular of Hispanic identity, *pochos*—too ethnic to be fully assimilated and too Americanized to be properly Mexican—their Spanish eroded by a generation or two of middle-class aspiration. What they eventually would learn about me would only add to their reticence: I was the writer who spoke like their grandparents, a gringo who, instead of marrying up, had given his name to a *wetback!*

Why Latinos ruled youth baseball in Monterey Park while the city's new majority scarcely participated is not something for which I have a neat answer. The sport is hugely popular in the Far East, not just as played by the pros but as an activity exactly like the one I was signing up Max for. Teams from Taiwan, Japan, and South Korea had combined, by that point, for twenty-two Little League World Series titles (compared to eight, in the same period, for the United States). Baseball *is* Asian. What I suspect, at the risk of propagating a caricature, is that the Asian immigrants of Monterey Park had traveled so far and sacrificed so much, always for the future of their children, that every hour was measured by its potential for advancement. The kids I knew from Max's school were booked solid on Saturdays—piano, math, Chinese lessons—and the commitments that baseball would have demanded were a frivolity their families did not believe they could afford. For Mexican Americans, especially those with roots in East L.A., the Monterey Park Sports Club represented just the opposite: mobility, status, an antidote to the dysfunctions of the barrio next door.

Some of these issues were familiar to me already, dynamics I had learned to negotiate as an *L.A. Times* apprentice, stationed in the old, twice-a-week San Gabriel Valley section. The San Gabriel, a twenty-five-mile stretch of subdivisions and smog between downtown and the desert, was L.A.'s other sprawling valley, less prosperous, more prosaic than the San Fernando. Or as James Ellroy, whose mother's strangled body was dumped here in 1958, has written: "The San Gabriel Valley was the rat's ass of Los Angeles County." Monterey Park was at the far west end, the only cushion between the valley's three dozen frumpy townships and East L.A., the cradle of Chicano power, a community whose population, at 98 percent Latino, was thought to be the most segregated in the state. From the outset Monterey Park fancied itself a bulwark, "a handsome little city" that, in 1924, was composed of "all Caucasians," according to the weekly *Monterey Park Progress*. That same year, the Chamber of Commerce publicly urged real estate agents to preserve Monterey Park "for the white race only," to exercise civic pride in their trans-actions by refusing to rent or sell to "undesirables." In a show of unity, twenty-five thousand people turned out for a Ku Klux Klan rally on Valley Boulevard, complete with white robes and a giant electric cross. For most of its existence, the city was best known as the birthplace of Laura Scudder's potato chips, an early sponsor of *The Lawrence Welk Show.*

Monterey Park, when I first saw it, was still hickish—there was no bookstore or cineplex or performing arts center—but it was also in the grip of its Asianification, a cultural revolution so unfamiliar, so sudden and thorough, that it was nearly complete before anyone grasped what was happening. Leery of communist China's rising clout and enticed by changes in U.S. immigration policy, jet-age ex-iles from Hong Kong and Taipei had begun pouring in—a profes-sional class, with money to invest, that was not about to huddle in L.A.'s cramped and seedy Chinatown. They were being lured to Monterey Park by a Guilin-born, Oregon State–educated civil engineer named Frederic Hsieh, who recognized that the town's self-imposed blinders, its cultivation of a dowdy middle American air, had allowed property values to become artificially depressed. He began snatching up land, millions upon millions of dollars of un-derutilized real estate, and urging others to do the same. In an over-seas advertising blitz, now a fixture of Monterey Park folklore, Hsieh promoted his would-be boomtown as the "Chinese Beverly Hills." In the 1970s, the Asian population jumped from 7,000, to 19,000. In the 1980s, it jumped again, from 19,000 to 34,000. A 7.7-square-mile community had become home to three Chinese newspapers, twenty-six banks, most of them Chinese-owned, more than fifty Chinese real estate agencies, and hundreds of Chinese restaurants, bakeries, video stores, and curio shops. As the pace accelerated, Monterey Park bristled with rumors and banalities, some specious, some undeniable, about Chinese drivers, about Chinese accents, about courtesies and aesthetics, and resistance caving in to satchels of cash. Developers employed *feng shui* masters to align their projects—doorways, staircases, street directions—with the cosmos. Superstitious home buyers petitioned city hall, at $500 a pop, to change addresses bearing ominous numbers (four = death) to auspicious combinations (eight = prosperity). A councilwoman, one of the last Anglos to be elected, called it the "rape of Monterey Park."

They put up a fight, those old-timers, at least long enough to make headlines. They tried to pass ordinances declaring English the city's official language, which failed, and requiring business signs to include at least two-thirds Roman characters, which succeeded. They battled for a moratorium on commercial and multifamily construction. They printed bumper stickers that read "Will the Last American to Leave Monterey Park Please Bring the Flag?" For all the fury, though, their protests proved to be more death rattle than xenophobic backlash. White folks were packing up—in many cases cashing in—grousing about the changeover and yet, by refusing to stick around, also encouraging it. The city was not growing especially fast; if anything, it resembled a revolving door, the exodus making room for the influx. There was nothing quite like it, a petri dish for a generation of demographers and political scientists: the first city on the North American mainland with an Asian majority, the first U.S. city governed by an Asian majority on its council, the first city with a female Chinese-American mayor. At the *L.A. Times,* where a team of reporters chronicled those superlatives, we called it "America's first suburban Chinatown."

Writing about Monterey Park was more or less my break at the paper, before gangs, before metro or national, my first chance to prove that I could wheedle myself into a place I did not belong. I explored it the way that in my off hours I was exploring the Spanish-speaking world, eating, drinking, flirting, risking, looking for a connection that would make me seem more humane than just another reporter. I discovered Shaoxing wine and three-snake soup and a newfangled entertainment system called karaoke. One night I was invited to the home of a Chinese real estate tycoon for a potluck. After the scotch had loosened his guests, a coterie of high-flying professionals, our host broke out the karaoke machine. As the microphone made its way around, I smiled at the bouncy Cantonese pop songs, the occasional Beatles or Sinatra number belted out in flawless English. When it was my turn, I held up my hands in protest. "No, no, no, no, please," I said. The second time I was offered the mike, I waved it off again and mumbled something about being an observer, not a performer. By the third pass, it was clear that I was not playing by Chinese sing-along rules. "I, really, uh, don't—" I hemmed. But I was drowned out by groans and boos. I could sense my cheeks getting flushed, my scalp starting to tingle. Besides fretting about my ability to carry a tune, I had the more practical hurdle of being a soloist without a catalog. For some reason, there was no video screen, no lyrics to follow. "—uh, really, know any songs." Everyone was crowing, calling for more Chivas. It was mortification versus dishonor. With panic setting in, I drew the pity of one guest, an American who did missionary work in Hong Kong. He offered to whisper the words in my ear if I could find the courage to sing them. What choice did I have? My rescuer cupped his hand. There was not even background music.

"*Aaa—*" I began. My voice quavered through the amp. "*—maaaz—*" Sweat was rolling off my eyebrows. "*—eee-ing—*" I was losing muscular control of my face. "*—grace.*"

It was lunacy. I was singing a Christian hymn, a cappella, to a flock of immigrant millionaires on the Gold Mountain of Monterey Park. They were so tickled by my distress, they demanded an encore. Before I could be excused, I had to give them "Yankee Doodle."

As a story, Monterey Park was fascinating, but as a place to live, not worth a second thought. I was in Echo Park, next to The Sunset, in the Latino epicenter of L.A., right where I imagined a young single journalist with a smidgen of Spanish should be. My mailing address said "Los Angeles," and my area code was 213. Suburbia, Asian or not, was for the fat and comfortable, the timid and hidebound. Moving to Monterey Park would have been like admitting defeat. A decade later, there I was, at home.

The town, as I had come to see it, was bougie enough to preserve what remained of Max's innocence—test scores were high, crime rates were low—but a long way from airbrushed. On the thoroughfares of Garvey and Atlantic and Garfield, I could surf the futuristic mash of acupuncture parlors and casino excursion agencies, drift through the ginseng and taro and sandalwood, trip on the doughnut shop that served pad thai noodles, the Alpha Beta supermarket that had been reincarnated as the two-story, pagoda-roofed Shun Fat supermarket. I found an honest mechanic from Malaysia and an adorable chiropractor from Vietnam. Max's favorite teacher, Ms. Fang, was the daughter of a Taiwanese army colonel who had shepherded his family to California, when she was seven, on Christmas Day. Up in the hills, where the neighborhood turned more Japanese and Hawaiian, I could retreat to the fogeyishness of a 1961 cul-de-sac ("beautiful, close-in Monterey Park Estates," the original ads trumpeted) with a view stretching from the skyscrapers of downtown on the west to the camel humps of Catalina Island, twenty-two miles offshore, on the south. Even people who know L.A. are surprised by what you can see from my backyard. Max and I shot baskets in the driveway, threw each other pop-ups in the street. He became best friends with a boy named Alex, who was half Filipino and half East Indian. As they grew older, they would call each other "Blackness" and "Cream." Monterey Park allowed me to shelter Max without playing it safe. From the day we moved in, I have been the only white guy on our block. Max, I guess, was a close second.

The next I heard from the league, maybe two or three weeks after I had registered Max, I was being told to pick up my equipment. "I'm sorry," I said, taken aback, "you're saying I'm a coach?"

The lady who had been assigned to call me seemed almost as puzzled as I was. "Didn't you want to coach?" she asked.

"No, no, no, I mean, yes, yes," I said. "It's just that—oh, never mind. Where am I supposed to go?" She directed me to La Loma. The park turned out to be two minutes away, and I had never seen it, never even known it was there. I took Max with me. We drove down our hill to Fulton Avenue, a sliver of side street on the way to nowhere, then took our first left, up a grassy embankment, into the rises and bends of this hidden arena. I parked on what might be described as the mezzanine level of La Loma, above the street but below any of the fields. There was a merry-go-round and a couple of barbecue pits but still no sign of a diamond, of any plot flat enough to hold two teams. Max spotted the stairs before I did and scrambled for the top. "C'mon, Dad," he called. I followed, gripping the handrail as I looked over my shoulder, watching the ground disappear below. The steps seemed to go on forever, clinging to a slant of sea lavender and lantana, jagging through a forest of privet and pepper. It was all so wonderfully impractical, to enter a municipal park as if acting out a scene from *Jack and the Beanstalk*. Halfway up, I was gasping.

The largest of the diamonds, what was called Upper La Loma, was splayed across the crest. Home plate was closest to the ledge, poised to float off into the horizon, and the outfield, 290 feet away at its deepest point, was on the inland side, which dead-ended into Chuy's Nursery, a grove of palms and vines that filled the barren space under the towers that hoisted the high-voltage cables of Southern California Edison. It was a natural stadium, geologically perfect, the slopes on the third-base and first-base lines forming a right angle behind the backstop and the home run fence curling through a wall of green. The effect was at once lush and windswept: high enough to feel exposed and still camouflaged enough to remain private. "Goddamn," I whispered. "Who knew?" I walked across the dirt, from left to right, to peek over the other side, and there, maybe twenty feet below, down a rear set of stairs, was an even more secluded field, a long quad tucked into a stand of ficus and oleander.

At the far end was a diamond known as Lower La Loma, about half the size of the one above, and where its outfield ended, closer to my vantage, the grass merged into a T-Ball field. They were all empty at the moment, but it dawned on me that under the right circumstances, you could stand there and watch three games going on at once, five-year-olds lost in clover at this corner, ten-year-olds spitting seeds at the other, fifteen-year-olds brandishing metal spikes up top. Without really thinking it out, I knew instantly that I would guide Max through that circuit, that in this one extraordinary park I would see him grow into a young man.

My roster showed thirteen names, including Max and his sidekick Alex, who had asked to be teamed with us. I would have to call the other families and introduce myself: Mr. Katz? Coach Katz? Jesse? I settled on Coach Jesse, a little queer but with the right balance, I hoped, of kindliness and authority. I needed every tool I could get. With title or without, I began to realize how unprepared I was to actually do this, to be not just a teacher of the game, for which my qualifications were at best untested, but also a source of inspiration and a builder of character and the arbiter of a thousand little wrongs and slights.

I found myself entrusted with a dozen tiny people, miniature works in progress: kids with gloves on backward, shoes untied, noses running, hats covering their eyes, all of whom, at any given time, might be squeezing their knees and tugging their flies. At our first practice, I suggested that we run the bases; one child tripped and belly flopped; then another, a chain-reaction pileup at every bag. I was so accustomed to Max's pace and temperament, I had no idea how to tailor my lessons for an entire team, to keep everyone busy and encouraged at once. A few parents offered to help, which I was grateful for, but I also came to recognize that adults, no matter how well-meaning, tended to complicate my job with their own anxieties and ambitions. They pored over my lineup as if reading smoke signals from the Sistine Chapel: Who were my favorites? Where was I playing Max? Why was so-and-so's son batting first? Why was theirs stuck in the outfield? No score was kept in T-Ball, but all the grown-ups seemed to know exactly which team had won and which team had lost. I thought that Coach Jesse, if nothing else, should try to defuse those preoccupations, to be as egalitarian as possible. As much as I wanted our team to shine—and for Max to be the brightest of all—I vowed to give every player a shot at every position, at every spot in the order, regardless of how clumsy or clueless. It *was* just T-Ball. Every family had paid the same fee. I figured it was my responsibility to make certain nobody felt shorted.

Even so, I was not immune to the pressures of putting on a show. At every game my audience crowded the backstop, camcorders on standby, jockeying to bear witness to their child's debut—that first hit, to many of the moms and dads, no less momentous than the first step or the first word. As the coach, I was expected to pitch. We used the tee only after three misses. I would get down on one knee, a few paces away, and hold the ball up like a scoop of vanilla, hoping to draw my batter's attention. The idea was to keep it simple, no motion, no spin, just cock from the elbow and float my wrist forward. I could hear the chants: *C'mon now . . . don't be scared . . . just relax . . . stay focused . . . choke up . . . keep your eye on the ball . . . take the bat off your shoulder . . . bend your knees . . . raise your elbow . . . that's right . . . hit one for me,* papito!

I wanted to make my players look good, to serve them up a nice easy pitch, just as Abel had done for Max, except that at that very instant, right as I was about to let it go, all the hope, all my doubts, all that projected angst, would somehow take possession of my arm. My shoulder would grow leaden. My fingers would turn numb. It was like shooting pool and muffing the break, the cue ball squibbing lamely across the felt. "Watch out!" I would cry. None of my kids ever budged. Pitchers, in their experience, were supposed to be allies, not saboteurs. I plunked them in the ribs, in the belly, in the back, in the thigh, and, on two or three occasions, squarely in the nuts. My throws, fortunately, were soft and the T-Ball was spongy, but not enough to ease my dismay. If I beaned Max, which I did, he and I could laugh it off later. If I beaned his teammates—and by the end of the season few had escaped my errant arm—that was another matter: I was tampering with someone else's memories. I wondered if there was a coach's equivalent to the Hippocratic oath. I might not ever be the Joe Torre of Monterey Park, but the least I could do was to do no harm.

As I reacquainted myself with the tribulations of Little League, I began to form some theories about human nature, about the traits that unite and divide us, that dictate our propensities and aversions. The great difference among the parents I was meeting had little to do with race or religion, language or culture. We were not split among liberals and conservatives, the rich and the poor. It was the question of restraint versus latitude. Do you subscribe to the notion that structure—order, formality, regulation—frees the spirit? Or quashes it? Do you prize independence for your child—creativity, dissent—or do your values favor obedience, duty over individuality? It may be that I was making false distinctions. In later years, I would start to understand the ways in which those categories could overlap without contradicting. At the moment, though, it was a helpful tool for making sense of my foray into La Loma society. I discovered that I had endeared myself to some of the parents—the milder families, you might call them—who were happy just to be in the park, to be around baseball, and did not expect me to forge their kids into prodigies. I became known in those circles as the Patient Coach, accommodating, even-keeled, nonjudgmental. It seemed normal to me, but much was made of the fact that I never yelled. The same qualities put me in conflict with the other kind of Monterey Park Sports Club family, folks who were looking for rigor, for a degree of achievement and acclaim that perhaps did not exist in the rest of their lives. Those people wanted their kids to be pushed, punished even, and when they happened to land on my team—under the direction of the Soft Coach—their contempt was hardly concealed.

In our second year, Max and I moved up to the Rookie division, which was for seven- and eight-year-olds, our first taste of something that resembled real baseball. I was relieved to learn that my players would be doing their own pitching, until it became apparent that none of them was any better suited than I had been in T-Ball. Our games turned into ponderous walkathons, demoralizing to be a part of and excruciating to watch. Max was as erratic as anyone I put on the mound. His pitches skidded into the dirt a foot before the plate or sailed a foot over the umpire's head. He would walk the bases loaded, then start walking in runs. To keep Rookie games from unraveling, the league imposed a four-run limit per team per inning, and more than once, Max gave them all up on consecutive walks—seven bases on balls in a row—without ever recording an out. He was just as flummoxed with the bat. The season was sixteen games. It took him fifteen to get his first hit. I studied him for signs of despair: Had I rushed him into competition, set him up for a collision with failure? If Max was overmatched, what business did I have instructing anyone else's kid?

I started giving a stump speech that season, reminding my players that years later nobody would remember how our team performed. Scores and standings were not necessarily within our control, anyway. What would be remembered was how it *felt* to be on our team—the joy of suiting up, of testing limits, of honoring tradition, of cheering one another on. That was the only measure of success that mattered. I mainly believed it. As the losses mounted, one of the dads, the father of our most promising player, pulled me aside and suggested that I cut the tutti-frutti crap. "I don't know what you think you're doing," he told me, "but these kids need to learn baseball." He was built like a caveman, with arms that spilled from his tank top like brontosaurus steaks. I had picked his son first in the draft, after securing spots for Max and Alex, but even that kid was struggling, as if afraid that every swing or throw would earn him a dressing-down.

"I guess, you know, I'd like them to do better," I said. "But— sheesh—look around." We had one kid with such severe vision problems that he had to shake his head from side to side to focus. (I always thought he was telling me no, but he was just trying to see who I was.) We had another kid who was merely cross-eyed, which I found easier to overlook after I met his mom, who had pneumatic tits and moonlighted as a stripper. We also had an enormously fat boy and two bashful sisters and a stubborn Korean kid named Stanley, who could not have cared less about baseball but whose father thought he needed fresh air. "Seriously," I said. "You're kind of at the mercy of the cards you're dealt."

"No, you have to demand more," he told me. "You're too easy on these kids. Be the damn coach."

With half the season to go, he pulled his son. I never saw them again. It would have been easy to dismiss him as a jackass dad, another glory hound living through his kid, but the losses were weighing on me, too. I hated leading any kid to slaughter. As the summer dragged on, I began to wonder if he was right, if the values I had tried to impart—fairness, humor, tolerance—had doomed my team. If I was dooming Max.

It took another year and two new players to show me how to be the coach I wanted to be. Jonathan Muñoz was the first, a pitcher of imposing stature and innate grace, coveted by every team. Even at eight, he was that exceptional, a full head taller than Max and armed with a fastball that topped fifty miles per hour, which, when thrown from thirty-eight feet away, made him look frighteningly like Nolan Ryan. But Jonathan was also reserved and sensitive, a classical musician, home-schooled according to the principles of the Calvary Chapel. His father, Jose, an L.A. County health inspector, had devoted himself to making up for the lapses of his own dad, a bartender who worked nights. He always had time for Jonathan, for anyone at La Loma who needed a hand. He was the tallest man in the park but a gentle soul, with a floppy safari hat and a toothy smile and a *mijo* or *mija* for every child, Latino or not. Another parent might have put Jonathan on a fast track, enlisting a private coach or shopping him to a year-round travel team. Because Jose had watched me lose—Jonathan had inflicted some of our beatings—he knew that, even in adversity, I would never belittle his son. When we returned for our second year of Rookie ball, the Muñoz family made clear that Jonathan would be playing for me.

The other charm was Carlos Zuñiga, a fourteen-year-old in a second-grader's body. If his condition had a medical term, I never learned it. He was a skeleton, frail and chilled, with speech impairments and a chunky hearing aid wrapped around each ear. "Hungry . . . wanna go home . . . watch TV," Carlos would say every time I saw him. His mother, Dorothy, a schoolteacher in East L.A., wanted him to live as unrestricted a life as possible, and she had enrolled him in baseball against the wishes of Carlos's father, her ex, who feared his son would get hurt or ridiculed. It was one of the beauties of a "rec" league that no child was rejected, and it was heartening to learn that the goons in charge of La Loma were not merely allowing Carlos to play but assigning him to a tamer division with kids half his age. I was just a little surprised to see his registration form mixed up with my paperwork. I already had drafted my team, and Carlos was not on it. All of a sudden he was. I had no idea how the Monterey Park Sports Club went about its business, but I knew that someone, aware of my reputation for leniency, had made me the patsy.

With Jonathan throwing, I was afraid to put anyone else's child behind the plate, so I taught Max to be a catcher. I bought him his first jockstrap and cup, a delicate purchase that required multiple trips to Big 5 before he found one that did not look like a codpiece. I decided against breaking the news to him that the rest of his catcher's gear—face mask, chest protector, shin guards—was known, in baseball parlance, as the "tools of ignorance." Max never became Jonathan's buddy; he was too much of a wisecracker, and Jonathan much too earnest. But they were what I like to think of as consummate teammates, feeding off each other, dueling for respect, refusing to let the other down. By example, Jonathan propelled Max in ways I was unable to, and Max, like a sparring partner, at least kept Jonathan from getting complacent. We won the championship that season, from last to first in a single year, although by championship I mean we were the best of the Monterey Park Sports Club's four Rookie teams. I had hoped for more of a contest in the finale, but the other team was hobbled. Its star pitcher, a boy named Chubby, had been playing Mission Impossible on the La Loma slopes a day before the big game and impaled his thigh on an acacia bush.

What I remember most from that season were not the trophies we hoisted or the championship T-shirts we draped on the kids but the sight of Carlos: parading out of the dugout, thumping and waving his bat, daring every pitcher to blow one by him. He was a ham. Nobody expected him to hit, so he gave us the lampoon version of a slugger, at once acquiescing to his infirmity and subverting it. As the ball approached, he would lose his nerve and bail out of the batter's box, flailing from a safe distance. I started accompanying him to the plate and drawing a line in the dirt with my heel, an arrow straight from his front foot to the pitcher. "Don't step away," I would tell him. "Step forward." Carlos would grunt, then go back to his theatrics. He must have struck out twenty or thirty times that way, game after game, week after week, glancing at me after each miss to make sure I was still in on the joke. I would flash him a thumbs-up. *You can do it, Carlitos.* He would grin and pound the plate some more. Then one day, like celestial bodies crossing paths in the void, bat somehow managed to make contact with ball. Maybe, given enough swings, it was bound to happen, a mathematical inevitability. I choose to believe that, even if just for a moment, he gave himself permission to try. *Run, Carlitos, run!* Everyone was screaming, on both sides of the field. Dorothy was in tears. We were witnessing something glorious and irrevocable—a grounder up the middle, all his. I got to first base almost as fast as Carlos did and wrapped him in my arms.

Any adult who has firsthand experience in youth sports, as the parent of a player, as a coach, as the spouse of a coach, which is to say tens of millions of otherwise functional Americans, knows that the amount of time commandeered by their child's team is beyond all reason or explanation. Getting to the park in advance of, say, a 5 P.M. practice, especially if you have a Los Angeles–grade commute, requires a career that can be neglected on short notice and for months at a stretch. A 7:30 P.M. game can kill off dinner, homework, and the prospect of sex in one fell swoop. Add in multiple sports (I had begun coaching Max's basketball team every winter) or multiple kids (I had exercised discretion in at least this department) and your life, to a degree that noninitiates tend to find sanctimonious, revolves around opening ceremonies and fund-raisers and snack duty and stain removal. As I cycled through the seasons, I came to find that I actually enjoyed surrendering my calendar to those commitments, sign-ups in February, tryouts in March, first pitch in April, team picnic in May, playoffs in June, trophies in July. I was locking in Max, ensuring that at least three or four days a week I would get to choose him over everything. I could delay work, avoid chores, sidestep Freddy, retreat from Raynelda, dodge *any* obligation that was daunting or disagreeable—and best of all, under the cloak of baseball, I could disguise whatever self-serving motives I harbored. I was just being a good dad.

After my second summer at La Loma, I left the *L.A. Times* for *Los Angeles* magazine. I had wanted to expand my repertoire as a storyteller but also to escape the daily requisites of a newspaper; at a monthly, I figured, it would be easier to sneak off to the park. After my third summer at La Loma, our championship season, I told Raynelda our marriage was done. It had taken me a long time to get to that point, maybe longer than it should have. We really had tried—a relationship born in a cantina, rushed into action, cleaved by a stepson, and conducted almost entirely in Spanish had lasted thirteen years! If you multiplied that by the degree of difficulty, Raynelda and I had practically grown old together. I hated to admit defeat about anything, and even as our frustration with each other mounted, I thought that giving up would somehow reveal me for a fraud: If I was going to be worthy of my barrio pass, of being an honorary Chicano, how would it look to be spurning the immigrant girl who had turned to me for sanctuary?

We had bridged so many gaps, mended so many breaches, but the one we could not get past was our children, the two boys, separated by a decade and half the Americas, whose bedrooms were across the hall from us, one door open, the other door shut. Even in

Monterey Park nobody could get through to Freddy, not me, not his mom. He flunked out of Mark Keppel, the high school Max would be attending one day, and he found nothing to take its place, except weed and sleep. Mystery summonses came for him in our mailbox: failures to appear, fines gone delinquent. For years I had been anticipating his eighteenth birthday, holding on, trusting that if I could just make it until Freddy was a legal adult, I would at last be granted some leverage. *Respect the rules of the house or live somewhere else.* But the date came and went, then another birthday after that, and suddenly I understood that I had been fooling myself, that Freddy's inertia was always going to win out. He had nowhere else to go, nothing to look forward to, and his mom, who had cut the strings when she should not have, could not bring herself to do it when she had to. Freddy was her son, and that was that. It was loyal and tragic. I did not see it at the time, but Max, in a very direct way, was the beneficiary of all this, of the debacle we were living. What could go wrong with a child was not theoretical in our home. Neither was the cost of having a dad, whether biological and absent or custodial and disgruntled, who could not express love to his son. I would like to think that I would have been an attentive father to Max no matter the circumstances, but I have no doubt that I became the father to him that I am because of what I had to endure with Freddy, and what Freddy had to endure with me. I was making amends. Everything I did and felt for Max—and by extension everything I did and felt for La Loma—was magnified by the one boy I failed to reach.

I am not sure how I persuaded her to leave. One of us had to. I just asked. She agreed without a fight. Maybe she was acting on emotion, sick of my codes and judgments, dying to do as she pleased. For her sake and mine, I prefer to think of it as Raynelda at her most deliberative and generous: for her to concede that the perfect one, who after all was not so perfect, was still the parent with whom Max was most likely to thrive. If she had dug in her heels, we might still be together. I never could have moved out and left him behind. We sent Max to Portland for a week, and while he was with my parents, Raynelda found an apartment for her and Freddy a few minutes away. I rented a U-Haul. I thought Max had been exposed to enough already, without having to witness his mom pack up her things. Some years later, in a fit of maternal pique, Raynelda announced that we had tricked Max by taking such drastic measures in his absence, and she was holding me responsible for the deceit. She still never challenged our living arrangement, but she was letting me know, in her way, that the decision had been far from painless.

After my fourth summer at La Loma, I turned forty. I felt depleted, all those years as an intermediary, a fixer, trying to hold together what was falling apart. I needed to step away, to stop being so accommodating—patient, soft—and do something just for me. I decided on a birthday trip to Cuba, to see what remained of the revolution while Fidel was still alive, to wallow in music and rum and Hemingway fantasies and, if it must be spelled out, to exercise my Spanish, my Latin American know-how, in hopes of earning some female company. It had been a long time since I was single, since I had pursued Raynelda, and I had been hesitant to put myself back on the market. I had no idea what I wanted out of a relationship, if indeed I wanted one, and I was not yet prepared to navigate the minefields of dating in full view of Max. I am not sure what I thought I was protecting him from. Friends suggested that it might be good for me, for us, to begin allowing women into my life again, that by opening myself up I might demonstrate to Max that romance was still something to cherish. After everything we had weathered, though, I was determined that nothing should ever come between me and my boy, that he should never have to share me, to feel what Freddy had, to be second. Cuba, if I was lucky, would allow me to test the waters, even take a plunge, without having to worry about covering my tracks. I would be at a safe distance, on an embargoed island.

As a journalist, I could have traveled on a visa, made the whole journey legit, but I was not going as a journalist, and I was in no mood to be encumbered or beholden. I opted for the underground route, from L.A. to Havana via Cancún. I was planning to be gone for ten days, the longest I had ever been away from Max. I asked Raynelda to look after him—she agreed to return, temporarily, to the house—then I disappeared.

Cuba was a wreck: improvised, archaic, moldering, depraved, all the qualities that in my life after Portland I had learned to embrace. For a dollar I got to see the Cuban national baseball team play Japan at the Estadio Latinoamericano. The score escapes me, but I was riveted by a white owl, with a rat hooked in its talons, that kept swooping across the field in the middle of the game. The next day I took a bus from Havana to Trinidad, a five-and-a-half-hour ride through sugarcane. It was a colonial landmark, like a mini French Quarter, with zany colors and wrought-iron curlicues and an ancient slave-trade pulse. Next to the main plaza, across from the cathedral, was a wide terraced staircase, the Escalinata, which became an open-air dance hall after dark. I ordered a drink and sat on the ground, and before long I was talking to a chain-smoking playboy named Yiovanny. He had a silver ring in his left ear and a racing-stripe goatee. He reminded me of a Caribbean pirate. We had a beer together, and then he pointed out a slender young lady a few steps below. She was dazzling, a *café con leche* angel, with obsidian eyes and a dimpled chin. I had been in Trinidad for all of an hour. "She saw you come in," Yiovanny whispered conspiratorially.

If there were alarms going off, I ignored them. I did not ask myself why I was being singled out, what I had done right, other than look a lot like a rich foreigner, to catch her attention. I did not ask myself about the politics of playing along, if by allowing myself to mistake her availability for desire, I was about to turn myself into a stereotype, to celebrate the big four-O as an ugly American. All I knew was that everyone back in L.A. had told me to be careful and I wanted the opposite, to be immoderate and impulsive, to give myself a break for the first time in a long while. I sat down next to her and offered my hand. Like Yiovanny, she had a great crazy home-cooked name: Yannarys. She was twenty-three—dear Lord—and studying folkloric dance.

"I'm Jesse," I said.

"Yessy?" she repeated.

I asked if I could buy her a drink. She said yes, only not here, in public. That would raise suspicions—every dark female in the presence of a white traveler was presumed to be for hire, which she most adamantly was not—and since Yannarys was in Trinidad on a scholarship, an ingenue from the provinces being groomed for the cabarets and floor shows by the socialist machine, she could not afford to be taken note of by the cops. Normally she would not even be out, she explained, but her cousin was visiting, a judo champion named Yony, who was right behind her. He was built like the Incredible Hulk, except that instead of green he was the color of charcoal, and he had a speech impediment that made me think of Mike Tyson. "Start walking," Yannarys said, "and we'll catch up to you."

This was getting weird, maybe dangerous, three spontaneous friends, all with their mess of Ys, leading me down a cobblestone street, to points unknown, through a town I had yet to see in day-light. It might not have been a transaction in the crudest sense, but they were dangling access and adventure and the prospect of affection—the keys to Cuba's inner sanctum—and I was prepared, happily, to pick up the tab. A few minutes later, Yannarys was at my side, threading her fingers through mine. Whatever she saw in me, it felt good. As long as we were in the shadows, Yannarys stayed close. At intersections and under street lamps, she pulled away and looped her arm through Yony's. She went back and forth like this, me, him, me, him, until we reached a dingy ice-cream shop. It was closed, but the night watchman, and why there was a night watchman I have no idea, allowed us in and agreed to sell us cans of Bucanero beer, and why there was beer in an ice-cream shop I have no idea, either. I was just glad not to be in some government-run clip joint. Twice our host thought he heard police outside and whisked us into a storeroom, where we sat on overturned buckets and, with stifled giggles, continued our illicit party. By the time we stumbled out, it was 3 A.M. and the only place still open was a twenty-four-hour gas station on the road to the transnational highway. There was a jukebox and more to drink and, apparently, a libertine vibe that did not exist in the strange nineteenth-century caste system of Trinidad proper. I grabbed Yannarys under the fluorescent lights, and we danced to Elvis Crespo's *"Suavemente"* between fast-food tabletops, twirling past Yony and Yiovanny, all of us high and howling, feeding off our instant trust. Yannarys took a gulp of beer and pressed her lips against mine. I kissed her, and she filled my mouth. We swallowed and dripped and kissed again. *"Feliz cumpleaños,"* she said. It was juvenile, maybe even shrewd, yet as lovely a present as I could have asked for.

If Yannarys and I were to consummate our courtship, as I understood the rural mores from Yony and Yiovanny, we would have to get out of town, back to Havana. I asked for their blessing. They reminded me that Yannarys was young—this I had not forgotten—and made me promise to take good care of her, as if she were their lone asset and I was being allowed to appraise its worth. If we were stopped by anyone in uniform, I was to say that we were a couple, already engaged. If I failed to be convincing, Yannarys could be arrested. She turned out to be anything but a freak or a pro, just a wishful country girl, a natural *guajira,* taking the biggest chance of her life. We found a bedroom for rent, on the black market, and went shopping, for clothes, toiletries, jewelry, even though she never asked, never implied it was expected. I felt like I owed it to Yannarys, and if not to her, then to myself. I think she lived on $12 a month.

With only two nights left together, I could feel her melancholia starting to well. She told me that she loved me. I had been bold and indulgent. Now it was time to be careful. I told her that I loved her, too. *Te quiero.* I could say that and mean it. She wanted to know when I was coming back. That was going to be trickier. I explained that I wanted to very much, that maybe I would if I could get away again, but that I had a job and a son and a couple of teams to coach, and, well, I did not want to lie, to make a promise I could not keep. "You're the best thing that ever happened to me," Yannarys said. She was getting ready to cry. I wished that it were so. I could have been, maybe, if this was 1988 and not 2002, if I was still looking for love in The Sunset, determined to be anything but the unworldly boy that I was, and not a forty-year-old man who had already done this once and was just barely getting himself right. I had used my income and nationality and cultural aptitude to win her over, to give her hope, and now I wished I had the power to make her more realistic, to grant her a perspective that was not hers and that she could not have been expected to have. On our final night, I figured out how to use the phone in our room and called Max. I had not spoken to him since I had left.

"What's up, Daddy-O?" he said.

"I miss you, champ."

I had never felt so far away from him. I hung up and started to tremble. It was my turn to cry, a flood of exhaustion, of guilt, of confusion, of loss. Yannarys was certain I must have received terrible news. "What's wrong, baby? Tell me. Please. Is it your son?" All I could do was shake my head, choking on my sobs. The next morning I flagged a taxi, one of those time-warp Chevys that survived the Cold War. On the way to the airport, we stopped at the bus station and I bought Yannarys a return ticket to Trinidad. She made me swear I would call as soon as I got home. She did not actually have a phone (or a computer or an e-mail address or the ability to receive parcels or currency), but if I dialed the neighbors, they would see if she was around. I kissed her goodbye. She was still clinging to the illusion that I could be her rescuer, the broker of yet another green card. As I headed for the cab, she gave it one last try: "Tell your son that his new stepmother says hi." Oh, my. How could she have known that was exactly the wrong thing to say? I was trying to keep Max out of it, and she thought he might be her way in.

Yannarys meant no harm. This was serious business, survival. She could not afford to be just fucking around—and in that instant, I saw clearly just how little I could afford to be doing it, either. Dating, sex, love, remarriage: It could all wait. It would have to wait. Max did not need a dog for a dad or a pretty young thing filling in for his mom. I had shielded him from so much, extricated us from such a fiasco, and now that we were on our own, a couple of bachelors, this was no time to be trifling with that bond. I had a son to raise. My work had just begun.

Chapter

Four

BASEBALL WOULD BE STARTING IN A COUPLE OF MONTHS, our fifth La Loma season. Max and I were returning to Single A, the nine- and ten-year-old division. In our initial Single A season, we had made it to the championship series, only to be swept by a team of older, rougher kids. I was getting used to the idea of winning, of proving that nice guys need not finish last, and I was eager to come back for that second year, as we had in Rookies, to trade on our experience. I still had Jonathan, who had grown half a foot, and Carlos, who was in high school already and appeared to be shrinking. I would be getting back Colin Yee, a polite and fragile boy who hyperventilated every time he stepped into the batter's box—chest heaving, cheeks puffing—but who could throw a clothesline from right field to home. I would also have another year with Natalie Peña, as girlie of a girl as there was—she was forever trying to braid Max's hair in the dugout—and yet a stud at second, turning double plays with a flick of her glove. With my son calling the pitches and Alex, a speedster who was both goofy and daring, batting leadoff, I was rather certain, actually, that we were the team to beat. It was 2003. I had been back from Cuba only a month or two. The season could not start soon enough.

Every year there was a flyer, the signal that registration was under way. Thousands would get printed and distributed to the schools. I never knew where they came from, how they got there, who had the authority to decide when baseball was going to be played. One would just arrive in Max's backpack every February, like some Groundhog Day ritual, a reminder that spring was near. Only this year February came and went without a flyer. "Are you sure you didn't get one?" I asked Max.

He was in fourth grade and developing an admirable regard for the esoterica of the game. His favorite Dodger, or ex-Dodger at that point, was a journeyman relief pitcher named Mike Fetters, not because Fetters was particularly good but because he had one of the most outlandish windups we had ever seen. The guy threw only seventy-nine innings in his L.A. stint, but they gave Max years of delight: Fetters standing sideways on the rubber, Fetters huffing like a weight lifter before the clean and jerk, Fetters scowling, Fetters snapping his head ninety degrees toward the plate—a motion so abrupt and unnatural, it could have been borrowed from *The Exorcist*. On one of Max's annual trips to Portland, my mom arranged for him to throw out the first pitch at a Beavers game. Max claimed that he was going to do it Fetters-style, a performance he worked on for hours in our driveway. "Look, Dad! Who am I?" he would say, snorting and grimacing and wrenching his neck. When at last he found himself in the stadium, in front of a crowd that *The Oregonian* put at 7,534, the enormity of the occasion sunk in. It is the only pitch he has ever thrown that I was not on hand to see, but from what I am told, Max played it straight. At any rate, if there had been a flyer, he would have known.

Basketball season was in progress, and I started asking around the gyms, hoping someone would have the answer. Mostly I got smirks. Even though both programs fell under the banner of the Monterey Park Sports Club, they functioned as separate entities—separate leadership, separate finances—and I was about to learn why. The basketball commissioner had a slow, deliberate Mister Rogers kind of demeanor. He worked for a Rocketdyne supplier, designing flight systems, and communicated to his coaches via intricately tabbed spreadsheets. The league reflected him. Basketball families tended to be more refined, more affluent, and compared to La Loma's enrollment, relatively more Asian. A lot of the top players, in fact, spent the rest of the year in an exclusive Japanese-American league, the Community Youth Council, which was formed in the aftermath of the internment camps that tarnished World War II–era California. Each CYC team followed strict—and if anyone were to mount a challenge, probably indefensible—racial quotas. They were, for that reason, unwritten, but the way it was explained to me, five of the eight players had to be of Japanese ancestry; two could be of Asian, if non-Japanese, descent; and one was allowed to be of any background: the *hakujin* exemption. Max once was offered that lone slot on a team that Alex (who qualified for a pan-Asian opening) played for, but we hesitated, unsure about making a year-round commitment, and there was never again a vacancy.

The Monterey Park Sports Club's baseball program, by contrast, was considered makeshift and brusque, haphazard even on its best day. That was a pretty fair assessment, too, of the man I had understood to be the commissioner, Bob Pasos, a payroll clerk who was crusty and patronizing and shaped like a keg. He had been running La Loma since I first arrived, except that he sometimes claimed not to be running it. Whenever things went haywire—if umpires failed to show or raffle prizes vanished—he acted as though he were the one inconvenienced, put out by the avalanche of complaints. "If you think you can do better," he would say to anyone within earshot, "be my guest." At the end of the previous season, in 2002, hundreds of people had gathered on the upper field for the closing ceremony, only to find that the trophies had never been delivered. As the muttering began to sound more like mutiny, Bob spotted me at the edge of the grass, rolling my eyes. I was still a puzzle to him, not anyone he cared to welcome into the fold, but he knew by then I was a writer. "I need you to go up there, man, and say something," he told me through clenched teeth. "You'll find the right words." I am not sure why I agreed. I guess I was flattered. The old guard had recognized something in me, a magnanimity, a susceptibility, that served its interests. I cleared my throat and stepped toward the crowd. Not only had the trophies been bungled, nobody had bothered to set up a PA. That was Monterey Park baseball for you. I had to stand there, alone, at the pitcher's mound, and shout my apology, covering for a league that was still playing me for a chump.

Weeks ticked by. No flyer, not even a hint. I kept pestering. Baseball had to start soon. *It did, right?* I sought out another of the Monterey Park Sports Club's lieutenants, a disarmingly soft-spoken bruiser named Frank Piña. He was a more gracious figure than Bob—Frank's grandson had been on my T-Ball team, and the whole family agreed that the child, who was sallow and slight, seemed to respond to my relaxed approach—but he also had a more complicated hand in the league. Frank appeared to run whatever Bob chose not to. He processed registration forms, his wife managed the snack bar, they stored equipment at their home in the off-season. Bob, in turn, made sure the Monterey Park Sports Club bought its uniforms every year from the same East L.A. apparel shop, a bargain-basement operation in which Frank happened to have an interest. As far as I knew, nobody ever questioned that arrangement. Frank always promised a fair price. Had someone wanted to point out the potential for conflict—the pitfalls of a charitable organization awarding contracts to its own officers—they would have discovered that Frank also served on Monterey Park's Recreation and Parks Commission, appointed by city hall to help monitor the league he was at least partly in charge of. I did not grasp all the ramifications myself at the time. I just wanted to get back to La Loma. "You don't know how much that park means to me and

Max," I told Frank. I expected him to be equally preoccupied. Instead he seemed wary of my insistence. "Maybe what we need," Frank said, "is to just skip a year."

I was stunned. That was not an option. Max was a kid, still learning the game, growing into his body—a year was an eternity for him. We had too much invested to take a hiatus. We had a championship to win! It would be a while before I caught on, but once I realized how thoroughly the Monterey Park Sports Club had been trampled, I think I understood: Nobody wanted a meddler, a newcomer whose allegiances were untested, to go rooting around in their dirt.

A month had been lost. Sign-ups should have been completed already, and now it was looking as though they might never begin. I felt like I was the only guy in town who cared about this bumbling little baseball league. Where was the outrage, the urgency? How could it be allowed to simply slink into extinction? I called up Alex's dad, Todd Ullah, and invited him over for a beer. Our children had brought us together—every season of baseball and basketball since the boys were in kindergarten, Todd had volunteered as my assistant—but in time our conversations traveled beyond sports. I considered him my first Monterey Park friend. Todd had grown up in black Detroit, a jazz trumpeter with a 1970s fro. He could play the soul brother, once even touring with Stevie Wonder's band, but his real name was Athaur Rahman Ullah and his parents owned a restaurant called Kashmir. With a doctorate in education from UCLA, Todd recently had been promoted to the upper echelons of the Los Angeles Unified School District, overseeing the science curriculum for the city's sixty-plus high schools and ninety or so middle schools. For someone who handled tens of millions of dollars in public funds, he was hilariously absentminded. He had four children, all with names that started with A, and if he wanted to get the attention of Alex, his youngest, he usually had to scroll through the other three before he arrived at a match.

Sitting at my kitchen table, I laid out what I believed to be true about the league—that it was in shambles, even if we did not yet know to what extent; that the culprits were all running for cover, even if we could not precisely assess blame; that a season, a crown, a tradition, was about to be lost and the chances of salvaging it were shrinking with each passing day. Getting mixed up in La Loma's internal machinations no doubt would come at a price. We would be tested in ways we could not possibly anticipate. But look at us: We were professionals, a Ph.D. and a reporter, with stable incomes and, if we pushed our luck, flexible schedules. Who better to pull this off? "I might regret saying this," I told Todd, "but I really think it's up to you and me." Before Todd could object, I cracked a couple more beers. We found ourselves reminiscing, about the four years we had already spent together at La Loma—Todd went back further, his older kids having played there before I came to town—about our own Little League memories. We talked about taking Max and Alex to another program, in a neighboring city. We could always find a park someplace else. What we treasured, though, was not just the game, not just the opportunity to watch our boys compete and progress. Monterey Park was home. La Loma, for better or worse, had become ours. "If we skip this season," Todd said, "we may never have baseball here again." We drank in silence. That pretty much settled it.

There was something a bit presumptuous, even comical, about us two, a Muslim and a Jew, coming to the rescue of a Mexican league in a Chinese city. Nobody invited us. Nobody elected us. I was commissioner by default. Todd was my deputy. It was like taking over a ghost ship. Before he left that night, we decided our first order of business was to create the flyer. We had no permits for the park. We had no money in the bank. We had no rules or bylaws or articles of incorporation. But if we announced that sign-ups were about to begin, the season would exist, at least on paper. That would buy us the time we needed to figure out how to make it real. I designed the flyer on my computer. I picked May 10 as opening day. The wording came out a little cocky: BASEBALL IS BACK AND BETTER THAN EVER.

I am not sure when I broke the news to my boss. I think I

waited until it was too late to turn back. If he objected, I wanted the stakes to be high—the blood of the league to be, in a manner of speaking, on his hands. "I need to tell you something," I began, "but you have to promise first not to kill me." Kit Rachlis had long hair and a speckled beard and silver wire-rim glasses, which gave him a bit of a late-1980s Eric Clapton semblance. He was wise about words and even wiser about writers, about our peculiar mix of obsessiveness and doubt and ego. The summer I joined him at *Los Angeles* magazine he brought his daughter, Austen, to La Loma to catch one of Max's games. We waited for an umpire, but none showed, and Austen, who played softball for her high school team, ended up having to officiate. "Everyone came up to me afterward and told me I was the best umpire they'd had all season," she would later recall, "so I guess we knew something wasn't quite right." Whenever I do anything of dubious merit—miss a deadline, fall for a cliché—Kit drops his chin, slides his frames down his nose, and arches a paternal eyebrow. I usually get it at least once per story. Now I was inviting that look again, pushing the boundaries of his forbearance. "Son," he said. It was half a question, half a scold. I tried not to squirm, but finally I laughed and so did he, both of us overcome by the absurdity, the irreversibility, of what I was about to undertake. Then Kit nudged his glasses back up. He was no longer smiling. "If I find out you're running for the Monterey Park City Council," he said, "we're going to have to talk."

I might as well have declared my candidacy. For all the breakdowns that Todd and I were going to have to repair, the debts to be repaid, the equipment to be replaced, the paperwork to be recovered, what we really needed to do was to restore confidence, to sell the idea of the Monterey Park Sports Club and, as its stewards, ourselves. The previous year, only 225 kids had signed up, barely enough to field three or four teams in each of the five age divisions. If more families lost faith, we would be skipping a season, whether we chose to or not. I found myself lobbying for baseball the way I coached Carlos, with an almost blind disregard for what was realistic. I was, on some level, spinning an elaborate lie—trying to inspire a community to step forward, to be its best, even if that meant overstating the odds of success.

The Monterey Park Sports Club had no office or kiosk, but it had voice mail, a number that for years had been the only way to get information about the league. I dialed it, to record an outgoing message. The line was disconnected. How could that be?, We had just printed it on twenty thousand flyers—spent a tedious night sorting them into stacks of twenty for elementary school classes and stacks of thirty-six for middle-school classes, then lined up volunteers to crisscross the four school districts that shared jurisdiction in the city—and I had not even thought to check if it was working. A journalist should have known better. I called Pacific Bell. Our account was in collections, delinquent for months. I put the $166.21 on my credit card, which I already had used to cover the $422.18 in printing charges, and told myself things would get better. I recorded a greeting, in English and Spanish, then checked for messages a dozen times a day. I authorized city hall to give out my home number. I did not want to miss anyone, lose any opportunity to make an impression. My way of speaking, in either language, my writer's vocabulary and grammar, set me apart, but I also thought it had the power to bring people to me, to articulate the things about our league that most of them intuitively felt. *La Loma unites us. La Loma redeems us.* I spent hours on those telephonic performances, trying to prove I was up to the task and yet not above it. A mom would call, wanting to know what days of the week her child was likely to have practice, and I would end up waxing about me and Max, about our wondrous park, about how baseball was not merely about baseball but also about love and belonging and second chances.

On a Saturday morning in March, Todd and I set up a table at the civic center, in the same spot, outside the gym, where I had first enrolled Max. It was still the thick of basketball season, and as crowds brushed past us, I was met again with pitying grins. Taking on baseball, everyone seemed to know, was a suicide mission, and few of them could figure out why I would willingly sacrifice myself. I heard a lot of "You're a better man than I." Which, of course, is not what people mean when they say it. One dad I was friendly with, a geologist for the county who had coached his boys in both sports, agreed to help with sign-ups but warned me to expect little else of him. "I just don't have as much faith in human nature as you do," he said, slapping me on the back. I spent four hours at it that day, greeting, explaining, cajoling, pleading. As a reporter I had made a career of subjecting myself to uncomfortable circumstances—as a husband, a traveler, a student, too—but always with the objective of deciphering someone else's life, another culture, an environment outside my own. My stories were vicarious adventures. This was a new, uncharacteristic role: Instead of going along for the ride, I was the one on view, exposing myself to scrutiny and skepticism. It was strange to be judged in this way, to be sized up as a leader. Was I fair? Was I committed? Was I different enough from my predecessors yet enough like everyone else? Becoming commissioner felt like a referendum—on me, on my place in Monterey Park. By the time we left, we had twelve players in our league. One was Max. One was Alex. We returned the next Saturday. We registered seventeen.

I had expected to face resistance, but this seemed more like obstruction. I thought I was doing the right thing, putting my credibility, my own money, on the line, and nobody seemed at all convinced. It was beginning to dawn on me that behind my back I was being maligned, that there were some La Loma *veteranos* not just wary of me but rooting for me to fail, who were counting on it, who did not want to be shown up or, worse, turned in. I could almost hear the whispers. *Who the hell does this* puto *think he is?* I needed somebody to vouch for me, a Monterey Park Sports Club insider who was clean but who also had the clout to keep the shady ones from undermining my campaign. That could mean only one person. I made a pilgrimage to the living room couch of Chris Contreras, and once I learned the drill, I never failed to return without offering him a twenty-four-ounce Bud Light for each fist.

You would have taken Chris for a baseball guy: the bravado, the

belly, the barbed tribal tattoo around the biceps. His dad had been
a milkman, and as a kid, Chris used to accompany him on his deliv-
ery route, rising in the darkness and rambling through the barrio in
a refrigerated Divco. He grew up to be a car customizer, cruising
Whittier Boulevard in a lowrider Karmann Ghia, and now in his
late thirties, he ran his own limousine service. Everyone knew
Chris, and from what I could see, everyone owed him a favor. We
called him the mayor of Sherwood Circle, the only street he had ever
lived on. For all his indelicacies, though, Chris's heart was with the
Monterey Park Sports Club's basketball program, not just with the
game, which he loved to coach, but also with the relatively more sophisticated tendencies of the families it attracted. His front yard was
a showcase of Japanese gardening, with a granite Buddha surrounded
by sagos and bonsais, which he watered compulsively with a hose
fed by modified industrial-gauge pipes. On his laptop he had built
a database of famous grave sites—his own homage to Hollywood
noir—with photographs of hundreds of headstones. To show off, he
once took me to the Home of Peace Memorial Park, an obscure Jewish
cemetery in East L.A., where he pulled up at the tomb of a certain
Jerome Howard. I shrugged. He took a swig of warm beer and
waited. Only when I saw the pennies on the ground, spelling out
"nyuk nyuk nyuk," did I get it. We were visiting Curly.

Chris was being trained to run basketball—in another year he
would be commissioner—and his wife, Valerie, who worked for the
credit union at Disney, was the league's treasurer. "If I knew you
guys had my back," I said one night on the couch, "it would make
all the difference." Chris sent me out for another pair of cans, and
when I returned, he agreed to loan me $1,000 in start-up money
from the basketball coffers. Valerie offered to set up a checking
account for baseball and handle our finances. I was elated and humbled. I promised to personally deliver to them every dollar I took in.
"I swear," I said, "I won't let you down." I had to trust them. Why
they trusted me, I am not entirely sure, except that I think Chris is
smarter than he lets on, a natural-born satirist in a lunch-bucket
world, and he appreciated having a friend whose business was

words. I asked him about it once. "I always thought you were all right," he said. "A bit gay, but all right."

Almost every night Todd and I returned to the kitchen table, trading horror stories, performing triage. Everything had to be created from scratch: our registration forms, our coaching applications, our rule book, our schedule. We had to start awarding contracts—for uniforms, for umpires—before we had any income, before we even knew if we would have enough kids to justify a season. Equipment had to be inventoried and replaced. We found only enough for half the teams we were hoping to field. When we tried to charge more gear to the Monterey Park Sports Club's account, the good people at Jeffs Sporting Goods told us they were sorry but the league had burned them so many times, we would have to pay for everything in advance. I had another relationship to salvage, this one with the professional franchise I had spent my entire childhood waiting to root for, the Los Angeles Dodgers. The team every year offered our league a discounted ticket plan, as it did other youth organizations, granting us $12 seats for $7. As fundraisers go, it was an easy sell, better than wrapping paper or cookie dough, and if managed properly, it could generate thousands of dollars in just a few weeks. As I was discovering, that was a big if, the previous season's Dodger Day having been superbly botched. The Monterey Park Sports Club had failed to collect the money on time—or done something with the money instead of handing it over to the Dodgers—and all the tickets that had been reserved for us had been snatched back by the team's sales department. The league was given a new date, but not everyone who had placed an order was able to reschedule, and dozens of families ended up with tickets they could not use or, in some cases, claimed never to have received them. The Dodgers were miffed, reluctant to do business with us again, and of the few people I had so far signed up, several were insisting on credit for having been jerked around the year before. As an incentive, the old regime had promised a satin Dodger warm-up jacket to the kid who placed the biggest order—a seven-year-old boy, I learned, had sold more than a hundred tickets—but his prize, naturally, had never arrived. His mom called me. "Now that you're the commissioner," she said, "what are you going to do about it?"

As if I did not have enough on my plate, I decided my boldest stroke, the signature of my inaugural season, would be to erect scoreboards on La Loma's upper and lower diamonds. We had some antiquated ones, rectangles of painted sheet metal on which you could manually hang numbers, but they were rusty and pocked, and as long as I had been at the park, I had never seen them put to use. I noticed that each bore the slogan "Have a Coke and a Smile." A little Internet sleuthing established that to be from a 1979 ad campaign, and I figured I could shame the Coca-Cola people into updating their sponsorship. I took pictures and sent them off with a letter, explaining that the Monterey Park Sports Club was a racially and economically diverse program, open to any child without regard to skill or experience, and that the scoreboards, in their current state, "do not present an image that is flattering to either of our organizations." Surely a savvy executive would take the bait and hook us up with something state of the art. I waited, then phoned, working my way up the chain of command. When a representative finally got back to me, she pointed out that Coke, just the year before, had furnished our snack bar with a fridge. That was news to me, but okay, fair enough. That still left us without scoreboards. The Coke lady coughed. The fridge had been loaned to the Monterey Park Sports Club on the condition that we commit to regular deliveries of Coca-Cola products, and needless to say, the league had reneged. If we wanted to hold on to it, I would have to get my order in, and fast.

"So, let me see if I have this right," I said. "I contacted you about scoreboards, and you're using that as an opportunity to put the screws on me for some refrigeration unit I know nothing about?"

"Maybe if you can demonstrate that you're a good customer and build up a track record with us," she said, "we'll consider getting more involved."

I wanted to scream. I did not know if I was more pissed at Coke for the strings it was attaching or at the bozos who had welched on this lousy scheme or at myself for failing to see any of it coming.

"Just take the damn fridge," I said.

The snack bar. That was a whole other deal, one more riddle atop our kooky little hill. The city, a few years earlier, had spent $350,000 on a new facility, which had cinder-block walls and a corrugated roof set at space-age angles. One side housed bathrooms, the other side a meeting room, and in the middle was a stainless-steel kitchen. It was ours to use, free, during the season, yet I was told that the snack bar had never turned a profit. That was insane. You could go to Sam's Club and buy a thirty-two-pack of water for $4.49, then sell each bottle for a buck. Profit: 600 percent. To just throw up your hands and say, *Oh, well, too bad, didn't work,* struck me as offensive, not just to the city, which had used tax dollars on our behalf, but also to all the parents who were expected to volunteer in that place—and who were threatened with having their children benched if they skipped out on their shift. Under the Katz administration, to the extent that such a thing could be said to exist, we were going to run this as a business. I wanted to hire a manager and offer a $150-a-week salary, the only paid position in our organization. It would have to be somebody whose word—and math—I would never question, and since that more or less drained the pool of candidates, I offered the job to Raynelda's nephew Christiám, who was twenty-three and, though it may sound inconsistent, living in my garage.

Despite my breakup with Raynelda, I was still a benefactor of the Gutiérrez clan, the underwriter of countless journeys, chief attaché of their U.S. welcome wagon. I had been translating documents and hosting parties, cosigning loans and dispensing hand-me-downs from the day most of them arrived. They invited me to their weddings and birthdays and graduations, even after Raynelda found a new boyfriend. I was honored to always be *cuñado* to her siblings and *tío* to her nieces and nephews. The family shared many of Raynelda's sorrows—her sisters, the three who were here, had all migrated with children and no fathers, and they had all worked the cantinas of Echo Park upon their arrival—but after a few years of American life, they had begun to cluster into two camps: half of them still barflies, half of them born-agains.

Fredesvinda was the empress of the drinking faction. Raven-haired and crimson-lipped, with a rose tattoo on her collarbone, Freda had married a bartender she met at a Mexican dance hall, and together they bought one of Sunset Boulevard's saltier watering holes, the Hollyway. Rechristened the New Hollyway, it ballooned under their management, eventually growing so debauched—drugs, prostitution, shootings, including the murder of an off-duty transit officer who was being served after hours—that a community group, the Echo Park Security Association, declared the bar "Problem #1" in its newsletter and a few of its members conducted some amateur surveillance. I knew one of the volunteer spies. He was a reporter at the *L.A. Times*. Because I was still an occasional customer, I thought it best to stay neutral. Freda lost the place, but she and her husband kept reinvesting in new joints, trying to stay one step ahead of the liquor police. They had a bar at home, more of a shrine really, all mahogany and brass and mirrors, right at the foyer. They were living in Monterey Park, too, on the other side of La Loma from us, and it was almost impossible to get through the front door without rubbing against the lacquered countertop. "Brother-in-law," Freda would say to me, running her hand over the bottles like a naughty Vanna White, "what is your pleasure?"

My mother-in-law stayed with Freda in those days, and I can only imagine how she rationalized the arrangement. After the ordeal of her crossing, Thelma had found salvation in a fundamentalist sect of tongue speakers, and she punctuated every sentence with a resounding *"¡gloria a Dios!"* She was stately and proud, and even though her material needs were subsidized by drink, Thelma was set on delivering her children from the sins and curses that had hampered their lives. When my marriage began to falter, when Raynelda's nights out grew later and more reckless, she urged me to put her daughter in check. "You need to be the man of your house," Thelma told me. I respected her and always addressed her as *madre*, but I found Thelma to be a slightly calculating ally. She was intrigued by my name and background and a little too eager to introduce me to her pastor, as if I were a prize, her very own Chosen Person, to be offered up for divine credit. If we left Max in her care on a Saturday night, I had to pick him up first thing Sunday morning or Thelma would whisk him to her temple. I had no objection to Max being exposed to a variety of faiths, but in that circus of yelps and jerks and gibberish, I knew she was praying for his lost Hebrew soul. Once, while he was suffering through a pesky bout of diarrhea, Thelma performed something akin to an exorcism, commanding Satan to release his hold on Max's lower intestine. The poor boy had no choice but to play along, lying still as she rubbed her trembling hands across his abdomen, although I must say that when I asked him about it later, he did concede that his condition seemed to have improved.

The youngest of Raynelda's siblings was Nestor, the only one who did not share the same father. His dad was a Managua civil servant, a kind, subdued white-collar functionary who had tutored Nestor endlessly as a little boy, and that gave Nestor a direction that eluded the rest of the family. Despite being uprooted and smuggled and plunged into a baffling new culture at the eve of adolescence, Nestor was astonishingly sober and studious, as if he lived in a protective cocoon that only he could perceive. I would see him at the kitchen table while music blared and glasses clinked, performing algorithms nobody possibly could have deciphered, and I would marvel at his resolve, at his utter sureness that every sacrifice would be redeemed. When years later he graduated from UCLA, with a doctorate in chemistry, it was at once miraculous and, by then, almost routine.

Raynelda's only other brother was Abersio, the Sandinista. He was about my age, thickset and boisterous, with an understandably conflicted view of America. For most of his life, he had raged against Yankee imperialism—he had overthrown a U.S.-backed

dictator, then fought off a U.S.-backed counterinsurgency—but
when the Sandinista government finally crumbled, with Daniel
Ortega's defeat in 1990, Nicaragua again became sympathetic to
U.S. interests. Abersio was suddenly a warrior in a country at peace,
a revolutionary without a revolution. He knew that the United
States was his best shot for a new beginning, but that was a hard
thing to admit, that he was going to seek his future here, in the
belly of his oppressor, especially since the only work he could find at
first was as a security guard: a Latin revolutionary guarding Yankee
imperialist shit.

"My crazy family," Christiám would always say, and we would
laugh and groan in unison, a pair of survivors, my retreat paving
the way for his. He was Abersio's oldest son, a baby of the revolution, born exactly nine months after the Sandinistas toppled
Somoza, and he tended to get the brunt of his father's aggravation.
When my marriage ended, Christiám and his younger brother,
Leslie, were living with their dad in East L.A., and they were hopeful that with only Max and me left in the house, we could offer
them some of our breathing space. At Abersio's request, I had
actually sponsored Christiám and Leslie on their visa applications—
they were the only Gutiérrezes, to my knowledge, to enter this
country with papers—and I was obligated to them, legally, in
ways that I was not to their cousins. I agreed to take in Christiám,
at no cost, but I had to pass on Leslie. I could deal with only one
boarder at a time. Raynelda, as I recall, was rather pissy about the
whole idea: I had just shown her and Freddy the door, and now I
was opening it again to another member of her family. I had some
reservations of my own about cycling Gutiérrezes through the
house, but Christiám was different, maybe not as introspective as
Nestor—he worked with his hands, carpentry, painting, drywall—
but every bit as dutiful. He had been raised mostly by his mom,
who was of Afro-Latin descent, and had inherited her complexion
and curls to a degree that, up here, he could easily pass for a kid
from South Central. Max was fascinated by Christiám, by how
foreign he looked in our home and how respectfully he conducted

himself, and Christiám treated Max like a child prodigy, seeing in him all that he had lost out on as a boy in Nicaragua. I considered myself lucky to have Christiám in both of our lives. I felt bad for Leslie, but Raynelda agreed to rent him a corner of her apartment— one brother on each side of the Katz divide.

Putting Christiám in charge of the snack bar was, I am well aware, a glaring case of nepotism, just the sort of back-scratching I was pledging to stamp out. Except I never thought I was doing him a favor. Christiám was coming to my aid. He already had a full-time job, and I was adding forty hours of slave-wage labor to his week: shopping, cleaning, pumping nacho cheese. I no longer needed to advise Raynelda of my commitments to La Loma. With Christiám's loyalty, though, all three of us boys were going to be engaged in its resuscitation. "Whatever you say, Uncle," he would tell me in Spanish, and though I would have been just as happy if he addressed me in familiar terms, it was impossible not to note that the "you" always came out as "*usted.*"

I created a to-do list every day, but no matter how many items I crossed off, the list never shrank. The base paths were out of alignment. Home plate was sodden and warped. Netting was torn. Lights were burned out. The hot dog machine was missing. Some families were still waiting on last season's trophies. The city was asking for proof of liability insurance. We needed a key to the rest room. I was trying to hire a parent I knew to build us a website— he had done one for the basketball program—but he kept dragging his heels. When I learned a few years later that he was a registered sex offender, I was grateful for his inattention. I became a regular at Office Depot, compiling the basics of our filing system. Every application, along with the receipt, was slid into a clear plastic sleeve. The sleeves were sorted into five age divisions. The five age divisions were ordered alphabetically. Then each slippery stack was threaded into an enormous three-ring binder, which I lugged around wherever I went. From the information in the binder, I helped Todd build a spreadsheet, reading aloud the names and the birth dates while he navigated Excel. It was cumbersome and redundant, but we realized we would need a master list that could be printed out later, to run tryouts and the draft. By the end of the week, I was back in front of the gym, giving my word, vowing to make things right.

Whether my genuflections to Chris were paying off or I was merely starting to engender sympathy, it felt like progress: forty-eight kids on our third Saturday, thirty-one a week after that. A month had passed, and we had 109 players, a substantial number and still not even close. The younger divisions were the strongest. Half our applications were for T-Ball. I found that those were the parents who gravitated to my style, who ate up my spiels about compassion and encouragement. "They don't know any better," I told Todd. "The league hasn't had a chance to alienate them yet." He was looking as overwhelmed as I was. "Don't worry," Todd said, "there's still time for that." Whenever someone bought in—the fee that year was $75—I felt both jubilant and sheepish. I had collected more than $8,000, and so far I had delivered nothing in return.

I was in the market not just for players but for coaches, the ambassadors of our program. A good one could do so much: instill optimism, quell rancor, protect us from theft and injury and violence. A lousy one could sabotage the entire league. We had about a dozen returning from the previous season—some I approved of, some I was crossing my fingers on—but I probably would have to drum up a dozen more or risk assembling teams with no one to lead them. I wish I could say that I approached this task with the utmost diligence. Parents were handing over their children to us, paying us to be surrogates, and it would have been nice to have been able to reassure them that every coach had passed some kind of training or vetting. What I was discovering, though, was that the Monterey Park Sports Club, for all its deficits, was for many potential volunteers a symbol of their own recovery. No matter where you came from or what mistakes you were haunted by, La Loma was proof of doing right by your child, of being straight on at least one irrefutable thing. There was a coach with a marijuana leaf tattooed on her hand—nothing phantom about that!—and another who could polish off a twelve-pack during a game, his beers disguised in tin sleeves cut from old soda cans. One confessed to having a felony in his past, for being an accessory to a murder. One had lost her husband to AIDS. The registration table became my recruitment booth, the place to appraise candidates and weigh their petitions for clemency. As long as they had a pulse—and, to ease my mind, a child in the league—they were eligible. We were beggars, not choosers.

That was how I ended up with David Sanchez. He was a Monterey Park Sports Club basketball referee, a few years younger than me, with a trim mustache and puppy-dog eyes. I had seen him in action before, thought him to be consistent and convincing on the court, and when he offered to help with baseball, I put him on sign-up duty. When I learned that he did not have a kid, I briefly fretted—being a parent, though no guarantee of probity, at least provided an incentive not to screw with the league—but then he told me about his niece, an eleven-year-old named Francine. She wanted to play baseball, and if we needed coaches, he would be happy to take her team. It was early April. Our enrollment had crept up to 168, but we were still struggling to fill the older divisions, Double A and Triple A, which had been hit hard by defections. Being a coach at that level took a bit more starch. There was stealing and balking and dropped third strikes, not to mention puberty, to contend with. "Man, if you're serious about that," I said, "you are my hero."

A week or so later, David stopped by my house. He was in a bind. His electric bill had gone unpaid, and he needed $80 to keep the lights from being cut. He did not have time to get to his bank, an out-of-the-way credit union, and Edison was demanding cash. If he wrote a check to the league, could I front him the money? "I hate putting you on the spot like this," he said, "but I promise I'm good for it." It goes without saying that the Monterey Park Sports Club, a 501(c)(3) charity, should not be in the business of floating personal loans. I know that now, and I knew it then, but I was just as eager as he was to curry favor, to gain converts. Besides, we had already accepted thousands of dollars without verifying funds, and unlike the folks who had written those checks, David was on our side of the table, giving of himself. I reached into a paper bag, one that I had yet to deliver to Chris and Valerie, and handed him four $20 bills. "If you want to postdate your check, to give yourself a little more time, that's no problem," I told him. David shook his head. "No, don't worry," he said. "The money's all there."

I was not worried. I had plenty to keep me occupied. I got a call from an angry mom, wanting to know why I had allowed her ex-husband's girlfriend to register their two sons, and then when I issued a refund to the dad, I got an angry call from the girlfriend, wanting to know why her boyfriend's kids had been kicked out of the league. I had one coach lose all his paperwork on the freeway—his kid had rolled down a window, and at sixty-five miles per hour, everything was sucked off the seat. People were asking what color the uniforms were going to be, when the games were going to be, how big the trophies were going to be, if the batting helmets were going to have face guards, if the snack bar was going to have a deep fryer, if the infield-fly rule was going to be enforced. My phone rang one morning, and a man named Bill introduced himself. He was with a company called Blockbuster and wanted to know when he could pick up the $350 needed to process the permits for our fireworks stand. "Fireworks stand?" I asked. "I'm sorry, but I don't think we're really interested."

"Heh, heh, heh," Bill chuckled. "I'm afraid you really don't have a choice."

"What now?"

"There is a balance on your account."

"Our account? Wait, don't tell me—we haven't been good customers?"

"It's about six thousand dollars you owe."

"Nice."

The politics of the Southern California fireworks trade was a tragicomedy of its own. Dozens of municipalities, including the City of Los Angeles, had in recent years banned all fireworks, even sparklers and smoke bombs. The region was just too populous, the landscape too dry, to endorse the sale of anything with a fuse. To maintain their toehold, pyrotechnic conglomerates such as Blockbuster relied on nonprofit organizations such as the Monterey Park Sports Club as proxies. Fireworks could be justified as a fundraising opportunity, a way for a cash-strapped Little League to make ends meet. The fireworks lobby had even meddled in a few local San Gabriel Valley elections, bankrolling pro-fireworks ballot measures to defy the prohibitionists. Monterey Park at one time had come close to joining the ban—our own fire chief recommended it— but the city council took pity on the two dozen service groups that had qualified for annual sales permits and voted not to deprive us of all that revenue. If only it had. The way Bill explained it, Blockbuster delivered us about $20,000 worth of fireworks every Fourth of July. We had one week to sell it all on consignment, then pay Blockbuster the wholesale cost, which was 50 percent. There were other fees and rentals, though, plus sales tax to calculate, and if you were not careful, or honest, you might not have enough left over to cover your obligations. The Monterey Park Sports Club—surprise— had been screwing up for years. Our debt to Blockbuster used to be worse, $24,676.25 at one point, and as such, it was hard to know exactly whom to finger. I asked Bill why, if we were so negligent, he had continued to do business with us. He gave me a long answer, some of which had to do with preserving Blockbuster's access to Monterey Park, but the bottom line was this: It was cheaper to wait for a sap—er, a scrupulous commissioner—to come along than to sue our pathetic little operation. "I've been hoping," Bill said, "for someone like you."

I plopped myself down on Chris's couch. My head was hurting. A part of me wanted to quit. "Beverage?" I offered. Chris scowled. "You know this fuckhead David Sanchez?" he asked. *Oh, please,* I prayed, *please do not say what I think you are about to say.* It had only been a week. In that time, David had been busy, offering Chris a pair of primo court-level Lakers seats, and at a budget price, just $100 each. Chris had bit—David was a referee in the league that he was helping to run, after all—handed over the money, then gone to Staples Center with one of his kids, to celebrate the boy's birthday, and waited outside for David to deliver the tickets. He never did. When Chris finally tracked him down, David spun an elaborate apology and promised to score him even better seats. To make good, though, he would need a little help. Money was tight. If he could write Chris a check for, say, $80, could Chris front him the cash? This, you had to admit, was smooth. David had just buggered Chris and was pumping him for more. The check did not merely bounce; the account no longer existed. At least Chris had been lax with his own money—the $280 came from his pocket. I had some explaining to do. "Um, I think we have a situation," I said.

We waited for Chris's wife to log on to the Monterey Park Sports Club's account, to confirm what we already knew. How did I get so stupid? I had dipped into the league's purse, into funds I had pledged to defend, and handed over our money to the first person who asked. Maybe it was only $80, but it was a test, my own, not a mess I inherited, and I had failed it. I had bent the rules and played favorites. I had fallen for the same bland temptations I was supposed to be rooting out. "We need to think fast," I said. I could save the self-flagellation for later. David had to be stopped. "Where else are we vulnerable?" I remembered the day he had worked the sign-up table—he must have been licking his chops. Valerie tallied our deposits again. They more or less matched the number of registrants. If he had skimmed, thankfully, it was not much. *Think, think.* What was the old reporter's admonishment? *Follow the money.* "Oh, shit!" I announced. "Dodger tickets."

I had contacted the Dodgers a few weeks before, introducing myself to a nice young saleswoman named Carly. I assured her that the Monterey Park Sports Club was for real this year, and if she gave me a chance, I would make up for our spotty history. (I decided not to mention that a year earlier I had written a *Los Angeles* magazine cover story, a first-person lament, about what a soulless, corporate shell the Dodgers had become under Rupert Murdoch: As a journalist I had no compunctions about taking the team to task, but as a commissioner I was compelled to be a booster.) Carly agreed to reserve 1,200 seats for us, for a game later that summer. I told her that we had set our opening day as a deadline—we would need to collect $14,400 by then—and that I would deliver the Dodgers their share, $8,400, within a week of that. Those were heady numbers for a league as desiccated as ours, on the eve of a season that might never be, but we had no choice other than to lurch forward, pretending that everything would work out. If we could not count on our cut of that revenue, which was built into my budget already, we would be putting the season in jeopardy, regardless. The mechanics of handling so much money and keeping track of so many tickets was unwieldy, a chore that would have to be farmed out in advance. If we tried to do it all in a single day, at the ceremony, we would trigger a colossal logjam. I instructed each coach to select a team rep (*team mom,* I decided, was no longer a viable term, even if most of them were, in fact, moms), and I summoned them to the snack bar. I explained that they were being charged with a thankless but noble mission, to serve as fund-raiser liaisons. No other parent would be authorized to collect or submit Dodger money, just that one team rep, on behalf of her one team. It would help us avoid a logistical nightmare, but it was still a lot of cash and a lot of trust: a bad combination. If anyone could see that, it would be David Sanchez.

I dug through my three-ring binder and pulled out phone numbers as fast as I could. We needed to get to his team. Valerie made the first call. "Too late," she said. Instead of designating a team rep, David had done just what I feared, rounding up his players and telling their parents how important it was to get their ticket orders in early. He explained that the league preferred cash, but he could take a check, and since there might be confusion over whether to make it payable to the L.A. Dodgers or the Monterey Park Sports Club, the best option was to leave it blank. We made a list of who had given him what, in all more than $400. I took the liberty of calling Francine's mom. I was not in a very diplomatic mood. "You know," I said, "her uncle has really put us in a bad spot."

"What do you mean, 'her uncle'?" Francine's mom said.

"What do you mean, 'what do you mean'?"

"She has several uncles, and none of them are involved in baseball."

"David Sanchez—her uncle, her coach—he's a damn thief!"

"I'm sorry to tell you this," Francine's mom said, "but Francine does not have an uncle named David Sanchez."

Before I was just angry. Now I was creeped out. Francine's mom knew of David—his brother had been a high school chum of her husband's—but there was no relation, no connection, no reason for anyone to suspect that he was piggybacking on their family. This was the work of a practiced con man. By posing as Uncle Dave, he had gained access to the league, to our money. I, the practiced reporter, had simply taken his word. I was getting ready to call the police, but first I needed to speak to David, to confront my betrayer, to absolve myself. He answered right away. "How could you do this to us?" I growled. "Especially since you *knew*. You knew we were trying to win people back to this league. You knew I was putting my neck on the line." His voice was low and hurt. He said it was all a mistake, a misunderstanding. "I'll pay you back," he said. "Just don't call the cops. Please." He sounded like he was starting to cry. He was still trying to play me. I never did learn what his demons were—he had once done time, I discovered, for burglary— but I figured money was just a symptom. I was gratified to have been left with a grandiose line to send him off with. "What you did," I said, "can never be repaid." I filed a report with Monterey Park detectives—David would later plead out to a thirty-two-month sentence—then I went to my computer and drew up another flyer. It would have been easier to pretend that nothing had happened. The last thing we needed was more public embarrassment. But if I was going to be a different sort of commissioner, if I was ever going to restore the integrity of this program, I would have to start by acknowledging my own flaws. "ALERT!" I wrote in giant block letters. "Please be advised that David Sanchez is not affiliated with the Monterey Park Sports Club." I printed it out and posted it at La Loma.

As we limped toward opening day, I kept holding out for more kids, an extra coach, a few more bodies, anything to complete a team, to round out a division. We did five Saturdays of sign-ups at the gym, plus two Sundays at the park, then we added another Saturday and pushed everything back a week. I taped notices to storefronts. I made house calls to stragglers. I wrote an "article" about the Monterey Park Sports Club's resurgence and "placed" it in the *Cascades,* the city's freebie newsletter. By May we had surpassed the previous year's enrollment—a moral victory, if nothing else—and kept on going right up until the first pitch. The season would start with 275 players, on twenty-four teams. It felt like we had spent an entire season just to get there.

Chapter

Five

STANDING AT THE PITCHER'S MOUND, WITH A MICROPHONE
this time, I surveyed the faces around me—coaches and kids in the
outfield, spouses and siblings and grandparents behind the
backstop—some hostile, others leery, a few merely uncertain. They
were at La Loma not just because it was opening day, an obligation
on the 2003 calendar, but because *I* had assembled them, coaxed
them back to a park that was dying, and challenged them to believe
in it. Everything up to this point had been hypothetical, offstage.
From here on out I was, publicly, officially, the commissioner:
Whatever happened, it would be on me.

To thaw the crowd, I recounted the story of my first Beavers
game, including its pitiable culmination, except that I cast it in the
most sentimental light I could conjure, a riff on fatherhood and
innocence. "And really, I think, that's why each of us, in our own
way, is here today," I said, scanning the diamond vainly for a nod or

a smile. "We're here because we love our children. We want them to be part of something bigger than just themselves, part of a team, part of a league, part of a healthy community." Anyone who had known me in my life prior to L.A. would have been bemused by my piety, my metamorphosis from dad to coach to baseball conservationist. In high school, in college, nobody would have ever predicted me back in uniform, much less geeked out in a tackle-twill, button-down Monterey Park Sports Club jersey and matching cap, with "Commissioner" embroidered on the side. I was the least likely guy to be waving an American flag, more likely to be defending somebody's right to burn one, yet I had spent hours the night before teetering on a saggy ladder, cinching star-spangled banners and streamers to every panel of chain link at La Loma. Instead of chafing at the middle-classness of Little League, I was promoting it. A lifetime away from the diamonds of my youth, I was upholding the organized part of sports again.

I am not too sure what Max thought of all this, about his dad becoming such a devout figure in the park. His life had not changed much since we had been living solo. I hesitate to call myself a single dad, given that Raynelda was not out of the picture, but I had always been the parent at parent-teacher conferences, the one who woke Max up and got him dressed, who packed his lunch and checked his homework and tucked him in, and I was still his primary caregiver. A precocious little boy at La Loma named Sebastian, whose own father had a fairly narrow view of gender roles, took note of our habits and started addressing me as Max's "man-mom." What had changed was the degree to which my commitments, my notions of accountability and service, were now on display. I was raising not just Max, ministering not just to his team, but making myself responsible for all of La Loma—for people who did not necessarily feel the same responsibility toward me. When I first explained to Max that the league was in ruins, that we were in danger of losing a season, he gave me the same look my editor had: "And you just couldn't take that as an answer, Dad?"

I was doing a good bit of running in those days—the

L.A. Marathon was another, less jaunty response to my fortieth birthday—and I would often train with Max, who paced me on his bike. We would follow the path around the Hollywood Reservoir, a forested loop at the crown of the 101 Freeway that sustained an improbable menagerie of deer and turtles and woodpeckers and bunnies, and log nine or twelve or fifteen miles together, Max prodding me any time my age began to catch up. One drizzly afternoon, an hour, maybe two, into our trek, he jolted me with the kind of meddlesome question that you secretly hope for from your child. "Is it true, Dad," he asked, "that you don't believe in God?" Well, I thought, here we go, a chance to steer my son onto some weighty terrain, to draw the distinction between spirituality and religious doctrine, to explain how I can be the first male in untold generations of Katzes to do without a bar mitzvah and nonetheless be considered Jewish. "The way I look at it, I guess, is that God is not some external force up in the sky but something that lives inside each of us," I managed to grunt. I stole a few lines from Richard Bach's slim parable *Illusions: The Adventures of a Reluctant Messiah,* about how humans only scratch the surface of what we are capable of, about how the ability to transcend our limits could qualify as divine. "But you're right," I said, "I'm probably a heathen by most people's standards."

I glanced at Max and realized he was not listening. He already knew the answer. I was being set up. "In that case," he asked suavely, like a lawyer who has caught a witness in a lie, "why are you wearing a picture of God?"

It took me a second to make the connection, to remember that the back of my T-shirt bore the image of the *Virgen de Guadalupe* and that below, in Spanish, it read, "My life is in your hands." I had bought the shirt a decade earlier, at a swap meet in Texas, in preparation for a series of articles in which I would go undercover as a migrant worker in an Ozark poultry factory. I had little hope of passing for a Mexican, but anything I could do to muddle my identity struck me as an advantage. Raynelda gave me a buzz cut. I removed my emerald ring. I traveled to the Rio Grande Valley and got drunk with a friend from the *Brownsville Herald,* slept on his couch, then presented myself, in my smelly and wrinkled God shirt, to the labor contractor who would send me north, on "the chicken trail." Max had been too young to remember that story, but he was old enough now to bust my chops, to see how hard I was trying to be someone other than the person I was born. He probably knew more about adaptability, about the cultural and linguistic nimbleness that sociologists like to call "code switching," than I ever would. "Well, jeez, c'mon, you know," I panted.

"I'm just sayin'," Max said.

Before I played catch with Max, before Dad played catch with me, Mom taught me to hit. She dressed me in a smart little pinstripe suit and stuck a cap on my head, then marched me out to the curb and peppered me with Wiffle balls. I swung hard, eyes closed, spinning around like a Gyro Wheel. I was not Max. Mom was not me. None of that mattered. "You were a boy," she would tell me later. "Boys played baseball."

Her name was Vera, a foreign name, chosen for her by foreign parents in a country torn by war, except that she was an American mom, brassy and vogue, with a dark brown bob that curled sharply forward at the bottom, tapering into a pair of sickles. She practiced modern dance and wore ponchos and puffed sweet cigarillos, but she hated sunglasses. It was wrong, she always told me, to hide your eyes. At Christmas—we lighted the menorah *and* decorated a tree—she fashioned ornaments out of walnuts, carefully splitting them, replacing the meat with coins, and gluing the shells back together with a loop of red velvet ribbon sandwiched between the halves, just so that I could bust them open again and reap the treasure. She stripped and waxed the wood floors even though we were renters. She scripted dinner parties from Julia Child cookbooks, then strapped her hips to gyrating belts at the Johnie Johnson Figure Salon. The only thing that appeared to hold Mom back was her inability to drive. Twice she failed the test, unable to visualize the angles, the cut to the right followed by the cut to the left, looking over her shoulder, in reverse, that would have allowed her to parallel park. On her final try, the instructor admonished her, a line that she delights in repeating: "Missus Katz, you don't exude confidence."

When all that changed, when she shed her groovy hausfrau skin and stepped onto the public stage, it happened so abruptly, so instinctively, that in my imagination I see Mom unzipping herself, like some quick-change Looney Tunes character, and getting down to work. It was 1968, a portentous year, the climax of the civil rights movement and the turning point in Vietnam. I had started kindergarten, and Dad, as he would forever be, was consumed by the issues of his studio. Mom was thirty-four, with a sociology degree from Brooklyn College that was going to waste and genes that were programmed, long ago and far away, for political action. She rode the bus downtown, to the Portland outpost of Robert F. Kennedy's presidential bid. "I can only give a few hours," she announced. They put her to work licking envelopes. Mom was taken not just by the Kennedy mystique but by his devotion to the poor and the powerless, never more so than when he traveled to the Central Valley of California to embrace a frail César Chávez at the conclusion of the union leader's harrowing twenty-five-day fast. It was a show of principle, of faith in the capacity of an unequal society to mend its ways, not a photo op; if anything, breaking bread with Chicano farm workers was going to cost Bobby Kennedy votes. Mom took me on picket lines, to wave BOYCOTT GRAPES signs outside the Safeway we used to shop at, and I remember adults brushing past us and grumbling, "What kind of parent would drag a kid out to something like this?"

To the extent that she had considered having another child, the prospect more or less ended there. Although she was not religious or a believer in destiny, Mom had to admit that something "got triggered" by the changes that were sweeping America, patterns, echoes, commitments, the responsibility to give something back— to "repair the world," as Jews have phrased it for centuries. "When I was in eighth grade, in Mrs. Gallucci's English class, we were told to write what we wanted to have put on our tombstones, and mine was, 'She made a difference,'" Mom explained. "I didn't want to be in a grave with a lie written on it." In the anguish that followed RFK's assassination, she volunteered to chair the Oregon branch of the Kennedy Action Corps, a movement launched by former campaign workers, in chapters across the country, to continue his fight. I found some of their old stationery not long ago. Our home number was printed on the masthead.

She never did learn to drive, but I think I can say, without the embellishments of a son, that Mom would become the most accomplished woman in the history of Portland government, the "feisty" queen bee of her adopted city, as *Washington Post* columnist David Broder periodically called her. What strikes me, looking back, is not just the heights to which she rose but how ballsy it was for a woman of her day to even think she might gain entry to the political arena. Before she could govern, Mom literally had to push her way through the door. Perkins Pub, a businessman's hangout in the basement of the Lipman Wolfe department store, refused to serve women; Mom helped stage a sit-in, seizing every table and hunkering down with brown bag lunches. The City Club of Portland, another male-only redoubt, met every Friday at the Benson Hotel; Mom picketed outside for two years, occasionally waving a rolling pin or donning a colander as a helmet. In 1972, she ran for state representative, on a budget of something like $6,000. Her lawn signs were all homemade, wooden rectangles silk-screened in a neighbor's basement, with stakes at each end, affixed with nuts and wing bolts. After she won, I helped retrieve the signs and noticed that several had been defaced: KATZ was turned into KUNTZ. I was accustomed to being teased about my name—"Kitty Katz" was big during those years— but this, even to my prepubescent ear, implied something darker.

The Oregon Legislature proved to be the ultimate smoke-filled room, a bibulous den of lobbyists and ranchers, none of whom knew what to make of the women's libber, with the wide gauchos and Noo Yawk accent, who lived in an apartment with a starving artist and a longhair son. She was for gun control: The Second Amendment diehards, out in the rural counties, used her picture for target practice. She was for gay rights: The Posse Comitatus, a Klan-like band of survivalists, named her in some kind of New Testament fatwa, which Mom might have dismissed, except that I was a latchkey kid by then, and so for my protection, she reported the threats to the police. "It was hard to tell if it was the woman thing or the Jewish thing or a combination of both," she would say, "but there was resistance. I was an outsider at first."

Up to the day I left Portland, she awoke at four forty-five every morning to newspapers, talk radio, and coffee and kept going for the next seventeen or eighteen hours, convinced she would have to work twice as hard as her male colleagues to be taken seriously. She had no hobbies, no diversions or indulgences to dull her focus or, it might be said, to soften her brio. In her level of preparation, her mastery of detail, her faith that good government could vanquish hypocrisy and greed, Mom was a public servant in the most ideal-istic sense of the term. I was in college when she was elected speaker, only the second woman in the nation to preside over a state assembly. She happily became a symbol of what she called the "feminization of power," the supposition that women, as caregivers and peace-makers, were more likely to rule by consensus than by testosterone. "I learned that everyone needs something," Mom explained. "Every-one wants to be loved and respected. You figure out what you can give them, and as you give power to people you trust, the power expands and good things happen."

In 1992, after twenty years in the legislature, Mom ran for mayor. It was in some ways a less consequential position—potholes and parades instead of land use and education reform. But the office was also more about her, her vision, her persona, and with me off on some incomprehensible Hispanic trip down in L.A., she gave herself even more completely to the job. The great livable city, the Portland of microbrews and solar-powered parking meters and bookstores so enormous that they came with a map—the town that was luring Californians north—flourished during her tenure. They were both late bloomers, Mom and Portland, and she was determined that her investment live on. "I was the mother," she told me. "This was my child."

Even with the flapping flags and the flowery speeches, my first opening day was not the triumph I had wished for. The problem lay with our uniform vendor, an overgrown bully named Adrian Magallon. Adrian's shop was the one that the Monterey Park Sports Club had always favored, an arrangement that I should have been more suspicious of. Uniforms were the league's single greatest expense, about a third of the operating budget and the easiest way to squander whatever goodwill we might have kindled. We were clothing 275 children—there was something very direct, even intimate, about that—and parents had little tolerance for anything ragtag. As a longtime coach, with three boys of his own in the league, Adrian presented us with another dilemma: If there was ever a problem on the field, a disputed call, say, or an unverified player, would the Monterey Park Sports Club be tempted to side with him, knowing that we had a financial relationship to preserve? I discussed it with Todd, debated whether to sever all ties with the previous regime or try to salvage this one business connection. To be honest, we were not sure we could afford anyone else. Todd solicited bids from several other shops, mainstream sporting goods retailers, which all responded testily to him. They were the same ones the Monterey Park Sports Club had always used as straw men, to allow Adrian to come in as the low bidder, and they were weary of the charade. If we re-upped with him, the price would surely be right, and if anything went awry, we still had Adrian's emissary, Frank Piña, our very own Rec and Parks commissioner, to look out for us.

I asked Todd to negotiate the terms, to remind Adrian just how important it was for us to make a good impression this year. Adrian told Todd not to worry. We were like family, Monterey Park Sports Club *compadres*. He would take care of us. There was just one small thing he needed in return, a brotherly favor—that we pay him his $9,000 up front and in cash. I look back now and wonder if I simply had "sucker" stamped on my forehead. Why was I always so willing to assume the best of people, to first give them the chance to disappoint me and then make my judgment? Journalists were supposed to be professional cynics, and I seemed to be wandering through life as if it were perpetually the Summer of Love.

Less than twenty-four hours before the first pitch, Adrian dropped off our order: wrong sizes, arbitrary colors, mangled spellings, undercounts of belts and caps and socks. Then he skipped out on the ceremony. Close to a hundred kids, I would say, were not properly attired that morning, forced to traipse around La Loma in a hodgepodge of street clothes and mismatched uniforms. After my little Beavers yarn, I had to stay at the mike and apologize—again for somebody else's lapses—and beg for a chance to make good. I felt sick. I had promised better and instead bought into the organization's pathology. As deplorable as my encounter with David Sanchez was, I could at least dismiss him as an aberration. I had fallen for his scam. Adrian, on the other hand, had been living off the Monterey Park Sports Club's teat for years, selling us shoddy gear and winking at his children's registration fees; while our fireworks debt was being run up, I also came to learn, he was among those who had signed for the merchandise on behalf of the league. He was not an intruder. He was us.

Todd visited the shop. Adrian refused to see him. I put Chris on the case. Adrian blew him off. We turned to Frank. "Adrian is Adrian," he told us. I had to carry around a notebook just to keep track of all the complaints and corrections. A week went by and then another. Dozens of kids were playing in jeans and T-shirts. After five or six games, some families simply went out and bought their own uniforms, then handed me the bill. We had no leverage, other than to appeal to Adrian's conscience. I found myself wondering if he had really been that hard up for money or if he had asked for it in advance for just this reason. I thought of writing the whole thing off. As my dad was given to say, education is expensive. Maybe I would have gotten over it, maybe I could have avoided the grief of a showdown, except that Adrian had found a way to rub in his disregard: While the rest of the league had been furnished with cheapie mesh pullovers, the Dodgers and Angels logos all being hand-sketched knockoffs, he had outfitted his own team in custom, top-of-the-line pinstriped uniforms, both home and road styles, and with a bullshit name, the Dukes.

He was supposed to be the coach, but Adrian was rarely at the park, not even showing up for games. When finally I did see him, he acted as if nothing was wrong. He expected me to go along with the lie. Everyone always had: If you looked the other way, you never had to answer for your own misdeeds. "What's up, Katz?" he said, swaggering past me. I was so angry, I could not speak. I had botched a few tests up to that point, but I realized then that this was one I had to get right. Adrian was the status quo, or what remained of it. He was beefy and arrogant, with a swelled neck and flared nostrils and chiseled hair, and he walked La Loma as if it were a prison yard. He was calling me out. The park was watching. If I failed to stand up to him, I would forever be his bitch.

In the process of putting ourselves in charge, Todd and I had gone about assembling a board of directors, mostly coaches and spouses, a dozen or so altogether. Some, like Jonathan Muñoz's dad, shared our sensibilities. Others had tougher veneers, such as Omar Robles, a union steward at a Coca-Cola bottling plant (whom I had enlisted, without luck, in my scoreboard campaign), and Carmen Delgado, a coed softball babe with a brood of kids (the youngest of them that boy I confounded, Sebastian) who sported a Harley-Davidson decal on the rear of her minivan. I did not delegate much to any of them. This was my show, and if I was going to assume the risks of it flopping, I wanted everything under my direction. What the board gave me mostly was credibility and cover or, as I told Todd, only half in jest, the "illusion of consensus." Before I could oust Adrian, I was going to need their backing. I prepared a letter: "We have been forced, regrettably, to conclude that you are, at the least, indifferent and, at worst, hostile to the best interests of the Monterey Park Sports Club." I asked each of them to sign it. It was important, I thought, to establish that the organization, in its new incarnation, was talking, not just the finicky commissioner. This could not be a feud between me and Adrian. It was a fight for the soul of La Loma. There was another perception that had me worried, a question of my own cultural limberness and validity. Every battle, I was coming to realize, had the unfortunate dimension of pitting me against a villain of Hispanic descent. That was not what I had signed up for. I was supposed to be down for *la raza,* an ethnic and linguistic confederate, not a self-righteous *gabacho* on a crusade to clean up a Mexican park. For my own conscience, I needed those other names on Adrian's letter.

The name that mattered the most to me was Carmen's. She was in some ways a female version of Chris: sassy, ribald, mercurial, even pugnacious, and yet also profoundly empathetic and nurturing. It took me a while to make the connection, but they were, in fact, related; Carmen's mother-in-law and Chris's mother-in-law were sisters. Carmen was fond of calling herself a man hater, dismissing her husband, a prosperous accountant, as "the bio." It took me a while to unscramble that one, too—shorthand for her children's biological father. When it came to her tiny 'Bash, though, Carmen doted and fussed, blowing his nose and probing his ears and plying him with cold milk. Born with a cleft lip and palate, as well as a slew of musculoskeletal disorders, he had endured repeated surgeries by the time Carmen started coaching him in T-Ball, and if he sometimes cried when called out at first base, he was also capable of charming the entire park with a vaudevillian jig or a flutter of bedroom eyes. "Look at my handsome man," Carmen would purr, bathing his wobbly head in kisses. She had grown up in what passed for the ghetto of Monterey Park, a backwoodsy pocket on the eastern fringe of La Loma, and graduated from Keppel, the school that had booted Freddy and that awaited Max. Her dad was a neighborhood roughneck, a prowler and a hype who wasted away while she was a teenager, and I had heard her mention that her brother, who still lived in their childhood home, regularly kicked it with my predecessor, the cavalier Bob Pasos, whose two boys were still in the league. In other words, Carmen could undermine me just as easily as she could lend me cred. If her allegiances were tested—and if she had foreseen that as a possibility, I suspect, she would have been reluctant to volunteer—I was less than certain how she would choose.

"Missus Delgado, may I have a moment with you?" I asked one afternoon, leading her into the equipment room. She wore jeans and a Pepperdine sweatshirt, which is where her husband had earned his M.B.A., and a humongous diamond on her left hand. Her fingernails were long and sculpted, and when she smiled, the corners of her eyes burst into crinkles, like a bullet on shatterproof glass. I gave her the letter. It was full of terms—"decency," "trust," "professionalism," "obligation"—not often associated with our league. Maybe that kind of talk would scare her off. Maybe, if I was lucky, it was just what she had been waiting to hear. Carmen put the paper down and shook her head. "You're crazy," she said. I did not know her well enough to be able to gauge whether that was good or bad.

"I might be," I said.

"I'm a behind-the-scenes type of person," Carmen said.

"This is important."

"Low-pro."

"If you sign it, everyone will."

Carmen reached into her purse.

I offered my pen.

"Why, thank you—" she said.

"You're doing the right thing."

"—Mister Commissioner."

Now we had to find Adrian. I checked the schedule for his next game. Hopefully, he would show. I made copies of the letter. One I sent, via certified mail, to Adrian's shop. Another I delivered to city hall. A third I gave to Todd, to present directly to our antagonist. It was a Monday night, and the Dukes were playing late. We would corner him as soon as it was over and inform him that the Monterey Park Sports Club had found him in default of his contract, that we would be billing him for any costs we had incurred, and that we were removing him, effective immediately, as a coach. "Do you think we should let the police know?" Todd asked me. "They might be able to send a squad car by the park, or at least have one on standby." He was worried, rightfully so.

"That may be asking for even more trouble," I said, thinking of all my years on the gang beat, roaming the streets unaccompanied. "Whatever he does, I think we're going to have to stand there and take it."

"You don't know how he's going to react."

"What's the worst he can do?"

"Well, my friend," Todd said with an exaggerated gulp, "it's been good knowing you."

For some reason I was late getting to Adrian's game. It must have finished early, or else I got waylaid attending to some other mis-adventure on the lower field. I have no recollection, either, of where Max was, but then, that was one of the reasons La Loma was worth defending. My ten-year-old son could be running around almost anywhere on that hill, even at an hour when he should probably be in bed, and I could be assured that he was insulated from the dangers that lurked in most parks after dark. Predators were unheard of. Whatever perils existed in La Loma, they were of our own making. By the time I worked my way up to the top, Todd was already in the equipment room with Adrian. I could hear their voices even before I swung open the door, Adrian defiant and Todd sermonizing in the modulated rhetoric of a school bureaucrat. I knew Todd to be almost cartoonish in his enthusiasms, bug-eyed and tongue-tied, like a Bengali Elmer Fudd. If we wanted to catch a movie, he called it "going to the show," and afterward if we stopped for a margarita at our favorite twenty-four-hour Mexican dive, he was sure to give himself at least one crippling brain freeze. Under stress, though, Todd had reverted to full Dr. Ullah mode, with his flash drive on a lanyard and silk polo shirt buttoned to the neck, expounding on "processes" and "time frames" and "outcomes." I felt bad about making him start without me.

"You little fuck," Adrian spit. He had turned away from Todd and was pointing a thick finger at my chest. If the room had been smoldering before, my arrival was a stream of lighter fluid. The letter was on the table. Adrian had refused to look at it, even touch it. We disgusted him—all our smug, highfalutin talk, our nitpicking, our ungratefulness. He had saved us money, thousands of dollars, did we realize that? Now we were disparaging him, tattling to the city, messing with a man's livelihood. "How dare you?" he said, pushing his way through the chairs to face me, shoulder to shoulder. "How dare you fuckin' disrespect me like this?"

As somebody who has managed to live four decades without getting into a fistfight, I am occasionally torn over whether this makes me honorable or a wuss. The closest I ever came was in sixth grade, during recess at Chapman Elementary School. Out on the blacktop, a kid I had never seen before slugged me in the jaw and snatched a basketball from my hands, but I was so unacquainted with this kind of behavior—*What? Ouch. Did someone just beat me up?*—that by the time I recovered enough to weigh my options, he was nowhere to be found. I say this only to explain that I had no guard to raise against Adrian, no instinct for going *mano a mano* if he were to decide to knock out my teeth. When I was still in high school, learning my away around Portland's barrooms on a fraudulent driver's license—which required me to pass as a twenty-three-year-old Irishman—I once saw a dyspeptic old fellow smash a beer bottle against the wall, then feign innocence when the management tried to roust him. "I'm a lover," he kept protesting, "not a fighter." It was a tired old saw, the chorus of a forgotten Kinks song, if I am not mistaken, but I had borrowed the line a few times in my life, and as I resigned myself to absorbing Adrian's rage, I thought of it again. "I just wanted—"

"Fuck you."

"To let you know—"

"Fuck you."

"That it's, um, nothing personal."

"Fuck you."

"And that your kids—"

"Do *not* fuck with my kids!"

"Are still welcome to play."

Adrian puffed his chest and stamped out of the room, my letter to him wafting across the table in his wake. I looked at Todd, and he looked back at me. My head was pounding, my voice close to cracking, but a smirk was beginning to inch across the corner of my mouth. I took what felt like my first breath of the season. "Holy shit," I said. Todd was still trying to read me. "That went well?" he asked. It was my turn for a little bluster: "We lived to tell about it, didn't we?" We had stood up, and Adrian had backed down. It was one of those small acts of will that, I hoped, would reverberate far beyond a single day.

Chapter

Six

"REMEMBER, IT'S FOR THE KIDS." HARDLY A DAY WENT BY at La Loma that I did not hear someone say that—*for the kids, for the kids*—the mantra of youth sports. It was uttered, presumably, as an antidote to all the adult impulses that fueled an organization like ours, vanity and ambition and manhood and posterity, the inclination to turn our children's successes into reflections of us. The thought was nice, to put kids first, to imagine an environment in which they could play and learn and even compete without being subjected to grown-up egos. Little League, however, was not that place. Children rarely decided for themselves that baseball was a palliative, that its splendid juxtapositions—nature and geometry, timelessness and quantification—could be a source of continuity, of renewal. They did not often choose, on their own, to be paraded onto a field and conscripted by a coach, to be drilled and ranked and categorized. It was seldom their desire to turn the game into a performance, to be tested and corrected before an audience of dues-paying partisans, half imploring them to win, half clamoring for them to fail. They might in time discover the virtues of that experience. They might learn to embrace the routines and the protocols, the butterflies and the goose bumps. But it was almost always a parent who first prescribed it, who inculcated in those children the orthodoxy that baseball was fun.

At no point did adults exercise their influence more than in the draft, an unholy ritual of deal making, hairsplitting, arm-twisting, and backstabbing. Once the season got under way kids had a degree of sway over their own fate—they were the ones who played the games, after all—but so much of what would happen, the teams sunk, the titles clinched, was decided before a pitch had ever been thrown. Some coaches were blatant about their agendas, armed with scouting reports and videotape and mock projections of the selection order. They took winning a championship as a parental duty, like throwing a birthday party or springing for braces, a reward to which their child was entitled. Some coaches were more interested in the fraternal aspects of the job, using their picks to gratify coworkers and drinking buddies. It was a perquisite they believed they were owed, too: If they were going to be stuck at the park for three months, they were not about to spend it with strangers. Some coaches professed not to care—any kid would do—which was a sin all its own, condemning a dozen hopeful families to a season of shutouts and slaughters. You needed adversaries to keep the system honest.

The rules for choosing teams in the Monterey Park Sports Club were baroque and arcane and, it will come as no surprise, never put into writing. They were passed down from year to year in the form of oral history, subject to the remembrances and revisions of whoever happened to be in charge. I had sat through enough drafts to know the basics, but I soon would be forced to improvise my own interpretations, La Loma's lore insufficient to account for every crisis or conundrum. The ideal in youth sports is to establish parity, to create teams that mirror one another in talent as closely as possible.

Competitive balance promotes the perception of fairness, of coaches having equal access to the best players, and makes for a healthier, happier experience all around. The actual results might still be lopsided—it was impossible to legislate effort or acumen or luck—but as long as the process was sound and transparent, free of what was commonly bemoaned as "politics," it was easier to accept whatever happened on the field. At least that was my philosophy as commissioner. Not all coaches were as willing to suspend their self-interest, and I was, of course, still a coach.

The starting point for any draft was the freeze, the player or players a coach was allowed to secure before anyone else got a chance. How many freezes per team—and, just as important, how those freezes were counted—tended to be the hallmarks of a youth league, evidence of either a laissez-faire or a regulatory bent. Some programs imposed no control, allowing coaches to recruit their own teams and show up with rosters already intact. Kids got to be with their friends, parents with like-minded adults they could count on for baby-sitting or transportation. At La Loma we ran T-Ball that way. It was great, as long as the children never learned the score. The older the players, the more opportunity for a cutthroat coach to assemble a superpower and shred less zealous squads. At the other extreme were the reformers, organizations that eliminated freezes altogether. Some soccer leagues were like that, with the league itself rating players, even moving them around like puzzle pieces, until no team could be said to have an advantage. I appreciated the intention, but it did away with partnerships—relationships—and without those, frankly, where was the joy?

The Monterey Park Sports Club was somewhere in the middle, with directives that created the appearance of a level playing field but that were also open to manipulation. To determine the drafting order, we drew numbers from a hat—literally: someone would have to take off his cap and fill it with scraps of paper—a method that gave every coach the same shot at the number one pick. We continued to pick in numerical order through the first round, moving from lowest to highest; then, to compensate the coaches at the end, we dropped into the second round and snaked back, highest to lowest, and so on. Whenever I identified this formula as reverse serpentine, the room burst into sniggers—such a fancy label for the crude bartering that was sure to follow.

A new team, whether new to the league or just new to the age division, was allowed two freezes, one for the coach's child and one for an assistant coach's. Coaches' kids went in the second round, assistants' in the third, leaving the first round open to choose a top player from the pool of available talent. As a coach that suited me fine: Max and Alex were always guaranteed of being together, and I could still use my first pick to go after a superstar, like Jonathan. As commissioner, with responsibility for the success of all teams, I began to grasp the degree to which that system tipped the balance of power. If a coach's own child was not particularly skilled, or at least not as skilled as Max, my team gained a sizable advantage in the second round. If a coach was a novice and did not have an assistant to team up with or, rather, did not know which parents had kids worth teaming up with, he could never hope to land a kid in the third round as valuable as Todd's son. Essentially, we enabled coaches with the best genes and the shrewdest alliances to withhold the most proficient players from the talent pool and to secure them at discounted prices. Maybe that was just the nature of sports. Maybe parents who had cultivated their children's skills, who had invested time in the park, had earned a rightful advantage. Still, that was no consolation to the kids who found themselves, through no fault of their own, on a team coached by a parent without those advantages.

A week before the draft we held tryouts, which should have been called evaluations, since no child was too inept to make a team. This was one of the charms of our league, that every roster, even those of the eventual champions, was sure to be freighted with at least a couple of kids who looked as if they would disintegrate upon contact with the ball. I bought a packet of white shipping labels, which we numbered with a Sharpie and stuck on the back of each child's shirt. It took at least an hour to go through an entire age division, forty or fifty youngsters running the bases and fielding grounders and taking swings while the coaches, deadpan behind sunglasses and clip-boards, distilled each player into a grade. Most kids showed up for tryouts jittery, trying too hard to make an impression, but those who scarcely tried at all were the ones everyone watched for. Sand-bagging was a chronic syndrome among La Loma's best players: You could see them slogging through the drills in slow-mo, as if shot with a tranquilizer dart, chins sagging, feet dragging, some even going so far as to throw with the wrong hand or swing from the wrong side of the plate. I was never sure if those antics were ordered by a coach or by a parent or if the child had taken it upon himself to camouflage his skill. Technically, I suppose, it was cheating. I never asked anyone to do it myself. But it was hard to police—how do you command a kid to not suck?—and, anyway, pretty easy to see through, unless, of course, you were new to the park or to coaching, in which case this was just another disadvantage to add to your list.

Tryouts were supposed to be mandatory, but we had no way of enforcing that, either. The only remedy would be to scratch anyone who failed to show up, and in our league's precarious state, we did not have the luxury of shooing away the players we had just pleaded for. The hotshots seemed to understand this better than anyone, and rather than go through the trouble of tanking, they often stayed home, deliberately keeping their skills out of view. On draft night, coaches were required to choose first from the pool of players they had observed at tryouts. That seemed fair, to start with the talent that had been on display. The names of no-shows were set aside, to be dispensed randomly, again from the hat, after all the evaluated players had been parceled out. That was supposed to be the penalty—that a coach could not *choose* a player who had skipped tryouts—yet if a coach happened to be conspiring with one of those players, the penalty could actually be an edge. Although the coveted player was unavailable to the intended coach at the out-set, the kid was also unavailable to everyone else. Instead of getting snatched up in the first round, he remained in the penalty box, as it were, untouchable and more or less under the radar. The connivers occasionally hit the jackpot. A coach might have a solid eleven players on his roster already, and then in his final slot—out of the hat, eureka!—he lucks into the player he really wanted. If not, the scheme could still be pulled off with a trade, which we allowed for at the end of the night. It was always easier to swap for a last-round question mark, a kid who had revealed nothing, a kid in whom the other coaches had nothing invested, than for a first-round whiz whose value they had all witnessed for themselves.

No coach manipulated the draft as coldly as Omar, our resident Teamster. He was gruff and mercenary, with heavy jowls and narrow eyes and a porcupinelike goatee. His cell phone rang to the theme from *The Godfather*. Although I had some trepidation about his past—his hometown, San Diego, was tattooed across the back of his neck—Omar had a loyal following among La Loma's iffier families, many with absent or incarcerated dads, and he was always rolling up to the park with a truckload of wayward kids. By inviting him to serve on the board, I was probably granting him more pull than he had earned, but he had two boys of his own, one in Rookies and one in Double A, and he coached both of their teams, not just in our program but also in a Little League in the next town over. It was hard to argue with his commitments. In exchange for those good deeds, though, Omar expected to be rewarded with rosters that were to his liking, which excluded anyone who might soften his act: girls, Asians, fatties, pansies, asthmatics. Omar wanted kids who could rumble. His players were his dawgs.

Draft night, for him, was like union bargaining, a test of resolve, of gall. There was always some kid who needed to be on Omar's team—a car pool issue, a money issue, a custody issue—and invariably that kid had a friend or a cousin who needed to be kept off the streets and, well, Omar was pretty sure nobody wanted to be responsible for thwarting any of their chances to play. Other coaches schemed, but Omar was the only coach I ever found whose collaborators were willing to back him up with the threat of a strike. "The kid's already said he's not gonna play for nobody else," Omar would warn. "If you pick him, he's gonna drop. You'll be left with nothin'." That was usually enough to scare off a rival coach. If your first-round pick were to end up withdrawing, you would have to accept a replacement from the waiting list, and the odds of that player being a first-round talent were slim. It seemed prudent to grab the next best thing. "I'm not sayin' it's right," Omar would add. "It's just the way the kid is."

Every now and then, out of greed or principle, a coach would reject Omar's ultimatum and draft the kid anyway. Maybe the player had made it to tryouts and was just too good to pass up. Maybe the coach was so fed up with Omar that he was willing to martyr his own team just to defy him. I admired the guts that took, but the fallout hurt everybody—the saboteur, his players, Omar, the family that was counting on him to look out for their son. I remember once the boy's name was Gabriel. The next day his mom called and gave me an earful. "I don't know why everyone has to make this so difficult," she said. "It's not like we're asking for the world."

"Well, actually, ma'am," I said, "you're kind of the one making it difficult."

"I'm what?"

"Maybe I'm being old-fashioned, but it would be nice to think that every child who enrolls in our league would be happy just to play."

"No, I don't think you understand. I'm a single mom. I work. I can't get my son to the park. Omar's been like a father to him."

"Oh, I believe it. That's the Omar I know. But why go through this whole process—having tryouts, conducting a draft—if we're just going to disregard it all and let everyone be on whatever team they want?"

"This isn't everyone. It's my son. If you're not going to put him on Omar's team, then I'll need a refund."

"I wish he was on Omar's team. I really do. But it didn't work out that way. I'm sorry. I'll put a check in the mail tomorrow."

"So it's like that?" she said. For a second I caught myself: Was I being too harsh, too hasty to cut her loose? Her parting shot brought me back to reality. "And here I was," she said, "thinking this was supposed to be for the kids."

Even after the draft was settled, Omar was not done shaping his roster. He would begin calling onerous practices, on consecutive days, at inconvenient hours, in the hope of shedding any weaklings he had not been able to fob off on the other coaches. For every refund I issued to a family left off his team, I had to issue at least twice as many to families wishing to flee. It was no coincidence that whenever Omar scared a kid off, he always seemed to know of another player—often the very player, lo and behold, who had just withdrawn in protest—eager to fill the vacancy. Sometimes it was easier to relent, to give Omar a team in his image, than to have him stuck with players he would not or could not accommodate.

My first season as commissioner, Omar ended up with a seven-year-old boy named Alfonso. It was a bad match from the start, a quiet, droopy-eyed kid and a bristly, take-no-prisoners coach, with Alfonso never doing much to shine and Omar never giving him much of a chance. Every team played twice a week, for eight weeks, and it was customary for each coach, win or lose, to award a game ball to the child who had made the day's noteworthy contribution. With sixteen games to choose from, most coaches found a way to salute everyone on their roster and still have balls left over for the kids who consistently deserved them. Not Omar. As the season drew to a close, Alfonso's dad called me to complain: His son was the only player Omar had failed to recognize. "Wow, I dunno, that's, I guess, um, pretty unfortunate," I said. Alfonso's dad seemed to think I was being facetious. "I don't know what sort of values you're trying to promote here," he said, "but so far I'm not very impressed with you and your league."

I called Omar. "Did you really not give the kid a game ball?"

"He didn't earn one."

"You couldn't find something to applaud?"

"Not really."

"He never walked? He never got hit by a pitch?"

"Like I said, he never earned one."

"Lots of kids don't *earn* one."

"They do on my team."

I called back Alfonso's dad. "Look, I'm sorry, but Omar's got his own way of doing things. It's not the way I coach my team. It's not the way I would want most of our coaches to go about their business. But I've come to learn, there is a certain kind of parent that appreciates his approach. Hopefully, next year, your son will end up on a team that's a better fit for him."

"What about the game ball?"

"What about it?"

"You're saying it's okay that my son was the only kid who didn't get one?"

"I'm saying our league has no rule entitling every kid to a game ball and I'm not going to start orchestrating how coaches should dispense them."

"So you're condoning Omar's behavior?"

"No, actually, I'm pretty opposed to Omar's behavior. But I'm not sure I understand what it is you think I should do. Should he no longer get to coach *his* son because *your* son didn't get a game ball? Should I kick Omar out of the league because he acts like a dick sometimes? We're a volunteer organization, and believe me, I have to worry about coaches doing far worse things than Omar's ever been accused of."

"You're really something," Alfonso's dad said. "I thought this was supposed to be for the kids."

Nothing was more delicate than running my own draft, adjudicating the formation of Max's team. The first year I had to do that, to be a coach and a commissioner at the same time, the whole thing blew up on me—a conniption of spite and envy—and Omar, if he had possessed a scruple or two, could have saved my hide. That was our returning year of Single A, my season of destiny, the payoff for making La Loma viable again. I had almost my entire roster secured already, a conspicuous gang of ten-year-olds, and it was going to be next to impossible for a newly formed team, with just two nine-year-old freezes, to impede our march on the championship.

Retention—keeping players on the same roster from one season to the next—was yet another time-honored practice of the Monterey Park Sports Club that tampered with the evenness of the draft. Our rules allowed coaches to retain the same kids as long as they were in the same age division, which meant a team could stick together for two years before it had to disband and start over in the next division up. I cherished that constancy, the chance to see a core of returning players grow and flourish, and I had even traded away some very good ten-year-olds in our first year of Single A—including one very, very good ten-year-old—so that I would have more nine-year-olds and as such more players eligible to come back for that encore season. There was nothing devious about it. I had paid the price, even sealed my doom, getting pounded by the same ten-year-olds I had let go. Now that I was not just an advocate for my team but a defender of the league, nobody seemed to remember my sacrifice.

We were gathered in the La Loma equipment room, a warren of lost mitts and cobwebbed rafters and limestone sacks, the same place I would secure Carmen's signature and, later, square off with Adrian. There were five coaches in Single A that year, three of us with returning teams, the other two both newcomers I had recruited. As I recited the names of the ten-year-olds I was retaining, I was met with grumbles, then groans, then finally wails of protest. My team was stacked. The season would be a coronation. One of the new coaches, a tightly wound aerospace engineer named Gomez, was threatening to walk out. "This is unbelievable," he said. "What happened to all your talk about integrity?"

"I shouldn't have to apologize," I said. "I was in your shoes, starting from scratch, just a year ago."

"I still don't see how this is fair," said Gomez, who had signed up to coach his daughter and already was feeling disadvantaged about having a girl for his franchise player. "Do you really think my team is going to be able to compete with yours?"

"Well, no, not exactly," I said. "But that's not the point. I assembled my team according to the rules, the same rules that have always been in place. I'd also like to remind everybody that we lost last year. I'm not the champion of anything. Omar kicked my butt."

Everyone turned to Omar. He was wearing a grimace and a backward Padres cap. My dealings with the man were a source of endless drama, not merely because I was the boss and he was a headache but because his oldest son was a grade ahead of Max. Every other year we were in the same division together, rivals mostly but, when it suited our purposes, also allies. In my first year of Single A, Omar had beaten me to the punch and snared my prize, Jonathan Muñoz, and thus it was with Omar that I had been forced to make a deal, to trade the league's premier ten-year-old so that I could claim Jonathan as a nine-year-old and keep him for consecutive seasons. Omar had done me a favor, sort of. He was under no obligation to give me Jonathan. But with the player I had to relinquish, I ended up handing Omar the championship. Omar had since moved up to Double A but was still a board member, the only one versed in the intricacies of Single A, and I had asked him to sit in on our draft, to help mediate whatever conflicts my dual roles might create. This was his cue to step in and bail me out, to explain that our league, for all its imperfections, did have some policies and precedents. What was unfair was not the composition of my roster, no matter how unseemly it might look, but changing the rules on me because of it.

"C'mon, Omar," I said, "tell them. You were in my exact position last year." He folded his arms and raised his chin, crooking the corners of his mouth. He loved plugging his own cause—if you were on his team, like it or not, you knew you were on a *team*— but he hated acting as a referee, exercising judgment, being answerable. Especially if there was nothing in it for him. "Yo no espeaking inglés," Omar said. Everyone laughed. Spanglish did have its charms. I smiled, too, but I wanted to shout: *If not for me, there would be no draft, no damn league, you sonofabitches, and screwing with my team, badgering me into falling on the sword, is one hell of a thanks for bringing this park back to life.* I decided that self-pity was not the tone I wanted to strike, though, and anyway, Gomez was right about one thing—I had put a lot of effort into establishing my propriety, into proving the Monterey Park Sports Club was no longer the same beast. I am not sure whether people had higher expectations of me because of that or whether they sensed, in my conscientiousness, a weakness for them to exploit.

By tradition, we drafted the older players in each division first, in this case the ten-year-olds, and once they were all accounted for, we would start over with the nine-year-olds. That way a coach who was unlucky in one bracket got another shot in the next. Because my returning players were all considered freezes, beginning with the first round, I was already maxed out in that half of the draft. No matter what number I drew from the hat, the pool of ten-year-olds would be exhausted by the time my turn rolled around. That was as it should be. The new teams were entitled to divvy up the older players among themselves. Because I had no nine-year-olds, though, I was competing with everyone else in that bracket for the top pick. That was proving to be the sticking point. Nobody in the room thought I deserved anything that would improve my roster. "How about this," I said, wishing I could retract what I was proposing even before I got the words out. "I can't do anything about my ten-year-olds. They're all locked into place. But when we do the nine-year-olds, I'll agree to forfeit my right to the number one pick. If I get it, I'll put it back and draw again. I'll still get a pick in the first round—I'm entitled to that—but it won't be the number one kid." Either I had shown myself to be a chivalrous leader or the world's biggest stooge, but my offer seemed to placate the Single A mob. The draft could proceed.

I ran my fingers over the creased slips of paper and pressed one into my fist. It would kill me to draw number one, only to have to give it up. I unfolded the wad, square by square. It figured. "You've got to be kidding," I moaned. Any other number and my self-defeating stunt would have remained theoretical. The draft would have continued on its regular path. By drawing number one, I had to abide by our bargain. Now we were fiddling with the fate of my team. I put my winning hand aside and drew again. What else could it be? Number five. I would be drafting last.

The first few nine-year-olds to go were naturals, swift and wiry, and I would have snatched any of them up if given the chance. By the time we got to number five, the choices were less obvious, the drop-off that abrupt, and I settled on a courteous, slightly anxious boy with a buzz cut and big ears named Garrett Masada. He was a stone-cold basketball player—Todd knew him from the Asian leagues, where he had a reputation as a three-point specialist—but a baseball tenderfoot. I was partial to kids like that, with more finesse than brawn, players whom I thought to be temperate and respect-ful, which is to say, a roster of anti-Omars. Garrett, if nothing else, would be coachable. He wore a Dodger cap to our first practice and responded to all my instructions with a polite nod.

"You're going to be a big part of this team," I told Garrett. "I like your approach."

"I've never really played baseball before, coach," he said.

"Don't worry," I said, "I have a lot of confidence in you."

At the start of every season I always ran the same drill, lining my players up at home plate and pitching them a semideflated bas-ketball. They loved swinging at such a big floppy target—even the weakest hitter was not going to miss that—and it taught them to drive the bat through the ball rather than halting at the first sign of resistance. Without air the basketball rarely traveled beyond the infield, which gave me an opportunity to also discuss the impor-tance of running out every dribbler or pop-up instead of slowing down to watch the ball's path. It was a gimmicky exercise but a good one, and I used it to signal that being on a Coach Jesse team was a different sort of experience. When Garrett's turn came, I curled the basketball in my right arm and sent a soft underhand bloop toward the plate. Garrett eyed it hungrily, then stepped and swung. The ball was supposed to cushion the bat—a nine-inch globe of synthetic leather swallowing a two-and-a-quarter-inch barrel of aluminum alloy—but somehow, in Garrett's case, it acted more like a trampoline. I had never had this happen before, and it has never happened since: The instant he made contact with the ball, the bat bounced right back, ricocheting into Garrett's face. Rather than sprinting to first, he stood there, dazed, with a hand over his nose, blood streaming through his fingers.

That turned out, regrettably, to be a fair preview of Garrett's first year of baseball. Todd kept our scorebook in those days, and Colin's dad, who was a high school government teacher, distilled all the hieroglyphs into stats. After the last game had been played, I would take the numbers and weave them into a personalized record of each kid's season, a mininarrative, suitable for framing. The ones who wowed were easier to do than the ones who bumbled, but I put the same effort and care into each certificate—about a week to finish the whole team. If you wrote it down, I liked to tell myself, it lasted forever. Even if Garrett had wanted to forget, I have a file in my computer that shows he batted .182 and struck out twenty-five times.

Garrett did get six hits that season, and the biggest of them, which came on a June afternoon, in the final inning of a game that saw us losing nine to six, I can recall without any notes. There were two outs, that I am sure of, and two runners on. Whatever hope we had, Garrett was it. *C'mon, now, Garrett, buddy, you can do it, hold your ground, be a hitter.* Did I really believe he was going to keep our rally alive? I knew that if Garrett stopped believing, my answer made no difference. He let a few pitches go by. He swung and missed. When he swung again, he connected, a shot into straightaway center, all the way to the deep grass, leaving me to wonder where *that* had been all season. *Way to go, kid, nice stroke, good job, that's a stand-up double, two ribbies, I knew you could do it.* The score was now nine to eight, and Garrett, safely on base, represented the tying run. This game, at this age, was all about the art of the impossible.

The other team called for time, and their coach, one of the Single A newcomers, trotted to the pitcher's mound. The entire infield huddled around him, whispering behind their gloves. I was still celebrating Garrett's hit, saluting myself for these grand lessons in faith and grit I was crafty enough to impart. The umpire signaled for play to resume. Garrett took a couple steps off the bag, watching for the pitcher's next move. But there was no move, no windup. The pitcher just stood there. Before Garrett recognized the trap, a poker-faced infielder walked right up and tagged him out. End of inning, end of game. It was the old hidden ball trick, a stunt from the if-you're-not-cheating-you're-not-trying department, something I had never seen attempted outside of one of the lesser *Bad News Bears* sequels. Setting aside the question of whether it was properly executed—a spirited discussion of balks and mounds and dead balls, including the nuances of MLB rule 5.11, spilled into the next several seasons—I could not fathom that a coach would instruct his team to steal a victory that way, that anyone would take pleasure in preying on such an easy mark. There were lessons in this, just not the ones I imagined. Garrett, to my relief, would continue to make a name for himself on the basketball court—I reaped the benefits of coaching him a couple of years later—but he never came back to baseball. It bothered me that I was unable to give him more reasons to return.

I still had a remarkable collection of players that year, kids I adored for their ingenuousness and resilience, and watching them blossom in their return to Single A, knowing how close we had come to disbanding, helped make up for all the nuisances. Jonathan was turning into a freak of nature, a ten-year-old man, free of flab or wiggles, with broad shoulders and a bulging Adam's apple and long pterodactyl arms. He arrived at the park as if checking in at the office, all buttoned, tucked, and laced, lugging his gear in a rolling equipment bag that was big enough to stow some of his teammates. Younger players stared at him, pointing and whispering, and for the first time I saw a few kids even ask Jonathan for his autograph. The attention flustered him. His family believed in humility and service, in never lording anything over anyone. Once I tried to pay him ten bucks for helping me distribute programs on opening day—about a thousand of them, over the course of an hour—but Jonathan gave me back the money as soon as I put it in his hand. "Thanks, coach," he said. "But it wouldn't be right."

On the mound he was more commanding than ever, the perfect merging of menace and elegance. As he launched into his windup, you could see the feet of his opponents shuffling, instinctively, seeking the safety of ground outside the batter's box. Those who summoned the courage to stick around for the pitch would flinch and duck and even close their eyes, waiting for the pop of Max's glove to signal that the ball had been delivered without resulting in their death or dismemberment. More than once Jonathan struck out the side on nine consecutive pitches—*pop, pop, pop, pop, pop, pop, pop, pop, pop*—a barrage so rhythmic, so methodical, that it was easy to forget we were supposed to be watching a duel, not an exhibition. As a coach I did not feel I had much to offer Jonathan, at least not in the way of instruction. His greatness was all his own, hardly a reflection of my insight or experience, and if anyone was going to tinker with his gifts, that person had better have a résumé more formidable than what anyone in the Monterey Park Sports Club could slap together. My obligation, as I saw it, to Jonathan, to his parents, was not to propel him to new heights but just the opposite—to keep him grounded, to provide a sane, unhurried environment in which he could enjoy what remained of being a kid. *Take your time. Nice and easy. Just relax. Stay within yourself.* If Jonathan was as special as I thought he was, he did not need me adding to the ambitions that would be hoisted upon his shoulders in the years ahead.

Compared to Jonathan, Max was increasingly the renegade, wry, ruffled, idiomatic, far less in awe of the authoritarian veneer that grown-ups stash their foibles and doubts behind. On our way to school one morning, he recounted a flippant remark he had made to a teacher the day before, the details of which escape me now, but it was irreverent enough that I felt the need to admonish him. Max rolled his eyes. "I can make adults laugh," he told me. "I know the ways of life." His hair was growing long and bushy, sprouting from his baseball cap like a nutmeg-colored Chia Pet. He wore three-quarter sleeves that flapped in the breeze and an oversized jersey that billowed from his belt. I have a picture of him, looking just like this, while being projected on the DodgerVision screen, twenty-six feet high and forty-six feet wide. As a fund-raising incentive, the Dodgers had offered to escort our top five sellers onto the field and introduce them before the game, and since I was the keeper of all ticket orders, I knew exactly how many Max needed to make the cut. It was not dishonest—I still had to pony up $264 for the privilege—but I decided it was about time that being commissioner earned me a perk. The club invited me down, too, and as I marched with Max across that cool Bermuda grass, around the crushed-brick base paths, along the spray-painted foul lines, it was hard to not want to run or jump or slide. When we reached home plate, Max turned to look at the bleachers, with that iconic zigzag roof, a good four hundred feet away. "Do you think I could hit one out of here?" he asked. "Maybe one day," I said. "Do you think *you* could hit one out of here?" he asked. Either he was more innocent than I realized or he was toying with me. "I'll let you figure that one out," I said.

If he had to choose a sport, Max probably would have said at the time that he liked basketball more; it was all performance—moves, fakes, style. Baseball was the odd sport in which the offense did not have the ball; it was about reactions—reflexes, repetition, readiness. In those days L.A. was a Lakers town. Shaq and Kobe were our divas. The Dodgers, a notch above mediocre, were characterless and interchangeable, the stars coming and going like bad sitcoms. Nobody was on a first-name basis with baseball players, anyway: Kevin? Shawn? Paul? Calling them Brownie, Greenie, or Dukie hardly added to their aura.

For his birthday that year, I bought Max another Louisville Slugger, this one with his full name, Nicarao and all, etched in the wood. He wanted to use it in a game, to be original, counterintuitive. It splintered on the first pitch. If he was not the phenom Jonathan was, Max was still more of an athlete than I ever could have hoped to be. He was hitting the ball as well as anyone in the league, his body like a bow and arrow, bat drawn back, weight coiled around his right thigh, left toe barely grazing the dirt, half flexed, half elastic, all poised to pivot and pounce. He started the season with an eighteen-game hitting streak and finished with a .620 average, including five doubles, seven triples, and one home run. I had no idea where he got it from, the carriage, the coordination, the ability to translate what I had loved, the imagery, the idea of baseball, into something demonstrable and consistent. It was not the Eastern European Jew in him, that was for sure. I came from tiny, hunched people—garment workers on my father's side, writers and socialists on my mother's—who knew of perseverance but not contests of strength or speed.

The answer, as awkward as it was to admit, had to lie somewhere in Central America, in Raynelda's genetic antecedents. She came from short, oppressed people, too, but they were stout and fierce, drinkers, fighters, dancers, lovers, for whom the body was an avenue to freedom, to absolution. Baseball was actually a cherished pastime in Nicaragua, the remnant of a century's worth of U.S. intervention. Dennis Martínez, the first Nicaraguan to play in the majors, is such a symbol of pride and unity that he has been routinely courted as a presidential candidate. In 1991, when he pitched a perfect game for the Montreal Expos at Dodger Stadium, the *L.A. Times* ran a picture of him weeping in the visitors' dugout. I asked the photographer to sign a print for me and gave it, as a Christmas present, to Raynelda's little brother, Nestor. I am not sure I fully grasped the irony of all this at the time, but it now seems unmistakable. I had been using baseball as a barricade, to shield Max from these volcanic Nicaraguans, and yet it was his connection to them—the Nicarao in him—that was giving him the capacity to excel. How much harder would it have been for me to coach him, or for him to be the son of the coach, if the game had not favored his gifts?

We ended that 2003 season in third place, with a record of seven wins, eight losses, and one tie. Our struggles were attributable to another abstruse, homegrown rule—to be fair, one of the Monterey Park Sports Club's wiser mandates—that required Single A teams to employ a nine-year-old pitcher at least three innings a week. It kept ten-year-olds from dominating the division and ensured that coaches would have an interest in developing younger arms. In Little League, as in the bigs, there was no such thing as too much pitching. A year before, when Jonathan was nine, I had been able to ignore the rule. He always pitched the maximum, six innings a week, which meant we were always in compliance with the minimum. Now that I was getting most of my pitching from ten-year-olds, I had to worry about that three-inning quota all the time, especially since the responsibility fell to my top nine-year-old, the dear, hapless Garrett Masada. I was not expecting miracles. He did not have to be an ace or a closer. He just had to get the ball near the plate, to keep us in the game. The first team Garrett pitched against was that of my draft night insurgent, Gomez. The first batter he faced was Gomez's daughter. On his first pitch Garrett beaned her. He hit another batter. Then he walked four straight. I tried him again the next week, to much the same effect. We still had time to work on his mechanics, and I still had a couple of other nine-year-olds to fall back on, but as the season crept along, it became clear that forfeiting the number one pick had cuffed my team of killer ten-year-olds—that my munificence, or spinelessness, or maybe it was egotism, had left us with a tragic flaw.

The coach who benefited the most from my sacrifice was the one who least needed the help. Her name was Lulu Magallon, and if that sounds familiar, it is because she was once married to the brother of our excommunicated uniform vendor Adrian. Lulu was even whiter than I was—pale, freckled, redheaded—but with the accent, the attitude, of a true East L.A. homegirl. She wore her polyester baseball shorts skintight and her T-shirts cinched at the waist, her lips painted strawberry and her hair strapped in place by an Angels visor. Women, to her, were bitches, and men were, well, bitches, too; woe be unto any who dared flirt with her. "Men are good for only one thing," she would holler across the field, "and most ain't even very good at that." In the same way that Omar had his following, so did Lulu, and I had to admit that, like him, she was good for the park—a brazen, foulmouthed single mom who backed up her act with an indisputable affection for the game. She had two kids in Single A, a boy named Donovan, who was Max's age, and a girl named Devynn, who was eleven already but permitted under league rules, which allowed for judicious doses of sexism, to remain in her brother's division. They were both gamers, agile and aggressive and, it seemed to me, more than a little fearful of incurring their mother's wrath.

Every other year, after Omar had won his championship and moved up to the next division, Lulu would replace him as my principal rival. I had dispensed with her our first season of Single A—she had berated Donnie, a lefty with a temperamental fastball, until he could no longer throw a strike—but now that she had drawn the number one pick, *my* pick, a kid who could throw strikes all day, it would be harder to fend her off. Before I realized it was in the works, she had also engineered a trade for the number three pick, who, despite being drafted onto Gomez's team, refused to go anywhere without number one and, as a result, had taken it upon himself to show up, a free agent, at Lulu's practices. He proved to be an even better pitcher than his buddy. All that ganging up on me and my überteam—and it was Lulu, as predatory a coach as there was at La Loma, to whom the spoils were falling. How was that any fairer? If this was all about the kids, why did it feel like Lulu was gearing up to kick my ass?

We met her in the finals, again thanks to Jonathan's arm. When he was on the mound, we were as awesome as everyone feared we would be, but then the next game I would have to fulfill my nine-year-old pitching requirement, and we would unravel like the yarn of a hardball stripped of its cowhide. If the championship were just a single game, I would have liked our chances. Lulu's team had lost only once all season—to us. In a best two out of three series, my team would be exposed. Jonathan would have to win the first game. The second game, with our nine-year-old on the mound, would be a disaster. In a game three, I would get to use Jonathan for another three innings—the one time a pitcher could exceed the weekly six-inning limit—then I would have to pray that Max could finish it off.

The opener was on a ninety-degree evening in late July, five months after Todd and I had staged our Monterey Park Sports Club coup. I was still laboring over that Magic Johnson story, which was due at the printer in a week, and it was getting impossible to pretend that my baseball life was not interfering with the cycle of the magazine. My nose had burned and peeled a couple of times already, and every pair of shoes I owned had turned the color of La Loma's soil. Bills were piled up on my kitchen table. Dishes were molding in the sink. I was living on a diet of Dodger Dogs and sopping my skull in bittersweet barleywines in order to get to sleep. I had spent the day in knots, brooding over my lineup, sketching out defensive assignments on the back of an envelope. In our league everyone batted—eleven, twelve, sometimes thirteen players—no matter how many were on your or your opponent's roster. Everyone also had to play the field—the minimum was two consecutive innings—even if that child failed to come to practice. As a coach, you had to have a plan, to accommodate them all, to comply with the rules and keep everyone content, and to still put your best team out there with the game on the line. Jonathan was magnificent as always, pitching a three-hitter, with fourteen strikeouts. That should have been enough to earn any team a win, except that Donnie pitched a one-hitter. Max looked edgy, like he was trying to win the game with every swing. He whiffed twice, ending his eighteen-game streak. We lost by a run.

Even for a wishful thinker like me, I knew we had missed our only shot. The next day, Lulu threw her nine-year-olds against us. My first two batters walked, including Natalie, who had not gotten a hit all season but was so stunning—tall and willowy and radiant, with dimples and brown hair flowing halfway down her back, like a Mexican-American Barbie—that few pitchers could keep their mind on the strike zone. Alex struck out, though, and Jonathan grounded out. Max was next. I could see he was disappointed about coming up empty in the first game. It had been his worst day

at the plate all season. This time he showed patience, letting a ball
go by, then a strike, then another ball. *That's right, Max-er. You see
it now. Pick the one you want.* When he finally uncorked, the result
was epic, a blast to deep, deep center, back, way back, that looked
as though it would never come down. He got all of it, with everything he had, the prettiest, solidest home run swing of his five years
at La Loma. A gasp swept through the bleachers. I clenched both
fists and crouched, waiting to leap from the dugout. That was my
son—Jew, Nicaraguan, or some new breed of kid beyond labels or
lineage—a Little Leaguer for the twenty-first century!

The ball was still in the air as Max rounded first, and it was then
that I realized the center fielder was also still running, peeking over
his shoulder, refusing to concede. I knew that boy, Nathaniel. He
had been Omar's nine-year-old pitcher the previous season, not a superstar but as dependable as any player in the league. How had he
found his way onto Lulu's roster? I remembered: Her assistant
coach was supposedly not returning, and so Lulu had allied herself
with the assistant coach from Omar's old squad, and together they
had formed this dubious hybrid team, half Lulu's kids and half
Omar's remnants, and somehow I had seen fit to give it my okay. It
was as if I was determined to win the hard way, the honorable way,
to show that I could take on all the schemers and still figure out how
to prevail. Ninety-nine times out of a hundred, Max's hit would
have emptied the bases. Ten-year-old boys do not make the catch
that Nathaniel did. I am not saying that we would have won if he
had failed to make it. But when he took one last step and lunged,
pulling the ball out of the sky, glove raised in triumph, it was clear
our season was done.

"Listen up," I shouted after the final out, dragging an ice chest
onto the field. "Gather 'round." My players were soiled and sweaty,
twenty games, maybe forty practices, a couple hundred hours of
baseball under our belts—double all that if you counted the previous year we had spent together—and yet they had come up just a
little short. Maybe one more hit, one fewer error. One slightly less
obliging commissioner. After so much preparation, that was all

that separated us from Lulu's team, which had already begun its victory party, with pizza and fireworks, on the opposite side of the field.

"What's in the cooler?" my kids kept asking. "We'll get to that in a minute," I said. I had been working on a new speech, a Little League version of the serenity prayer. "I know it sucks to lose. I don't like it, either. But we can only worry about the things that are within our control. We can't control the umpires. We can't control the draft. We can't always control the wins or the losses. What we can control is what's in here"—for dramatic effect I thumped my chest—"your heart, your desire, your commitment, your willingness to believe in yourself. Nobody can take that away from you, and nobody has. I don't want anybody on this team, not even for a second, to feel bad about what happened today."

On that note, I swung open the lid. I had spent the afternoon in my kitchen filling the cooler with water balloons, dozens of them, knowing the likelihood that we would be in need of consolation. Our side of the field, the loser's side, was suddenly pandemonium, so loud and delirious that Lulu's kids stopped their celebration to see what had gotten into us. I grabbed a balloon and went hunting for Max, stalking him through the scattering herd. The sun was down, but the night was balmy again, the park buzzing with moths and mosquitoes. I spotted that mop of hair under the lights. "Gotcha!" I yelled. I raised my arm. A balloon hit my back. Then another. I was getting ambushed, the water splashing my neck, soaking my jersey, sending muddy rivulets down my arms and legs. Whoever was doing it I could pay back later. I did not want Max to get away. Dripping, shivering, I heaved the balloon. It smacked him on the rear and bounced, harmlessly, onto the grass.

"Nice try, Pops," Max said. He bent down and grabbed it for himself, and now he was running, with a sly grin, back toward me.

Chapter

Seven

IT WAS A TENET OF REC BALL THAT EVERY PLAYER RECEIVED
a trophy: T-Ballers, teenagers, champion teams, laughingstock
teams, the Jonathan Muñozes, the Carlos Zuñigas, we were all
winners at closing ceremonies. I think most people find that an
endearing notion, for participation to bring the same reward as
superiority, but I am also aware that some people consider it ho-
kum, a namby-pamby practice that cheapens the accomplishments
of the victors.

This is where Omar comes in again. While my team was being
swept by Lulu's, he was battling for the Double A title on the upper
field against Bob Pasos. The mess left by Bob was far greater than
Omar's annoyances, but he had sons who still wanted to play, who
still wanted their dad to coach them, and I had made it a policy not
to punish kids for the sins of their fathers. These were two thuggish
teams, under the command of a couple of major-league instigators,

and all season long their games had been marred by taunts and cheap shots. Both Omar and Bob complained incessantly to the umpires, with moans and curses and pantomimed antics, as if the efforts of their players were not a sufficiently good show. Omar had the advantage, with a roster anchored by a pair of elite travel-ball kids—one of them being the same kid I had traded him the season before—but those boys had obligations to their year-round teams, and as our playoffs spilled deeper into the summer, Omar could see that their time on his roster was about to expire. It began to look as though the Double A championship would hinge on the particulars of the La Loma schedule.

I had set the first game of the Double A finals for a Monday, the second game for Wednesday, and the third, if necessary, for Saturday. Omar did not object when I issued the schedule, but then he got word, as he feared, that his star players were heading to Hawaii for a tournament that weekend, and so if the series was not yet decided, his team would enter the final game without their services. He growled to me about it, insisting I had screwed him by spreading the series across an entire week, but when I explained that the games were staggered for a reason—a convenience to all the coaches and assistant coaches who had children in more than one division—he withdrew his complaint. "I'll just have to sweep the first two games," Omar said. "You know my dawgs. Won't be a problem."

I was at that Monday game, along with Todd and Carmen, to make sure the "bad blood," whatever that was supposed to mean, between Omar and Bob did not spill onto the field. I was secretly rooting for Omar, hoping a win for him would help preempt a whole lot of bellyaching about the schedule, but Bob's younger boy chose that evening to pitch a masterpiece. I forget the score. The game was otherwise uneventful. But as soon as the final out was recorded, everyone on Omar's side of the bleachers turned on me, the scheduler who would deny them a championship, now that a third game was the only way for their team to recover. Todd and Carmen were trying to intercede, to keep the throng from surging, but I was getting swarmed: parents, players, Omar, his wife, all shouting and jostling, until I was wedged against the wall of the snack bar with my hands up, pleading for calm. "Please, everyone, let's not end up on the eleven o'clock news," I said.

"Why you wanna do these kids like that?" Omar snarled.

Levity was not working. I licked my lips and swallowed hard. How many times was I going to have to defend our rinky-dink organization? My own imperfect precepts and criteria? A part of me was getting ready to crack. "I—I—I—" I stammered. "I'm not doing anything to anyone."

Omar was adamant that I accelerate the schedule, allowing him to play on consecutive nights, with the final game on Wednesday. I had made him a board member, and he was expecting that to count for something. "We're ready to go tomorrow, man," he insisted. "You got a lot of pissed-off people here."

"You agreed to the schedule," I said. "Now you lost and you want to change the rules."

"Why are you taking Bob's side?"

"Oh, my God, that's the last person I'd want to defend."

"Well, that's what you're doing."

I was feeling better all of a sudden. Something about having my motives misread helped restore my backbone. "We're done," I announced. "The schedule is the schedule. End of discussion. I suggest everyone go home right now and get some rest." Leadership had always struck me as sort of a contrivance, a buzzword of business schools and boot camps. I was a nonconformist by nature, an observer by training. Being a leader—*follow the leader*—just sounded so banal to me, but I was learning. If I failed to, I was not going to survive at La Loma much longer.

Omar won the second game, forcing the Saturday tiebreaker. With his two best kids headed out of town, he told the rest of his players not to show up. It was outrageous, an affront to our league, an insult to his own team. But Omar would not budge. "Call it whatever you want," he said. "I ain't gonna waste my time." I told Bob that his team still needed to be there, in uniform, ready to play. He was not happy about that, but I was not going to award a forfeit without following my own procedures. I paid two umpires to be present. I watered the field and chalked it. Anything less, I believed, made me complicit in Omar's disdain. He never came, as I knew he would not, but two of his players did: a slow, hulking boy named Christian, the sort whom Omar tended to slight, and the oldest son of my consigliere Chris Contreras, a kid who had been loyal to Omar but decided it was more important to honor his commitments to the park. I thanked them both and told them they were courageous; then I apologized to Bob's team. "Since there's no game today," I said, "everyone's welcome to a free ice cream in the snack bar."

That might have been the end of it, except that a week later, at our closing ceremony, Omar outdid himself. As I readied the trophies at home plate—big, gaudy statuettes for the younger divisions, bobbleheads for the older ones—Omar's team lined up on the outfield grass in matching T-shirts. I was still pretty sore about everything that had happened, and so I was not all that curious about the wording silk-screened on the back, but when it was their turn to run in and be introduced, I was floored by what I was seeing: MONTEREY PARK SPORTS CLUB DOUBLE A CHAMPIONS. Somewhere in that lizard brain of his, between smugness and persecution, Omar had thought it plausible to declare his team the winner—to mock me, our park, an entire season, by printing up souvenirs.

The trophies themselves were close to being a fiasco, one more chapter of the league's history I did not wish to repeat. We had found a shop in El Sereno, another Eastside barrio, that was willing to do a rush job for $3,000, no tax, provided we paid in cash. If that suggests I had learned nothing from my transaction with Adrian, I did, in fact, approach the deal a bit differently. I gave only a $1,000 deposit, and I insisted that the trophies be ready on a Thursday, for a Saturday ceremony, giving me a chance to review the finished product before it was too late. The man who took my money was an old Mexican cowboy, with a gray mustache and chunky sideburns, who spoke little English. "Don't worry . . . no problem . . ." he kept saying. Those were just the sorts of opportunities I relished, to defy whatever assumptions might exist about me and respond in

Spanish, to prove myself an able participant. As with my years at The Sunset or my Cuban escapades, I can see how there might be some showiness to that kind of performance—*check me out, señor, aren't I the baddest gringo you ever met?*—but it still has never felt that way to me. The experience is more one of submission, of offering to surrender some of my fluency to help close any gaps—*don't you worry, señor, I'll meet you on your terms, adapt to your ways, 'cause we're all in this together*—which, in its pretense of humility, is still, I suppose, something of a boast. I can afford to be the one who gets stretched a bit further because, well, I can.

In either case, I gave him a list of players and teams, with instructions to engrave "Monterey Park Sports Club" across the top of each nameplate. He offered his hand. *"A sus órdenes,"* he said. I wanted to believe I had found a vendor who, despite his cut-rate practices, had gravitas, and so when I returned on Thursday and saw that all the trophies were finished and boxed, I applauded myself for having at last recognized someone of character. I pulled one out to admire his work, the heft of the marble slab, the gleam of the gold figurine, ten bucks of hardware reborn a majestic keepsake. Then I read the nameplate. My heart sank. I looked at another. They were all the same. My old Mexican cowboy had inscribed our trophies with *"Monterrey* Park," as if it were a city back home, not a suburb next door. I started to laugh. What could I even say? He had spelled it right, the way it was supposed to be in Spanish. It was us, the California usurpers, who had dropped the second *r* and bastardized the language. "I hate to tell you this," I said, "but that's not how you write the name of our town and, well, for the same reason, not how you write the name of our league." He furrowed his brow, as if he had never considered it could be anything else, but he did not protest or doubt me. He said he would fix it—twenty-four hours to redo 275 trophies—and as promised, they were ready. Whatever anxiety I suffered in that day of waiting was made up for by the knowledge that I had been right about the guy all along.

Spanish entered my life before I met Raynelda, before I even came to L.A. I learned it in the ashes of my great college romance, a tortured episode that explains more than I wish it did about how I got to be who I am. Her name was Susan. She was a photographer from San Francisco. She showed up at Bennington in hippie skirts and Ray-Ban Wayfarers, with bee-stung lips and hennaed hair, and though her ancestry was all-American, she had hung out in the Mission District, amid lowriders and *vatos locos,* and considered herself an authority on vegetarian burritos. She used to tell me that her most treasured possession was her passport; she was only nineteen and already had filled one up. I was infatuated. I had never left the country. What she saw in me I hesitate to guess, maybe attentiveness, or fidelity. I had to be the whitest boy she had ever gone out with, a wannabe journalist with an antique Royal typewriter who had read everything by Hunter S. Thompson and nothing by Borges or Neruda.

Although I had traveled three thousand miles to get there, Bennington was even more isolated than Portland. Wedged into the Green Mountains of southwestern Vermont, in the thick of maple and deer, the school had barely six hundred students—and no teams or mascots or stadiums. Its tuition was the highest in America, and its philosophy was "learning by doing," distinctions that tended to attract a refined breed of misfit. (Bret Easton Ellis started his Gen-X fable *Less Than Zero* in the nonfiction workshop I attended, and in my philosophy class I sat across from Princess Farahnaz, the shah of Iran's exiled daughter.) To force us out of seclusion, Bennington would shut down at Christmas for two and a half months, a time that was to be spent gaining firsthand experience in our field of study. It was called the Non-Resident Term. In our junior year, by which time we were a dependable couple, Susan announced that she was going to travel to Mexico, to take pictures and hone her Spanish. We had a friend at Bennington named CC who had grown up in the expat colony of San Miguel de Allende, her family among the earliest wave of northerners to fall under its spell. CC was an exponent of all things Mexican, a generous, flamboyant, bilingual artist in a bastion of New England ennui, and only too happy to host Susan for the winter. It made perfect sense—and it crushed me. Why would Susan want to go to a foreign place? So far away? So far from me?

My winter was to be spent interning for Jerry Brown, the former California governor, who was trying to resurrect his career at a think tank in Los Angeles. I suppose I should acknowledge that as my first trip to L.A., but I was so distraught about Susan, so afraid I would be left behind as she blazed new trails, that I scarcely lifted my head to see where I was. To console me, Susan invited me to join her in San Miguel for the final week of our break. It would be almost like a honeymoon, our first time in a hotel, then we could fly back to Bennington together. I counted the days as if I were marooned on an island, January, February, longing for my rescue. I fantasized incessantly about Susan. I hardly gave a thought to Mexico. San Miguel, as much of the world has since discovered, is a jewel, as full of color and spirit as any place on this planet. But after so many lonely weeks, after my first international flight and a bus ride to the central highlands, I was aware only of what intruded on my comfort. San Miguel was grimy and claustrophobic. There were flies, beggars, exhaust, the jeering cadences of a language I knew nothing of but that seemed to be saying *skinny white boy faggot punk* a thousand different ways. I was in a hurry to get my duffel bag up the hill that led through town, past the plaza and the church and the stares and the sneers, to the hotel that Susan had found for herself, which proved to be not quite a hotel but a $12-a-night boardinghouse with fussy plumbing. We fell onto the bed, and for a moment, everything was right again. I wanted to curl up and hold her forever. Susan had other plans. She was throwing on her clothes, checking her watch, anxious to take me out and share her adventure.

The unease I had felt earlier was now more like panic. I was disoriented, unsure of directions or distances. Where was a map? Which way was home? How far to the coast, to the edge of this land? It was dark outside, and deep in the Mexican interior, I was being swallowed up. "Let's get going," Susan insisted. "We'll have fun. I promise. Please?" I buried my face in a pillow. I needed some parameters, a reference point. I opened my mouth to explain, but all that came out was a gasp. My chest heaved, and my chin quivered. I knew I was immature and inexperienced. I had never thought of myself as so ridiculously vulnerable.

Susan went for a six-pack and, over the next hour or two, nursed me back to my senses. I stopped my sniveling in time for us to go out for a normal enough evening—for the remainder of the week we could have passed for the bohemian lovers we were supposed to be—but I was never quite the same. I was out of my element, before I had learned to enjoy the sensation, and Susan was fully in hers, an undaunted, cosmopolitan young American walking the sixteenth-century lanes with her camera and rebozo. I smiled and tried to live up to what was expected of her mate, but I had not come prepared for Mexico. I had no repertoire—no Spanish, no kinship. I ended up doing a lot of deferring. Susan translated for me. She apologized for me. She ordered my food and settled my bills. I never got scolded for being a drip. Susan was forgiving, and so was San Miguel. Still I hated being at the mercy of either one.

Back at Bennington, I vowed to make up for my poor showing, to make myself worthy of Susan's affections. I enrolled in a beginning Spanish course. For a beatnik college, the language program was severe: an hour of grammar every morning, an hour of literature every afternoon, and once a week, three hours of conversation. To my delight, and I think to Susan's dismay, Spanish came more readily to me than our travels would have predicted. It had an intuitiveness and grace, an internal logic, that made English seem like the invention of rodeo clowns. It was a language of faith (*esperar* meant both "to wait" and "to hope"), of empathy (to say "I'm sorry"—*lo siento*—was to say "I feel it"), of frankness (a jigsaw puzzle was a *rompecabezas*—literally, a head buster), and of mordant humor (*esposas* were both wives and handcuffs). Best of all, our own classmate, CC, was hired as the conversation instructor, which meant pitchers of *cerveza* and songs of *amor perdido* and endless conjugations of *chingar*. I loved the power of my new vocabulary, of being privy to a secret

code. Everything in your life could stay the same, but if you just renamed it—if a computer became a *computadora* or pregnant was
embarazada—you gained a new set of puns and malaprops, the keys
to a parallel world.

CC assigned me the task of translating my own name, of devis-
ing a Latino alter ego. Katz was easy, if done phonetically. A cat was
a *gato*. Jesse was more of an issue. The only name it corresponded to
was Jesús. Now, I have got to say I find it baffling that in one culture a man can share a name with Christ and have it be considered
a privilege, and in another culture he would be a candidate for the
loony bin. It is perfectly acceptable to be Hey-SOOS. I once saw a
Mexican poll that declared it the country's fifth most popular name
for boys, which comes to tens of thousands of little Jesús babies
every year. Nobody in the English-speaking world is named
Jesus—that is, GEE-zus. Nobody is *allowed* to be Jesus. I decided it
was probably not the best fit for me, no matter how it was pronounced. Fortunately, almost every Spanish name has a diminutive,
and Jesús, through a bit of linguistic alchemy, comes out as Chuy.
So there you had it: Jesse Katz, two generations after my dad's
father arrived at Ellis Island on the S.S. *Polonia*, was rechristened
Chuy Gatos. And why not? When he left Pinsk, Grandpa was
Aron Kieczkier. By the time he was allowed onto American soil, he
had been chopped and spliced into Katz.

As I immersed myself in the language, I also turned my attention to the news of Latin America, the cynosure at that time of danger and intrigue and radical chic. The Sandinistas had captured
liberal imaginations with their promises of literacy and land reform,
and flocks of international volunteers, the "sandalistas," were descending on Nicaragua to aid the revolution. If Ronald Reagan was
to be believed, Nicaragua was an imminent threat, a Soviet beach-
head, "only two days' drive from Brownsville, Texas." Under his
administration the CIA secretly funded and trained the Contras,
Nicaragua's right-wing rebels, while helping to suppress left-wing
revolts in Guatemala and El Salvador. Those civil wars became the
defining story of my college years, the flash point for activism and

immigration, journalism and art. I soaked it up, from Joan Didion's
Salvador to Gregory Nava's *El Norte* to the Clash's triple-disc *Sandinista!* I followed Bianca Jagger's work on behalf of human rights,
and I found myself thinking, damn, so Mick married a Nicaraguan?
I recalled, with sudden clarity, that the great Pittsburgh Pirates
right fielder Roberto Clemente had died on his way to Managua
after the earthquake of 1972, a mercy flight that he was chaperoning
to keep donations from falling into the corrupt hand of the Somozas.
I wanted a piece of all that, of the politics and the poetry, and I decided to turn my senior thesis into a critique of the U.S. media's
Central American coverage, how one man's freedom fighter could be
another man's terrorist. In pretty swift time, I had killed off that boy
who had boo-hooed in San Miguel. My final NRT would be capped
by a trip to Nicaragua.

It would be hard to exaggerate just how unattractive Chuy
Gatos was to Susan. If I thought I was redeeming myself, she
thought I was crowding her. Her plan that winter was to travel
through Central America with her camera, final destination Nicaragua. That was funny, I told her, because, well, see, I am going to be
in Nicaragua about the same time as you. The minute I said it,
Susan's face turned into a mask. I had learned something about
Spanish but not a thing about love.

"No, you're not!" she snapped.

"What?" I said.

"You're not going with me."

"You're kidding."

"You're copying me."

"Like, what—Nicaragua's not big enough for the both of us?"

"Well, I don't want to see you there."

I have no conscious memory of trying to sabotage our relationship. I still found Susan to be the most intriguing woman I had ever
known. When she ended it six months later, after I started work at
the *L.A. Times,* I was a wreck. I really had thought we might be a
couple all our lives. Naturally, I had doomed us: I was not just playing catch-up, I was competing with Susan, shedding her as my

guide. If she objected to my Nicaragua trip, then fuck it—I would show her. I would outdo her at her own game. I would be more fearless, more compassionate, more genuine. *Más* Latino.

I flew to Managua that February, about a week after Susan passed through. I had made arrangements to tag along with a factfinding tour from Portland, the kind in such vogue during the Sandinista revolution that P.J. O'Rourke, in *Holidays in Hell,* suggested that Nicaragua had more fact-finding tours than facts. Because of the U.S. clampdown, there were shortages of everything, water, power, food, toiletries, pencils, except maybe AK-47s and Flor de Caña rum. The Contra war was raging in the countryside, and in the capital, the ruins of that deadly earthquake, a decade earlier, were still teetering like dinosaur bones. I wandered through the soggy heat, past altars and trenches and bullet pocks and girl soldiers in snug olive uniforms. I met with the editor of *La Prensa,* the barely tolerated opposition newspaper, and I surveyed the aftermath of a rebel attack on a tobacco cooperative, where I found a charred nail in the soil and slipped it, a curio, into my pocket. I wanted to think of myself as daring and worldly just for being in Nicaragua, but in truth, I never got too close to anyone or anything. I imagined myself returning as a foreign correspondent, being more dexterous, more rakish, than the reporters I was scrutinizing, but as of yet, I was not even a decent tourist. When I got back to school, I wrote an essay, "The Tan American," about the ways in which I was moved by Nicaragua and the ways in which my thrills were destined to remain detached: "I could choose what I wanted to feel and who I wanted to be; and what I felt and who I pretended to be was never too involved or too passionate. It was all determined by convenience—in a country where no such luxury could be said to exist."

When I later took my first tentative steps into The Sunset, found myself in the sway of a barmaid from, of all places, Nicaragua, there was a lot I was still making up for: all those questions of access and validity, the humiliations and aspirations that had borne Chuy Gatos. It mattered that Raynelda was not just another American interpreter of the Latino experience but the source—an unvarnished, unassimilated, unapologetic Managua girl—that she could have been one of those teenage soldiers I ogled, that we had arrived in L.A. at almost exactly the same time, and yet even in her marginalized state, without papers or English or education, she belonged more to the city already than I did. After the wedding, I filled out Raynelda's and Freddy's I-130 forms, their petitions for legal status, and sent them off to the INS. When we got word that their residency had been approved, we discovered that they first would have to leave the United States—obtain their documents from the American consulate in their nation of origin—then reenter the country they already resided in, only this time at an official port. It was bureaucratic nonsense, superfluous and expensive, but when the three of us boarded that plane for Managua in 1991, a year still before we entertained the idea of Max, I think we each felt, for our own reasons, punchy and triumphant. I was Raynelda's trophy, the citizen who entitled her to free passage, and she was mine, proof that I was finally more than a dilettante, more than a witness. This was better than going back as a reporter. I was taking the plunge, in the most intimate sense, merging my identity, my name, soon my blood, with something that for me, only a short time earlier, had been excruciatingly alien.

From the start, I spoke only Spanish with Raynelda, and still, after all these years, that is how we choose to communicate. Although it suits her fine, I have no doubt that I have been the main beneficiary of that arrangement, that my language skills were the ones that were allowed to develop, and to the detriment of hers. I had to learn to articulate not just romantic desires but also the nuances of professional ambition and financial worry, holiday functions, legal quandaries, taxes, insurance, and car repair. I used to print out copies of my stories for her and, over dinner, attempt instant translations, line by line, word for word. I supplied the subtitles for movies and doctor's appointments, for the two or three trips a year my mom or dad made to see us. In time I had to figure out how to tell her that I was hurting and unhappy, to find the Spanish equivalents of "taken for granted" and "choosing sides" and "emotionally worn out."

When it came to Max, Raynelda stuck to her language and I reverted to mine. Maybe I was doing him a disservice, too, by not nurturing his command of Spanish, but I figured that could always come later, after his English was flawless. We lived among too many people who trafficked in homiespeak, and I could not bear for Max to sound like a Cheech & Chong routine. A number of my friends have done just the opposite with their kids, reinforcing Spanish at home to counter the predominant culture. I get that, and I wanted Max to be as perfectly bilingual as those children, but perhaps I did not trust that he would be perfect, that his mastery of English would not be compromised by the Nicaraguan jamboree under our roof. Raynelda tried to encourage his Spanish, and I encouraged her, but Max resisted, like a typical *pocho* kid, responding in English to whatever Spanish she aimed at him. This made for strangely disconnected conversations, mother and son each speaking a different language, at once acknowledging and ignoring the other's limitations. "Son of a bitch, where did this child come from?" Raynelda would groan. "Is he mine? Do I know him?"

Max would give her a weary sigh. "I understand you, Mom."

"Mahlm, Mahlm," she would repeat, filtering the word through the most vanilla accent she could muster. "I'm your *madrecita*, and don't you forget it." Then she would switch into an infantile patter. "And you're my little love, my handsome little precious love."

If I had not spoken Spanish, my presence at La Loma would have been sufficiently novel: a single white only-child Jewish dad with no connection to L.A. other than what I had invented for myself. By speaking Spanish, by using La Loma as a stage for my inclinations and affections, I ensured that I would be even more of an oddity—an outsider who acted like an insider—and it often required explanations of me that I was not entirely sure how to give. "Everyone always wants to know what your deal is," Carmen once said. "It's the whole mystery of Mister Katz." Like the old man at the trophy shop, I had a habit of pronouncing names according to the rules of proper Spanish, and I heard the snickers that first opening day when I decided to introduce all 275 players on the PA, and Martin became Mar-TEEN and Perez rolled off my tongue as PEHR-ess. I noticed that Jonathan's dad frequently signed their name *Munoz,* without the *ñ,* although I insisted on writing it correctly on Monterey Park Sports Club documents. I struck a deal with Liliana's, the famed *tamalería* on César Chávez Avenue, to supply us with red beef and green chili tamales every Saturday for the snack bar. I gave my friend Abel a hundred bucks to decorate the interior, money that went to baseball piñatas one year, to *papel picado* skeletons another, to fresh coats of Benjamin Moore Aztec Yellow paint the next. One of my board members, a straight arrow named Gary Verdugo, could finally bite his tongue no longer.

"This place is starting to look like a Tijuana whorehouse," he told me.

I told Abel. "Hmm," Abel said. "I think I'm going to take that as a compliment."

My literary comrade, Abel Salas was the most loyal of friends, with no business at La Loma other than to help me remake it into a place that mirrored our sense of L.A.'s beauty and quirks. We had met a decade earlier on the Rio Grande, during my Houston stint. Abel was a poet, an actor, a dancer, and a University of Texas runaway with a freelance gig in the Matamoros bureau of *El Heraldo,* the Spanish-language edition of the *Brownsville Herald.* He wore a ponytail and silver earrings and long pointy fingernails on his right hand, in the tradition of Bram Stoker's *Dracula.* As an American on the Mexican side of the river he liked to describe himself as a reverse *mojado*—he was working there without a permit or visa—and I instantly identified with the dichotomies, the cultural ambiguities, that he extolled. He was ABE-ul, he was ah-BELL. He was Abelito, he was Abeloco, he was Abelunatico. He once wrote a story about the knee-jerk perceptions of U.S. border agents and to test his theories attempted to cross into the state of his birth under various guises, as a ranch hand, as a corporate suit, as a street urchin. I still have never met anyone as fluid: Abel is the ultimate Chicano shape shifter, as deft about J.R.R. Tolkien and Stevie Nicks as he is about Emiliano Zapata and Flaco Jiménez. When I left Texas and returned to Los Angeles, he followed me west, persuaded by my descriptions of a brown city, polyglot, crossbred, transnational. He found a cottage in East L.A. and a job writing press releases for one of Hollywood's scarce Latino publicists. Just as Raynelda had, Abel offered me entry to the place I already lived, vouching for my downness, my internal kindredship, whenever we navigated its racial and linguistic divides. He called me Chewbacca, a twist on the whole Chuy riff, and since he had never been married or had children (unless you counted Almita, the daughter of a Latina power couple in Austin, for whom he had lent his seed), he felt like he had a stake in my role as a father, that we were, in his words, "Max's two dads."

Abel had no affinity for sports, but he understood the people of La Loma, saw them as his own, recognized all the ways in which baseball was our alibi, a pretext for wanting to be part of something even more essential. I put him in charge of wrangling a celebrity guest for that inaugural season, a recognizable name to throw out the first pitch and signal our new beginning. Abel used his gift for schmooze to secure a commitment from Luis J. Rodriguez, the writer and activist whose bestselling gang memoir *Always Running* is rumored to be the book most stolen from Southern California libraries. I had read it years earlier, in my days on the gang beat, and loved its faith in language, in writing as redemption, but I had forgotten that Luis was from right around here—that his old turf was Lomas, the same hood, I realized, too, that Carmen's family had come up in. "This is brilliant," I told Abel. "I think." I would need to sell it to my board, to convince everyone that a reformed hoodlum, one who had been shot at on nearby streets, who had been arrested by local cops, who had been tossed from Keppel just like Freddy, was the sort of image we should be projecting on opening day. Even Luis, who was running a bookshop and coffeehouse at the far end of the San Fernando Valley, wanted to make sure his presence would not be disruptive. "As you know," he told me, "this is like coming home."

As with the decor, the objections came from Gary, a basketball coach at Garfield High, the East L.A. landmark immortalized in *Stand and Deliver*, who wore sweat-stained T-shirts and a 1950s flattop. He and his wife were as dedicated as any parents in our league, but they preferred to think of La Loma in narrower terms, as a safe and ethnically neutral haven, rather than an extension of the ferment that surrounded us. They once tried to get me to post a prayer in the snack bar, one of those Little League invocations designed to slip a Christian message into the game. "God grant me wisdom/To tell a strike from a ball," it began. What about me made them think I would go for that? In Luis, whatever his merits, they saw a downer, a reminder of everything that families came to La Loma to avoid. We were a youth organization, promoters of teamwork and sportsmanship. "Isn't there somebody else we could get, somebody who might be more of a role model?" Gary asked.

"Such as?" I replied.

"Like a sports figure," Gary said. "A coach? A player? Someone with the Dodgers?"

"That's just so, so, I dunno—*predictable,*" I said. "I feel like we should be trying to reach for something more significant, more transcendent."

"That's funny. I thought we were trying to run a baseball program."

"Well, yes, of course, but most of these kids are never going to be baseball players. They need to dream and hope. I'm sure we have a few kids who are already on their way to becoming little Luis J. Rodriguezes, who are struggling out there, away from La Loma, with all the same issues, and he might be exactly the role model they need."

"Hey, whatever you say," Gary muttered. "You're the commissioner."

I told Luis we would buy several copies of his books and raffle them off, which meant some T-Baller might end up with a bedtime story about smoking *yesca* and packing *cuetes* and getting down with the *rucas*. Oh, well. It was still art. I liked that a man who looked a lot more like the children in our park than I did took the time to show up with tangible proof of his imagination, a creation to be autographed. The next year Abel scored me the Chicano R&B singer Little Willie G., formerly of Thee Midniters (we raffled his CDs); a year later, Abel delivered Lalo Alcaraz, creator of the nationally syndicated *La Cucaracha* comic strip (we raffled his sketches); a year after that, Abel rounded up the actor Jesse Borrego, who had been in *Fame* and *24* but was best known, at least on our side of town, as Cruz in the prison gang drama *Blood In, Blood Out* (we raffled his DVDs). Somewhere along the way, I realized I was no longer merely adapting to the culture of the Eastside, of L.A.'s Latino renaissance; I was introducing it, promoting it. I was changing, and Los Angeles, at the onset of the twenty-first century, was changing too, dismantling its caste system, shedding its years of separateness and denial. History was about to be made with the election of a Mexican-American mayor, to go with a Mexican-American sheriff and a Mexican-American city attorney. The most popular TV shows in L.A. were not *CSI* and *America's Got Talent* but the daily installments of *La Madrasta* and *La Fea Más Bella,* the boffo soaps distributed by the Univision empire. The most popular radio program in L.A.—actually, the most listened to in the nation—was not hosted by Howard Stern or Don Imus but by Eddie (Piolín) Sotelo, the morning deejay on La Nueva 101.9, who as a teenager was smuggled up from Mexico in the trunk of a car.

Latinos of Abel's generation were giving themselves permission to embrace their other half, the side that had been shamed and silenced, their Spanish, their Indianness. Abel told me the word for that was "retro-acculturation," and I liked it enough that I wrote it down and stuck it on my office wall. Whatever was to become of our baseball league, however flawed my tenure, I thought that we should at least be acknowledging the new L.A.—that if a white boy was going to rescue La Loma, he should start by honoring its mestizo soul.

Chapter

Eight

AS TAXING AS THAT FIRST SEASON WAS, I FOUND MYSELF
looking forward to a second year as commissioner, if only to prove,
like a September call-up who had fouled off a few in his debut, that
I had not yet taken my best cuts. I would finally have the luxury of
planning, a head start of months. I had money in the bank and keys
in my pocket, a computer full of templates and all the league's
equipment stored safely in my garage. I had found a new uniform
supplier, a square dealer from the Yucatán who called me Señor
Jesús. I had convinced Carmen's brother to build a chain-link
backstop on the T-Ball field in exchange for a twelve-pack of Corona,
and between Chris's mechanical aptitude and Abel's graphic finesse,
we had refurbished the old Coke scoreboards into sweet, old-timey
monuments. I called up Todd one afternoon, at the beginning of
2004, to share my excitement. "Man, we've come a long way," I said.
"I really think it's going to be easier this time around."

"I've been meaning to talk to you about that," Todd said.

"About what?"

"About running the league. I don't think I'm going to be able to help you out anymore."

"You're joking, right?"

"I wish I was," Todd said. Even though I had not seen it coming, I knew exactly what was up. The strain of juggling baseball with everything else, the time stolen from work, the hours of lost sleep, the family meals skipped, the household chores ignored—life, in season, was on hold. It was like developing an addiction, or taking a lover. I had hoped that the fall and winter would give us both a chance to recoup, but Todd had more people outside of La Loma to answer to. He had a taxpayer-funded job with one of the nation's most complex school systems, a district beset by poverty and language barriers, and he served at the pleasure of the L.A. Unified superintendent, Roy Romer, the former Colorado governor and DNC chair. Three of Todd's four kids were teenagers already, wrecking cars and testing curfews, and his wife, who had emigrated from the Philippines in the late 1960s, had just started work as an overnight doula and nanny. I was asking Todd to help me reform a messy little society, and he had a couple of his own he could barely keep up with. He was about to buy himself a convertible Porsche for his fiftieth birthday, but the weight of age and obligation was still pressing on his chest. "If something doesn't give," Todd said, "I swear I'm going to have a heart attack."

I had prided myself on my own ability to cope—the journalist's trick of appearing poised and pithy under the terrifying crush of deadline—but I was about to be challenged, too, in ways that would fast exceed my command. Max and I had just returned from a trip to Mexico with my mom, a gift for her seventieth birthday. We had spent New Year's in San Miguel, Mom's first visit to the town that had played such an unexpected role in redirecting my life. I took her to the markets, to the bullfights, to the churches, to Mama Mia—the same courtyard supper club that Susan had dragged me to on that first anguished night. Mom claimed to be charmed, but her comments were all spoken like a municipal planner: Where did the water come from? Who paid for the schools? What kind of ordinances regulated sewers, traffic, police?

"C'mon, Mom," I groaned. "It's Mexico. *MEH-hee-koh*. Its dysfunction is its charm."

What I did not know at the time, what Mom only revealed to me a few months later, was that during our trip something had begun to feel wrong inside. She had discomfort in her abdomen, and long after menopause, she was alarmed to find spotting in her underwear. When she told me this, it was because she had been to the doctor and was about to announce to *The Oregonian* that she was going to have surgery in April to remove a fibroid tumor from her uterus. Mom was in the final year of her third term as mayor—she had already decided she would retire at the end of 2004—but she was not about to let anyone think she was not in command. "The mayor said with a laugh that she feels fine and fully expects to maintain her busy schedule before the surgery and after her recovery," the paper reported. It served my purposes to believe that, to brush off the procedure as a routine feature of her age. Mom had survived breast cancer four years earlier and had managed somehow to make that recovery seem almost mundane. I hate to admit I was too swamped for this to be anything else, but I had thrown myself into baseball again so obsessively that I felt I would be jeopardizing the season if I left to be at her side.

The week she called me was the final Saturday of sign-ups, the final Sunday of tryouts. I had drafts to run and uniforms to order—and not for 275 kids, like the previous year, but 395. For all that had gone wrong that first season, word was spreading that the Monterey Park Sports Club was on the rise again, that this new guy, Katz, however excessive or nervy or unconventional he was, seemed to be sticking it out. Flipping through my old calendar, I am reminded that it was not just baseball that week: We were finishing up basketball, and I was coaching Max's team in the championship, a game we were about to lose badly to Chris. It was also my son's eleventh birthday, which meant I had a party to plan and a sleepover, with Alex, to chaperon. I was volunteering once a week at Central Juvenile Hall, teaching creative writing to young criminals. It was the anti–La Loma—stark, debilitating, full of kids who missed out on things like Little League—yet I went there, with pens and notebooks instead of gloves and balls, for many of the same reasons. With the time that remained for my day job, I was profiling a homeless encampment on the banks of the Los Angeles River, hanging out with thieves and addicts and a transvestite hooker named Seven. I was stretched so thin, giving so much, that I look back now and wonder if I was not actually running away, trying to escape myself, as I did after my parents divorced. By making time for everything I was ensuring I had no time for anyone, except, of course, Max. If I had been his buffer before, he was becoming mine, a reason not to date, the perfect excuse for cordoning off my private life in caution tape.

When the doctors finally went in to remove Mom's fibroid, they found it was big enough to necessitate a hysterectomy. As she had before, she downplayed the seriousness of the surgery, which is what you are supposed to do in situations of this nature, and which I mimicked, because again I had no choice. The season opened in nine days. In May she learned that a biopsy had turned up cancerous cells—hardly good news, but at least it pertained to tissue that had already been excised—and when a CT scan of her pelvis showed no sign of the disease, we knew, as we had all along, that she was in the clear. In early June, about three-quarters of the way through the season, she went for another exam. This time her gynecologist felt something odd, a hard mass that he was able to touch with his fingers. She told me his words: "Oh, my God." Two days later a new CT confirmed the worst. A tumor that had not been there a month ago was growing in her abdomen. It was the size of a tangerine already. Nodules, too numerous to count, had spread through her lungs. The cancer was rare, adenosarcoma of the reproductive system, and the prognosis was pretty close to incurable. When she called me to explain all this, her voice was shaky. She could no longer pretend. I wanted to be able to say something, to reassure her that we would get through this together, but all I could think of was the distance that separated us, not just the thousand miles but the fact that I had put it there. I had chosen to leave, to go in the opposite direction, to a place that was everything Portland was not and that Portland hoped never to become. I had been away for twenty-three years, more time than I had spent living in Portland, and to prove what—that I was fearless, that nothing and nobody could get to me? Now my mom was sick, and I was somewhere else.

Even then I did not budge. The notes I jotted down about her condition—"mixed müllerian," "sarcomatous overgrowth"—were on the same sheet of paper that I had used to write the phone number of our trophy vendor and the e-mail address of the coach who had stooped to the hidden-ball trick. I had playoffs to preside over and all-star games and fireworks and Max's last day of fifth grade. Mom was starting chemo. "I don't need for you to come up, honey," she told me the night before. "Take care of whatever you have to." I should have known—how could I have not?—that this is never what a mother means.

The poison that was supposed to attack her malignant cells invaded everything that was alive. After the first infusion, she tried to go straight back to work but threw up at city hall. She went home, to that fragile slate and salmon dollhouse, climbed the steep hardwood stairs to her bedroom, and spent the next twenty-four hours in a fog, vomiting, alone. My dad stopped by in the morning and rang the bell. He is remarried but still her most steadfast companion, better friends, I would say, than when they bought the house. She refused to open the door or answer the phone. Her esophagus had begun to bleed. Her lungs were filling with fluid, and her kidneys were shutting down. A police officer arrived in the afternoon. He was in charge of the mayor's transportation and security detail. She had a follow-up scheduled with her doctor but instead was put on a respirator and rushed to the intensive-care unit of Good Samaritan. My dad called me that evening. He had been to see her, sat on her bed and held her hand, in a maze of tubes and pumps and alarms. She had vowed to stay alive until I could get there. It was time now. Time to stop being the commissioner, to stop being a coach, to stop if just for a moment being a dad, and to start remembering how to be a son.

I had never thought of our relationship as being particularly troubled—we were not trapped in some long-running cycle of grievance and recrimination—but neither were we exceptionally close. I loved my mom. I was proud of everything she had achieved. But I could go a week or two or three without talking to her, months at a stretch without seeing her, and not really dwell on her absence. To the extent that we antagonized each other, it was more a question of temperature, the way we handled uncertainty and preparation. She had always been the voice of caution—the voice of the piñata—my reminder to plan, to save, to worry, and my life, at least as an adult, was about shedding those restrictions, about being less squeamish, less careful. "You, Mister Independent," she would call me. "Joe Cool."

Mom was typical, I suppose, of immigrants of her generation, uprooted by revolution, fascism, the Holocaust, and catapulted to a distant shore, to a nation that still opened its arms to the tired and the hungry. She was just a child when she landed in New York, when she decided for herself that she was no longer French or German or Russian but American, and I think that means something to her that it never could for me. When travel becomes exodus, when ethnicity is cause for extermination, adventure is not often what you choose to seek out. I had grown up knowing pieces of her story, but much of it she had forgotten and, over time, lost the curiosity to recall. When she got sick, I vowed to learn more, to honor her life and to help decipher mine. My questions eventually took me to Europe, to Paris, the setting for her earliest memories, and then across the Pyrenees, into Spain, the route she traveled to freedom. As I retraced her footsteps, I struggled to wrap my mind around the enormity of her journey, all the junctures at which she was rescued by the courage and conscience of strangers, the impulses she has handed down to me.

Mom began life as Vera Pistrak, and when I was a kid, that was no small source of embarrassment. To my juvenile ear, it sounded like a urinary infection, made worse by the fact that the Pistraks, whoever they might have been, were probably not in on the joke. Even today, when a bank or employer asks for my mother's maiden name, I choose to spell it out rather than try to pronounce it. In time I came to understand that she had inherited this unfortunate pedigree from Lazar Michailovich Pistrak, my grandfather, who was a Menshevik, a loyal comrade of the Russian Social Democratic Labor Party. As a student, in 1917, he joined in the revolutionary fervor that toppled the tsar. Later that year, when the Bolsheviks seized control and imposed communist rule, he was thrown in jail. With the help of my grandmother, Raissa, he bought his way out, and along with the Menshevik elite, they fled to Germany, where they reestablished their movement in exile. I would sometimes ask Mom, who was born in Düsseldorf, if this meant we were German. It was too hard for me to grasp that she had entered the world already a refugee, and was about to become one again. The year of her birth marked the rise of the Nazis, a new regime to fear. She was still an infant when Lazar, strolling in the park with his young family, was confronted by the Gestapo. Whatever warning was delivered, however imminent the danger to a Jewish socialist might have been in 1933, my grandparents raced home and packed their entire apartment. By morning they were on a train for France.

In Paris, the Mensheviks regrouped again, and my grandparents continued to plot and lament. Lazar was a dreamer, to the point of being untethered, perhaps even suicidal. He joined the French army—"a little boy with a wooden sword, looking for a fight," as my aunt Zena, Mom's older sister, remembers him—and disappeared for months at a time. Raissa, "emotionally starved and paralyzed by her fears," turned increasingly bitter. "We were never a family," says Zena, who grew up to become a psychiatrist, a profession she considered more a destiny than a choice. "We lived in a state of upheaval." When Mom was six, France fell to the Nazis. She huddled in air-raid shelters, waiting for the bombing to stop. If Paris had been an uneasy sanctuary for Jews before the war, it had by the summer of 1940 become a death trap. Mom remembers only fleeing, a single day to fill a rucksack and join the sea of humanity pouring south. What she did not know, what I only discovered in my rummaging, was that Lazar, as a political operative, an intellectual, had the pull to secure his family emergency haven in the United States. His name was on a list of 468 "world-famous writers, editors, labor leaders, former government officials, and ministers" submitted to the Roosevelt administration by the Jewish Labor Committee, a council of New York leftists. Should any of them be captured by the Nazis, the document warned, "they will face certain death, and their loss would be irreparable for the civilized world."

The JLC's archives are housed on the tenth floor of New York University's Bobst Library, close to the East Village tenement that would be Mom's first American address, and it was there that I found myself, not long ago, poring over spools of microfilm, looking for the Pistrak name. Of the 468 families in need of credentials, 352 were stranded in France, and of those, 149 were identified as Russian-Jewish. The list had several incarnations, first handwritten, then typed, in Russian, then in English, with addenda and corrections penciled in the margins. When I finally spotted him—"PISTRAK, Lazar: Well known Russian Socialist. Volunteer in the French army"—I felt an odd mix of pride and indignation. Within a few years of their arrival, he would leave Raissa and exit my mother's life, and yet his name had spared their lives; for all his paternal shortcomings, somebody had thought him worthy of saving. I kept looking for a document that might refer to Mom, and when I found one, it listed her by her diminutive, Verachka. That made me smile. I had only heard my grandmother call her that. Then I found another document, a shipping manifest that indicated the Pistraks would require a donation of $625.86 for their journey across the Atlantic. It referred to them as a family of "3½." I was stumped for a moment, until I realized that Mom was the basis for this uneven number. She was so young, so tiny still, she had come to America as a fraction.

Even with papers, there was no easy way out of occupied France.

Only one route offered Mom a chance, to creep through the Pyrenees, the vast range at the base of the Iberian peninsula. The climb itself was not insurmountable, an eight-mile trek over a two-thousand-foot pass, but for displaced city dwellers, already shaken and drained, the mountains were a frightful test. The last stop in France, Banyuls-sur-Mer, was a rugged wine-making enclave, home to generations of Catalonians who have terraced the hillsides with sweet Grenache grapes. Also nestled in those vineyards was the studio of Aristide Maillol, the grand modernist sculptor, who favored a craggy beard and a beret, and remained fixated, well into old age, on bronze casts of young nudes. He was already a septuagenarian when, to the chagrin of his long-suffering wife, he invited a fifteen-year-old Parisian named Dina Vierny to pose. Finding girls willing to disrobe for a grizzled artist in a remote agricultural town was no easy task, and for the last decade of Maillol's life, he worshiped her as both model and muse. Dina happened to be Moldavian-born, the daughter of Menshevik exiles herself, and when war broke out, she recognized the faces streaming into Banyuls, understood that they were her people, on the run.

Guided by instinct, she began ushering them to Maillol's studio, out in the middle of grape country, and after they had eaten and rested, she summoned the nerve to steer them through the fields and up the trails and over the mountains. Trafficking was ingrained in Catalan culture—clandestine paths crisscrossed the peaks—and once Maillol realized what Dina was up to, he apprised her of the best routes, teaching her to sidestep French customs agents and Spanish national guardsmen. For a couple of perilous months, until her arrest, Dina made the trip several times a week, shepherding a hundred, perhaps two hundred refugees to safety. As a signal to each wave of arrivals, she wore a rose-colored dress to the train depot. Nobody knew her name: They just knew to look for the Lady in Red.

Mom does not remember the Lady in Red, but my aunt does, and it was Zena who recently filled in a lot of these gaps for me. Who would have thought? My family was smuggled to freedom by a nubile Jewish *coyote*! I googled Dina Vierny and found an e-mail address for her at the Musée Maillol in Paris, which she had opened with a collection bequeathed to her by the sculptor's only child. She was eighty-nine now and apparently still running the place. I asked if she might be available for a meeting. "*Cher* Jesse Katz," she wrote back. "I will give you everything you need." I flew to Paris, my first time, anxious about what to say and how to act. I was doing research, but I was also my mother's proxy, a son as much as a writer. A handful of people had found Madame Vierny before me, other children of Jewish Labor Committee evacuees, but not many. Like my mom, few of Dina's beneficiaries ever learned who had helped them, and for their protection, Dina never asked who she was helping. Given her age, I would surely be one of the last. For the occasion, Dina wore a red dress, with a red sweater, and her long hair, braided in the back, showed traces of red tint. She could not have been more than four-foot-something, a wizened little thing who required oxygen when she traveled, but she was as spirited as anyone I have ever met, loud, funny, extravagant, profane. I had come with a tape recorder, but Dina was not much interested in sitting for an interview. This was a reunion, her vindication. She wanted us to eat, to drink, to celebrate the triumph of optimism over inhumanity. "My boy," she said, squeezing my hand between her rings and bracelets. "This is life."

Armed with Dina's maps and photos, I left the next day for Banyuls, a six-hour train ride down the Vermillion Coast. I had some trepidation about traversing the mountains without an escort, but as long as I was following Mom's path, I told myself, I was not really going it alone. I set out in the morning from the center of Banyuls, on the Mediterranean, and hiked south, through the outskirts of town, and into the vineyards, which seemed to stretch on forever, weaving through the foothills like strata on ancient stone. Mom made her escape in the darkness of a September morning, in the middle of harvest, when the grapes would have been fat and the fields rustling with peasants. She had to be silent, to conceal her identity, while Dina led the way up, scrambling in espadrilles over dirt and rock and brush—*cabra boja,* the locals called her. The mad goat. Happy to be doing it by daylight, I trudged on, the pink stucco of civilization shrinking behind me and the tenebrous ridges of prehistoric granite towering above. The terrain turned to forest, swirling with butterflies and bursting with thistle; then, as I climbed higher, it became stark and dry, an invitation to lizards and lichens. To think, sixty-odd years earlier, this trail represented survival, a future, the only way out. So much had changed and yet so little. It was not the Rio Grande, not Raynelda's odyssey, but the premise was the same, to get to America: to sneak over a line.

As I neared the summit, I found myself mulling the one piece of this story that Mom remembers, the only fragment that, for most of my life, I had any knowledge of or the capacity to understand. Somewhere shy of the frontier, out in the brier and scree, after Dina had pointed to Spain and scampered back to Banyuls, my grandfather became disoriented. Lazar would later enjoy a distinguished second act: He was a Soviet expert for the U.S. Information Agency and the author of what was considered the definitive biography of Khrushchev, *The Grand Tactician.* But for the time, he was on the losing side of history, a man without a country who was saddled with a family he did not much love. Not knowing which way to turn, if they were steps away from deliverance or starvation, asylum or capture, Lazar panicked. It was a storm of self-pity. He screamed and cursed—how badly had life fucked him that he was now wandering in circles, about to be consumed by these godforsaken borderlands?—and then, his unforgettable sin, he took it out on Verachka. Mom had been allowed to leave Paris with only one toy, a doll. It was a little boy, made of plastic and dressed in knit shorts, and she had not stopped clutching him, acting a mother to the most reliable male in her life. In his fury, Lazar ripped the doll from her hands. He must have felt so impotent, so disgraced. Mom began to whimper. Lazar was going to show her. He hurled that doll with all his might, off a ledge, down a gorge, out of sight.

New York was supposed to offer stability. No more war, no more running. Lazar and Raissa eventually found an apartment on 110th Street, in a building filled with other Menshevik luminaries, but without the external turmoil, without the demands of survival to bind them, my grandparents had no affection to fall back on. Lazar walked out when Mom was twelve. "I cried and cried," she said. "I don't know why I cried. I hardly knew him." He came back once, when she was sixteen, to buy her an ice cream. Then he disappeared from her life forever. My grandmother—Babushka, as I knew her—worked in the sweatshops, stitching beads onto ladies' handbags, and at home knitted sweaters for the navy. Although she would later dote on me, the grandchild who could do no wrong, she was steely and distant with her own daughters and quick to enforce her rule with a belt. Mom was often jittery and alone, struggling to learn English—her third language—and tiptoeing around their neighborhood, on the periphery of Spanish Harlem, where yet another strange new culture lurked. At night, if my grandmother was still in the factories, Mom would slip into Babushka's bed and listen to the screams and sirens out on Morningside Drive, and she would close her eyes and wish she had a normal family.

It was in those moments that she discovered the Dodgers, the steady rituals of baseball. By tuning the radio to WHN 1050, she could curl up with Red Barber, the team's Southern gentleman announcer, and root for the perennial bridesmaids, who toiled in the shadow of the Yankees and were forever having to "wait 'til next year." The Dodgers kept her company. They broke through her shell. They bound her to the outside world, to the world of men and sport and hope. When they introduced Jackie Robinson in 1947, an act of such simple but sublime bravery, they supplied Mom with her first hero. Jackie stealing home. Jackie getting heckled. Jackie winning the embrace of good-ol'-boy teammate Pee Wee Reese. He was brazen on the field and dignified off it, sure of the justness of his cause yet patient enough to give his country a chance to come around. She did not know any black people and was not about to get anywhere near the Apollo Theater, just a couple subway stops away, but for a scared little immigrant girl, intent on shedding her foreignness, Jackie's quest was universal. "In a way, he stood for everything I had to go through," she said. "It was about being accepted by America."

On the June day that I finally flew up to see her, my head was swirling with doubts and guilt. I kept thinking how sad it was that I had allowed myself to become this estranged—from my mom, from what had once been my home. It felt like an era was ending in Portland: Even if the chemo worked, I was reminded that my parents were not going to be around forever, that the experiment that had brought them out from New York was winding to a close. Sooner or later, they would be gone—and then what? So would the Katzes. These two remarkable people, who had uprooted their young family and, in separate ways, helped Portland evolve into what it is now, would be survived by a lone heir who had left the minute he became an adult. They had made Portland their own, and I had refused to be defined as their son. Dad picked me up from the airport and took me straight to the hospital. She looked small. An oxygen line was clipped to her nose. An IV drip was taped to her arm. A dialysis machine was drawing blood from a port in her chest. I bent down to hug her and felt mostly bones. She was maybe half of what she had been in Mexico. When I let go, we both had tears in our eyes. "How did I lose you?" she asked.

Something became clear to me at that moment, something I had been only vaguely aware of on the plane. All this time I thought I was running, disrupting patterns, subverting expectations, I was doing just what my parents had dedicated their lives to. I was investing myself in a community, in a culture, in a game, in a park—fixing, rescuing. I had come from someplace else, and yet I really had not traveled so far. I wiped my face with my sleeve. I am the way I am, I said, because you are the way you are. I did not want her to feel bad about that.

"This is your gift to me, Mom."

I stayed with her for forty-eight hours, then I did what I had trained myself to do and returned to L.A. for the playoffs. We were in our first year of Double A, headed for another showdown with

Omar. My mind should have been elsewhere, if not my presence, but I have to say I was relieved to be back at La Loma, on the grass, under the lights, in a familiar role. There were things I could remedy, situations I could affect. I was supposedly making a difference in the life of a child, several hundred of them actually, but it was my own life that needed the structure, the distraction, of baseball.

Omar had the returning team again, bigger, older, and, at least in his mind, the defending Double A champs. It would be hard, as it had been in Single A, to topple him in our first year, but just being in the finals once more, especially with Mom's ordeal, was a welcome consolation. I tried to convey that in my pregame huddle, to remind my team what was at stake. "Kids play years in this league, good kids, deserving kids, and for whatever reason, through no fault of their own, never make it this far," I said. "You could play sports for the rest of your life and never make it this far again. So no matter how nervous you might be, no matter how bad you want to win, make sure you stop, take a breath, look around, pinch yourself—and remember what it feels like to be eleven years old and playing for a championship in your park."

I scanned the faces in our circle. Half the team had tuned me out. Natalie was snapping her gum. Max was whispering to Alex. I guess I would have been doing the same at their age. Thank goodness for my right fielder, the ever-buoyant Colin. "Yes, sir!" he chirped.

To my surprise, we won that first game, six to four. Jonathan was strong, as usual, striking out twelve. But it was Colin's hitting that propelled us. The first year I coached him, he had gone hitless the entire season, an exercise in futility that never seemed to get him down. He barely had enough meat on his bones to budge the bat off his shoulder, yet he turned every trip to the plate into a celebration of fortitude, calling time with an outstretched palm, fidgeting and measuring and steeling himself, eyebrows bobbing with every dire, dizzying gasp. "There's always tomorrow, coach," he would say. Somewhere along the way, between Single A and Double A, Colin changed, not physically, because he was as slight as ever, but inside, in the presence, the steadiness, that had taken root. He still lacked the strength to hit the ball much beyond the infield, but he had grown surer of himself, of his ability to connect. Twice against Omar's top pitchers, Colin poked a couple of weak grounders, and each time, despite the resulting out, Max was able to score from third: Our RBI leader was a half-Chinese, half-Japanese Boy Scout whose parents forbade him to see even a PG movie.

To enter the second game and not be facing elimination was a luxury, maybe too much of one. We had margin for error, and we used it accordingly. Max was my pitcher and withered early: walks, balks, errors, wild pitches. I called for time and trotted out to see him. "How you doin', kiddo?" I asked.

"I can't pitch."

"Sure you can."

He looked at the ground.

I smoothed the dirt with my foot. "I'll pull you now," I told him, "but you're coming back out here tomorrow." My scorebook does not show how many runs were charged to him, but by the time it was over, we had coughed up seventeen. I knew Max felt responsible.

I had never experienced a tiebreaker before. Usually the team that won the opening game ended up sweeping the series—that was just how kids were, the way they assimilated the pressures of competition—but we had let Omar come storming back. I wondered if we had missed our shot. More than losing, I hated giving that guy a second chance. Because it was our third game of the week, Jonathan would be allowed to pitch three additional innings, which meant that for at least half the night we would be in contention. I decided to save him for the end. If we were going to stumble, I wanted to get it over with. I told Max he was starting again.

As unsettled as he had been the day before, he was nearly flawless in his return. I saw in him everything I had urged him to be, everything I had never been able to do myself. His left knee was coming up high, his thigh as flat and even as a tabletop. His right arm was extended behind his ear, elbow up, wrist away, fingers gripping the ball as if they were cobra fangs. Pitching, as best as I could tell, was not about throwing hard but about alignment and mechanics. You closed yourself sideways, then you sprung yourself open. You started tall, you finished long. Had I taught him this? Or had Max shown it to me? I had been so busy running the league, so rattled by my mom's illness, I could not even remember the last time we had played catch. After three innings, the score was one to one. Max could have continued. He was nowhere near the weekly limit. But I had Jonathan in the wings, ready to close it out. Omar later would tell me that I had erred, that Max was that good: I had failed to recognize what my own son was pulling off. It kills me to think he might have been right. Jonathan pitched a scoreless fourth inning. In the fifth, he got shelled. He was so solid, so consistent about getting the ball over the plate, Omar's kids knew, no matter how fast it came, they would get something to swing at. I had never considered that Jonathan might be anything less than intimidating. We went into the last inning down five to one.

I called a quick huddle. "Do not think for a second that this game is over," I said. "Only you guys, nobody else, get to decide how it ends." Max was up. He singled and stole second. Colin was next. He poked another of his infield dribblers, and this time he not only knocked in Max but made it safely to first. "What are you feeding this kid?" I said to his dad, Bill, who had taken over scorekeeping duties and had his face buried in the book, glasses lifted up to his brow, trying to pencil the action into three-quarter-inch squares. "Just goes to show you, coach," he said, shaking his head. Two of my kids waved at strike three, but another singled, driving in Colin. We were down to our last out. The tying run was at the plate.

I was happy to see that it was Christian Rios, one of the boys who had defied Omar the year before and shown up for the forfeit. His parents had requested that he be placed back in the draft, to be available to any team but Omar's, and because of how they handled that situation, I made it a point to pick up Christian for myself. "What position do you usually play?" I had asked him at the start of the season. Christian shrugged, then looked down. "Bench," he told me. He was a sweet kid, stocky yet soft. His dad had bought him an expensive new big-barrel bat, but Christian was trying so hard, trying to live up to his size, that he rarely made contact. There was no better time for him to finally just be himself. With a full count, Christian turned on a fastball. It flew off that fancy bat like a slingshot, a blast into the depths of center field that reminded me of Max's near home run in the Single A finals, the perfect meeting of determination, physics, and luck. *Take that, Omar, baby, and start printing up your bogus T-shirts again!* I was getting it done my way, the right way. As Christian's smash began to descend, I noticed a familiar silhouette dashing across the grass, glove open, a less welcome flashback from the previous season. It could not be happening—*please, no*—but it was, and I knew at that moment the game was over, our season finished. Nathaniel had seemed like such a gentle kid. He went to a Montessori school, after all. How did he keep ending up on the side of my rivals?

I called Mom to tell her the results. Losing another championship was trivial, but we had started talking more, and if we were going to erase some of the distance between us, baseball was a good place to start. Mom had set a new milestone for herself. "I asked my oncologist to keep me alive long enough to finish out my term," she said. That was only six months away. "Please, Mom, don't stop there," I told her. We were quiet for a moment.

"Are you going to do this again next year?" she asked.

"What? You mean baseball?"

"Yes."

"I don't know. I guess. Would you come down and see Max play?"

"Maybe," she said. "I want to try."

Chapter

Nine

STARTING THAT SEASON WITHOUT TODD—MY ASSISTANT
coach, my co-commissioner—left me with two vacancies to fill.
Picking a new coach seemed like the easier task, and at first I
thought it might even afford me an advantage. In all the time I was
allied with the Muñozes, Jose had always lent his help, as many parents did, pitching batting practice, coaching first base—a de facto
assistant—but I still had been forced to sell my soul to secure
Jonathan. Apart from Max, only Alex, as the son of my assistant of
record, was guaranteed a spot on the team. It was one thing to make
a deal for Jonathan when he was eight or nine, in the infancy of his
pitching career, but now that our boys were entering Double A, he
was just too mighty, too tempting, to expect someone else to pass
him over or cough him up. Certainly, as commissioner, nobody was
going to feel sorry for me or concede that I was entitled to the best
player in the league for another two years.

As much as I would miss his company, Todd had done us a favor. If Jose was my assistant, I could freeze the biggest prize in the draft, then use my first-round pick to go after Alex. It would be much easier to negotiate for him, if necessary. Alex played baseball like he danced—he took weekly hip-hop lessons—with lots of swift, funky, occasionally slapstick maneuvers. He could wreak havoc on the base paths, juking and taunting, provoking errors, manufacturing rallies, but he was more of a table setter than a plate clearer. I used to play him at shortstop—he had the range and slinkiness—but he developed some regrettable, herky-jerky tendencies and too often ended up dancing right over the ball. There were five Double A coaches that 2004 season, the year Omar would knock us out in the tiebreaker, and while I was in a good position to land a couple of quality twelve-year-olds, I was inclined to go young again, as I had in Single A, investing in eleven-year-olds and reaping the benefits in our follow-up season. Everyone at the draft knew I would use my top pick on Alex, and even if I drew last, I had taken comfort in the knowledge that the pool of eleven-year-olds included at least four who were as talented, if not more so; if I had to urge somebody to skip over Alex, to save him for me, it would hardly be considered a sacrifice. When I drew number two, I knew I was home free. Only one coach would have to pass him up.

"Okay, who's got number one?" I asked. I looked around the equipment room, hoping it was one of the nice-guy Asian coaches I had recruited that year, someone I would have no trouble convincing of the righteousness of my claim to Alex. The only coach with a smile, though, and frankly it was more of a leer, had outlined her lips in pencil, then filled them in, a Betty Boop mouth, fuller and redder than I had remembered it. "Lulu?" I said. "Really?"

She was way ahead of me, already calculating her leverage. "Hmm, I think I will choose . . ." Lulu said, milking the moment, ". . . let me see, ah, yes, I will take Alex Ullah in the first round."

I felt queasy. I was not good at feigning nonchalance. "Of course," I said, "we'll be making a trade."

"Maybe," Lulu said. "Maybe not."

With my pick, I chose a scrappy little catcher named Justin Carleton, also half Filipino, who was among the toughest hitters in the league to strike out. Although I had never coached him—he had spent his Single A years with Lulu—I admired his demeanor so much that on my first opening day it was him I selected to handle Luis Rodriguez's ceremonial pitch. The draft continued, Max in the second round, Jonathan in the third, Colin in the fourth, Natalie in the fifth, until every roster was full. "All right, Lulu," I said. "What's it going to be?" I figured she would demand one of my twelve-year-olds, probably my first-round pick. It would not be a fair exchange—Alex was just not that developed—but I was in no position to be choosy.

"I think I'll stick with what I have," Lulu said. "I like my team as it is."

"What? I'm sorry. Seriously. Who do I have to give up?"

"No, that's it," she said. "I'm good."

"Wait, wait, wait!" I said. Even if Todd was backing out on me, I had loyalties to him, a pledge to my son. Max and Alex had been teammates for five years; this draft, being the start of Double A, represented years six and seven. Had I gambled unwisely? Was I so impatient to win another championship, so greedy about reserving Jonathan for myself, that I had trifled with a treasured friendship? Or had Lulu just spotted weakness and moved in for the kill? "This is not right," I said. "Alex is my boy. He belongs with me. You know it."

"You've had him for a long time," Lulu said. "I think a change would do him good."

"But—." I was at a loss. Lulu was getting up to leave. The league's rule—unwritten, naturally—was that all trades had to be made on draft night, in that room, so that rosters did not get fiddled with in private. "You can't go yet," I said. "We have to resolve this here."

"I'm done," she said.

"Just so everyone knows, this is not over," I announced. "I'm reserving the right to make a trade at a future date. Executive privilege."

Lulu was out the door. "Call me," she said.

Now what? I hated to be such a crybaby, but without Alex alongside Max it almost was not worth coaching his team, let alone running the league. Max never demanded to be with Alex, never fretted about not being with him, but then, he did not really have to: It was understood. La Loma was our rock of stability, of continuity, year after year, season after season, and that included his original friend, his oldest teammate. They would play there together until they could play there no longer, and we were barely at the halfway point. As the adult, I was expected to honor and preserve this arrangement—as commissioner, I should have had the authority to enforce it—and instead I had screwed the whole thing up, put myself at the mercy of a witchy baseball mom who saw no reason to accommodate my sentimental tendencies. I called Lulu on her cell the next day. She was at work when she answered, at Adrian's shop. "Maybe we should talk later," I said. If I was going to bargain with her, I did not need to be doing it across enemy lines.

"It's okay," Lulu said. "He's my brother-in-law. But that doesn't mean I don't know he's an asshole."

Maybe there was still hope. "Look, I know you're kind of getting a kick out of making me squirm, and I guess I left myself open to it, but in all seriousness, do you understand how important this is to me?" I said. "Not me, exactly, but to Alex and Max? It's the reason why we're all here in the first place."

"I know that," Lulu said.

"Huh? I mean, wow. Okay. Um, then why did you snatch him away from me?"

"No reason," Lulu said. "We can make a trade—Alex for Justin."

"For real?"

"On one condition."

"Uh-oh."

"It's not so bad."

"I'll be the judge of that."

"That you take me out," Lulu said. "It doesn't have to be a big old fancy date. We can just go for drinks."

"I, um, well, you know, it's just that, I, um——." I had choked. It was useless to even try to invent an excuse.

"Think about it," Lulu said.

My next call was to Carmen. She seemed to enjoy watching me squirm almost as much as Lulu. "Don't be *escared*," she mewed, pretending to console me. Sometimes there were things you could say only in Spanglish. Carmen had become the solution to my other problem, finding a new co-commissioner, a title that in her case we could make gender-specific: Carmen was simply La Commish.

Asking her to fill in for Todd was a bit forward on my part. I had known her mainly as a parent and a volunteer, a fixture of the cloistered multigenerational society that had grown up around La Loma, people who had used the park as a lover's lane before they ever had kids to take there. We were not quite friends, and her children were the wrong ages to be Max's friends. But Carmen had shown me loyalty the year before, when I had taken on Adrian, loyalty I had not expected and was not sure I fully deserved, at least not yet, and just as important, she was—how to say this without diminishing the enormity of choreographing the domestic life of a family of six?— *available.* Carmen had to answer to her husband, naturally, but her juggling act was, compared to the rest of us, more or less self-contained. As long as the house was clean and dinner was waiting, she had the morning hours to herself, time I was not bashful about hijacking on behalf of the league. By eight forty-five, our kids off to school, we would be sitting down to coffee, making lists, swapping gossip, mapping out all the ways in which La Loma still needed guidance and healing. When finally I could put off my work no longer, I would leave Carmen with a stack of to-dos, calls, purchases, deliveries, tabulations, then we would reconnoiter at the end of the day, usually via texting. It was a technology I was new to—a text virgin, Carmen teased me—but I soon came to understand its power, how it allowed her to stay engaged in baseball, covertly if necessary, while still fulfilling her duties at home.

The cell was our first indication that becoming La Commish might have been more than she had bargained for. A month or two into that 2004 season, whenever their April or May statement arrived, Carmen's husband, Eddie, confronted her with the bill, a whopper, at least four or five hundred bucks. I was not the sole cause. Everyone at La Loma had Carmen's number, and as her responsibilities and authority increased, she became nearly as much of a troubleshooter as I was, her modest pool of family minutes forced to handle an extra twenty, thirty, forty calls a day. The same had happened to me the year before, but I had nobody to berate me. I just sucked it up—billing the league seemed like an unwise precedent—and hiked my plan to three thousand minutes. I should have warned Carmen, urged her to warn her husband before it was too late, but I was focused on teaching her to run the league with me, not on preserving the tranquillity of their marriage. Eddie was furious. He took Carmen's phone away. "I just got scolded," she said, calling me from their landline. She sounded like she had been crying. "I guess I don't know how to do anything right."

"Why do you say that?"

"It's what I keep hearing."

"Self-pity doesn't become you," I said.

"Stop," she said.

"It's true. This is just the cost of doing business. Don't be so hard on yourself."

"I don't know what to do."

"Besides," I added, "it has nothing to do with a cell phone."

Within a few days, predictably, she got it back—Eddie hated not being able to reach her more than he hated paying the bill—but the battle lines had been drawn. Baseball, me, the park, the hundreds of families who inhabited it: We were all under a cloud of suspicion, subversives, poised to undermine the hierarchy of the Delgado home. Eddie had grown up rough in East L.A., not quite as rough as Carmen, but even more than she, he had dedicated his life to surmounting every bit of that poverty, the taint of the barrio, and building himself a tidy, upper-middle-class life, the

Hispanic accountant in a big WASPy downtown firm. He and Carmen used to correct each other's grammar (she still said "seen"
instead of "saw," "nothing" when she meant "anything"), and after
the crisis of Sebastian's birth, which left his top lip pinned to his
nasal passages, it was Eddie who had insisted on plastic surgery
right away, to make their son as normal as possible. He was a year
or two younger than Carmen, and somewhat to her dismay, he
looked it, slender, fit, clean-shaven, blow-dried, with a closet of
creased and pressed business attire. Women often went out of their
way to tell her how lucky she was. Carmen agreed—compared to
most of the men in her life, Eddie oozed success—yet the more
time we spent together, the more I sensed her despair. La Loma
nourished something in her, something so powerful and liberating, I think she almost wished it had never been awoken.

When I first thought of enlisting Carmen, I had called her at
home and gotten Eddie, and he told me to try her cell, that she was
at Staples Center with a girlfriend, watching the Clippers. She
answered in the middle of the game—our conversation was interrupted by screams and buzzers and what had to be gulps of beer—
and in the commotion she said sure, why not: "I'd be willing to
help out." I tried to explain that it was more than helping out, that
I was asking for an extraordinary commitment, but even if she had
been able to hear me, if I had been able to impress upon her the
level of organization and creativity and gumption that would be required, my description still would have fallen short. It would have
been impossible for either one of us to have predicted how being La
Commish would change her, how for the first time in her life—
Carmen was, I believe, thirty-eight—she had begun to measure her
worth on her own terms, not as a wife or a mother or a daughter but
as a protagonist, on a public stage, in a role she was inventing day
by day.

Eddie was at the park, too, as a coach for his namesake, Lil'
Eddie. But he was systematic about it, clocking in for practices and
games, while Carmen lost track of time at La Loma. She cared
about texture and tone, the emotional caliber of the experience we

were helping to create. She lived for the exchange of greetings, the handshakes and hugs, the petty dramas, the suggestive puns, the picnic dinners, the ability, if just for a few hours, to breathe in the cut grass and the summer fog, and to exhale. Eddie was at first mystified and then annoyed and finally offended that she had the energy to attend to so many other people—demanding, undeserving people—and such a waning interest in the basic operations of their home. As the season progressed, our morning coffee sessions became as much about excavating their marriage as about reconstructing the league. Carmen, it seemed to me, had never been so happy or so sad. "He doesn't understand what I get out of the park," she would lament. "He only sees what's being taken away from him."

I am not sure at what point Carmen told me about her first child, the son before the other four, but I remember how quickly my surprise turned into something else, a cross between sorrow and solidarity. His name was Christopher, and he was eighteen already. His father was a bad boy, the embodiment of all the patterns that Carmen had vowed, after high school, to break. They had never married and he had shown no inclination to be a dad, and I found myself doing the math, calculating that Carmen had been a single mom, hoping for something better, at almost the same time that I had met Raynelda—that Eddie was being introduced to her son just as I was beginning to lose my way with Freddy.

The parallel did not end there: Even though Eddie had graciously accepted Christopher, raising him as his own, Christopher had never quite embraced him as his surrogate, never fully trusted the illusion of their four-bedroom, three-bathroom, two-story house or allowed himself to believe that he was as much a Delgado as his four younger siblings—a family of seven!—which he was not, having retained the name of a man he scarcely knew. Like Freddy, Christopher had gravitated to the streets, adopted an image that both eased and justified his anger, shaved his head and tattooed his left shoulder with the "L.A." logo, which I am pretty sure, in his case, had nothing to do with the Dodgers. To help keep him straight, Carmen asked if we could hire Christopher to prep the fields. I agreed to pay him ten bucks a day for the hour it took to water and chalk, but he quit after two weeks, convinced that we were playing him for a fool. I understood better, then, how much Carmen was hurting, how much she feared, for all the bourgeois trappings she now enjoyed, that she had lost the ability to save her oldest baby. One morning the cops raided their house, searching for evidence that might link him to the abduction and murder of a fifteen-year-old girl, a sensational crime that was being blamed on a gang from East L.A. They found nothing, but Eddie still had to pony up five grand for a lawyer, just in case. "He's had everything, every opportunity I never had," Carmen told me, "but there's still something missing, and I hate to say that I think it's that male figure, his real dad."

It must have been around this time that I told Carmen about Freddy, not just that I had a stepson racked by the same pangs but that his disaffection had proved at least as ruinous as Christopher's, perhaps more so, to him, to our home. The day of his accident, the day that Freddy turned my fears from abstract to imminent, he was fourteen and I was still the *L.A. Times* guy in Houston. We had left him alone for a few hours, on a gray Saturday in 1997, so that his mom and I could take Max to a barbecue cook-off on the grounds of the Astrodome, one of the highlights of the annual Livestock Show and Rodeo, which is to say the sort of quintessentially Texan extravaganza that reminded Freddy why he had never wanted to come in the first place. Raynelda had given him a few dollars and suggested he go to the movies. I had set the alarm and insisted he not return until we did. If it was not exactly parenting to be proud of, it was at least a truce, a way for three out of four of us to continue functioning as a unit.

We had been to the Astrodome before, a couple of years earlier, when the Dodgers and their Japanese sensation, Hideo Nomo, were in town. It was on its last legs as a ballpark—the Astros would soon move to a more intimate, throwback field—but there was still something awesome and absurd about the ambition of the place, the Eighth Wonder of the World, even if now we were just wandering the parking lot, gnawing on spareribs. After less than an hour, the sky turned leaden. An icy wind began strafing the asphalt, kicking up twisters of napkins and beer cups. I took Max, who was three, out of his stroller and tried to shield him in the folds of my jacket. "Let's get out of here," Raynelda said. We lived only a few minutes away, in a dated wedge of suburbia called Willowbend, which had a lot in common with Monterey Park, except that it was flat and swampy. Raynelda, as I recall, wanted to grab some warmer clothes and head out again, to keep the party going; I was lobbying to call it a day. The moment we pulled up, I knew nothing would be the same.

Red strobes were ricocheting everywhere, off the concrete driveway that Max only a few months earlier had ridden his bike down for the first time without training wheels, off the basketball hoop that Max would shimmy up and dangle from, tickled to have created so much distance between himself and the ground, off the smooth elm that Max used as a fort and a swing and a couch. Police were walking across our lawn, in and out of our house. I shivered at the familiarity. I had warned of this, written this story before.

"Your son's been shot!"

One of our neighbors was waving her arms, running our way, shouting at us through the car window. I remembered her as the lady I had tried to introduce myself to when we had moved in: Seeing a stranger at her door, she had left the chain on, speaking to me through the crack. I had hardly shared a word with her since, but I was certain she had not been overjoyed to have a family of L.A. exiles, mixed and blended and freighted with an angry Central American teenager, on her block.

"Shot!" she repeated. Then, as if she were not adequately conveying the gravity of the situation: "In the face!"

I began to climb out of the driver's seat, but my knees buckled and I had to brace myself against the wheel. I tried to speak, but I felt my belly clench. I managed only to wheeze. What happened? Who did this? We had just seen Freddy, alone, on his way to the theater. Was he already dead? I told myself to think like a reporter. I had a press pass, issued by the Texas Department of Public Safety, in my wallet. I should find a sergeant. I knew the protocol of the perimeter, the questions I was entitled to ask. I had not succeeded in being much of a dad to Freddy. The least I could do was get some answers about how badly I had failed. It was then that I saw the ambulance, parked in front of us the whole time, now ablaze and wailing. I jumped back in. I turned the key and punched the emergency blinkers. We could talk to the cops later. As long as Freddy was alive, if he was alive, my duty was to catch up to him. I drove through stop signs and red lights, onto the freeway, my route to the office, seventy, eighty, ninety miles per hour, each tick of the clock reducing the odds that Freddy could be saved. I craned my head to look at Max, strapped into the backseat, unusually quiet. At least he is young, I thought. I put my hand on Raynelda's thigh. "*Amor,*" I said. I always called her that, "love," no matter what crap had come between us. "I know—you know—that we're hoping for the best." My throat was a knot. "But you also need to prepare yourself." Did I even need to say this? "For the worst." She stared out the windshield. It was too soon for her to cry.

A TV crew was stationed outside the hospital, waiting for the body. What did they know? Why was this news? I was embarrassed by their voyeurism. I was embarrassed at myself for having given them something to film. Freddy was cinched to a gurney, hooked to tubes, swathed in cotton. Before we could get to him, he was swarmed by doctors and wheeled away, through sliding doors, past prying lenses, into the cold light of the emergency room. I clutched Max to my chest. Raynelda was still speechless. We were led down the hall, to a small office, with a vinyl couch and a potted plant. A nurse came in. The bullet had entered the bridge of Freddy's nose. It was still lodged in his skull. A nun came in. She asked if she could pray with us. I asked her to respect our privacy. A paramedic came in. He handed us a plastic bag with Freddy's possessions: gold earring, Velcro wallet, three dollars and change. "His last words," the paramedic said, "were 'Tell my mom I love her.' " The door was closed, and then we were alone.

During my mom's first campaign her supporters included

David and Elisabeth Linder, dyed-in-the-wool lefties with a story that mirrored her own—he a Brooklynite, she a refugee from Nazi-occupied Czechoslovakia. They were among the earliest families to open their home to her, up in the Northwest Portland hills, to invite their neighbors to meet this brash homemaker turned activist who had the audacity to believe in peace and justice. I had not known Ben, their youngest son, but I remembered hearing his name when I first visited Nicaragua, on the trip that cost me Susan. He was in his twenties, like me, except that he was helping the Sandinistas construct a hydroelectric plant on a remote mountain stream, to bring light to an impoverished village, and I was trying to out-Latino my college girlfriend. I felt envious, at the time, of his commitments, his idealism. He had sunk his teeth into something so purposeful, and I was barely nibbling around the edges. A couple of years later, while I was carousing in Echo Park, Benjamin Linder was killed, ambushed by the Contras. He was the first U.S. citizen, a noncombatant, to die in a civil war clandestinely orchestrated by his own government. My shock was tempered by a selfish thought: I was not Ben Linder. I was a journalist, apolitical, an observer, not an acolyte. Drinking at The Sunset, flirting with Raynelda, was thrill enough.

With Freddy's shooting, to my surprise, Ben's name came back to me. Nearly a decade had passed, the revolution was over, the Sandinistas had been ousted, the Contras had disarmed, and yet the legacy of conquest and colonialism, of Nicaragua's tortured past, was being played out under my roof. Maybe I had not engaged in the same magnitude of service—I was the sponsor of the Gutiérrez clan, not the pueblo of San José de Bocay—but on that winter day in the waiting room, wondering if Freddy was going to make it, I suddenly began to grasp the stakes of my cultural immersion. I was not Ben, but I had left Portland for a foreign place, for an identity that suited me, and now because of it, on my watch, blood had been spilled.

Freddy, from what I later pieced together, had slipped back into the house as soon as we turned the corner. He called some of his friends, fractured Latino kids like him, too recently arrived to feel welcome and too captivated by hip-hop dreams to appreciate the sacrifices that got them here. One of them—a boy named Jesús—brought over a .32-caliber semiautomatic Beretta, filched from his aunt's closet. They went through the kitchen and out the den, to our back patio, passing the gun around, mugging. They felt its weight, its precision, the compactness and finality of its power. When Freddy collapsed, and one of those boys had the good sense at least to call for help, they insisted there had been a drive-by; never mind that they were shielded by our house, hidden from the street. The cops split them up, told them each that someone was lying, and without much more fuss, the weapon surfaced, in the ashes of our fireplace. When he was questioned further, the boy named Jesús said that Freddy had been toying with it, looking down the barrel. Nobody expected it to go off, just a foot away, for that bullet to slam, at close to the speed of sound, into his head. The Beretta was made to kill him, instantly, unequivocally, and yet for reasons I usually give little credence to, fate, luck, miracle, it failed.

The shot pierced his nose more or less cleanly, just left of center, at the exact spot where a pair of eyeglasses might rest. If it had continued on course, there would have been no need for an ambulance; the trauma would have been catastrophic. The bullet, though, struck bone. It splintered. Fragments of lead burned through cartilage, careened across sinuses, tumbled into the cavities behind his eye sockets, and then stopped, out of steam, just short of Freddy's brain. There was no internal bleeding, no disfigurement, no injury to his motor skills or thought processes. Freddy was, at that moment, unable to see—the doctors were still reading his X-rays, assessing the damage to his optic nerves—but by the time we were escorted to his bedside, not more than an hour after our frantic chase, he was alive and conscious and otherwise unharmed.

Raynelda put her hand on his cheek. "Oh, baby," she said. "Baby, baby." She rested her head on his chest. I could feel her relief. No matter his condition, Freddy was still with us. He was intact, present. Raynelda's son had been returned to her, once again. Freddy started to giggle. It was weird, almost demonic, as if he were watching a movie none of us could see. I was aghast. After everything this kid had put us through, he had the temerity to laugh in our faces? He kept right on going, unable to help himself, and then it dawned on me that Freddy was flying, high by his own doing or from whatever chemicals had been slipped into his IV. Between snickers Freddy said something about having been shot—his phrasing was passive like that—an admission I took as unrehearsed and, because of the drugs, perhaps more truthful than he realized. When I later told Freddy what the cops were saying, that his hand had been on the gun, he conceded, maybe, that could also be true. Whatever happened, if it even matters, probably lies in the smokiest reaches of the adolescent brain. Maybe, there in the hospital, Freddy had played a semantic trick, an act of self-preservation, to distance himself from his own awful blunder. "I got shot" had to sound better to him than "I stupidly shot myself." Maybe, though, Freddy had been forthright from the start. Maybe one of his friends had actually been fiddling with the Beretta, and maybe, after it went off, that supposed friend had made the calculation that Freddy would not be around to contradict him, and maybe once the cops started asking questions and all that had sunk in, Freddy had wanted to prove himself a loyal soldier and agreed to go along with the lie. I suppose I could ask him again. In a decade, not much has changed: He still lives with his mom, ten minutes from us, still depends on her to finance and forgive his indifference, his afflictions. We are polite on the infrequent occasions when we need to be—he follows the Lakers and reveres Bob Marley, which affords us some easy chitchat—but I cannot say that I would trust his answer any more today or that a clearer picture of the accident would make up for anything.

That first night in the hospital, Raynelda and I slept in the waiting room, tried to, at any rate. We ended up on the linoleum floor, under the flicker of fluorescent lights, her back to my front, one of our jackets folded as a pillow and the other straining to keep us warm. The neighbors we knew best, a couple with a pair of boys close in age to ours, had offered to baby-sit Max. I was used to him running into our bed in the middle of the night, awakened by a dream or the urge to pee, and feeling his hot toes against my ribs as he tried to settle himself back to sleep. I needed to see him. In the morning, I found a McDonald's and brought a McMuffin back for Raynelda. I gave her a peck on the cheek and headed for home. It had been almost eighteen hours since we had left for the Astrodome, since our house became a hangout, then a crime scene. I needed to take care of that first.

By the front door I spotted a pair of latex gloves, discarded in haste. I tried the knob. It was unlocked. Without a key, the paramedics had been forced to leave the house open. In the kitchen I found torn packets of gauze and rubber syringe tips. I peeked into the den, saw the fireplace screen pulled aside, the smudge of charcoal on the carpet. I kept going, toward the back, outside, dreading what awaited and yet also drawn to it—or maybe drawn to the part of me that was no longer squeamish, that wanted to believe I had the reservoirs, the selflessness, to endure whatever could be heaped on me. *Let me face it. Let me spare his mother. Let me clean the mess, because I can, because I have to, because in my odd, restless dance between poverty and privilege, I am not at peace unless I am bridging those worlds.* On the cement platform that served as our patio, a damp nook where the ferns and mosquitoes grew large, I dropped to my knees. The stain was dark, almost black, but still sticky, as if a side of the barbecue sauce we had been licking off our fingers the day before had fallen to the ground. Tendrils had wrapped themselves around the base of a cheap folding lawn chair, the kind held together with plaid nylon straps, and I had a vision of Freddy slumped there, fire between his eyes, while his cohorts, strangers in my home, scrambled to come up with a story. No, she should not have to see this. No parent should. I went for a scouring pad and some Comet. I turned on the hose.

I went next door after that, to pick up Max. In those days he still raced to me like a puppy, tongue wagging, arms pumping, toddler feet at full pitter-patter, a stampede of enthusiasm that usually put him on a course straight for my groin. The trick was to scoop him up a step early, just before I got pummeled by an innocent elbow or shoulder, and use his momentum to hoist him into the air, suspended over my head, where I could both cherish him and govern him and pretend to take hungry bites of his stomach. *Mmm, tender. Grrr, needs salt. Ohhh, tastes like chicken.* This time, when Max made his beeline for me, I just pulled him to my chest and held him there, squeezing, nuzzling, breathing in his sweaty boyness.

I wanted to be able to tell him, if I could have found the words that a preschooler would have understood, that his future was not Freddy's, in part because his past was not Freddy's, and that as his father I would never allow it to be. I had a duty to block for him, to offer myself as his shield, his own personal body armor, not just because that is what a loving parent does but because I had, at least indirectly, put him in harm's way. By leading this damn contrarian life of mine, by believing there was no risk or burden I could not absorb, I was causing Max to experience things he should never have to know about. A gun had been fired in our home. The flesh of his brother—stepbrother, half brother, whatever, a child born to Max's mother, a child I had helped bring to this country—had been breached on our patio. I had washed it away, sanitized the horror, but Max was a sponge: He was seeing everything, taking it in, feeling more than I could know. If I had married a nice Jewish girl, as my mom sometimes nudged me to, Max would not exist, of course; maybe some other child, a different version of him, but not this kid, with all his beautiful syntheses and comminglings. Raynelda and I had made the perfect baby—to be fair, she had done the hard work—and yet the very thing that gave Max his attributes, that endowed him with such perspective and balance, was exposing him to unacceptable dangers. If I intervened too forcefully, I would be doing more damage, turning Max against his mother, against his own self. If I did not intervene forcefully enough, I would be falling short of the dad Max needed me to be for him.

We headed back to the hospital, retracing the route we had taken the day before, slowly now, without sirens. I told Max that his mom was waiting, that she would be so happy to see him again. "Is Freddy dead?" Max asked. I had neglected to address the most obvious question. "Oh, no, champ, don't worry, he's, uh, going to be—." I sighed. Freddy was alive; that much seemed certain. Beyond that, who could say? If only he could emerge humbled, whatever his condition, receptive at last to my counsel, to anyone's encouragement and care. I would never have wished it on him, but since it happened, maybe this bullet was his wake-up call, a blessing even. "—he's going to be happy to see you, too."

We met with doctors off and on for the rest of that afternoon, Raynelda still numb and Max clinging to my neck. The nerve behind Freddy's left eye had been severed. He was blind, the damage irreversible. He was blind in his right eye, too, but the surgeons thought the nerve on that side was merely being pinched; if they could get the swelling down in time, he might regain some function. They assigned us a social worker and referred us to the Lighthouse of Houston, a rehab center for the visually impaired. We were told about magnifying screens and jumbo keypads and talking clocks, and I think someone even mentioned Braille. It was a lot: this lost teenager of ours now on the verge of being a handicapped one, perhaps unable to fend for himself to a degree we had never previously imagined. We would know more in a few days. There was nothing to do but wait. I told Raynelda to come home with us. She agreed. I was pleased that the house appeared undisturbed now, no sign of the intrusions, of the torments, that had greeted my return. Raynelda got right into bed. I had not told her of the cleanup I had performed, and she did not bother to look around. I thought I was protecting her. She had already decided for herself she did not want to know.

"Let's let Mommy rest," I told Max. We sat on the couch and turned on the Nintendo. I had bought him the latest version that Christmas, the N64, and we had been working our way through Super Mario ever since, from the ice level to the fire level to the psychedelic rainbow level, but we still had not managed to defeat Bowser in the final cataclysmic showdown, with the earth disintegrating under our feet. Max was about to turn four and I was thirty-four, which in video game years made us roughly equals. "You go first, Daddy," Max said. I took the controller from him and kissed him on the head. His cheeks were flushed. I looked at his neck. Blotches were spreading from his ears to his throat. "Hey, champ, can you lift your shirt up for me real quick?" I asked. He grabbed the bottom of the hemline, unsure whether to raise it or hold it taut. He probably thought I was going to take another munch from his belly. "Just for a sec," I said. The blotches were turning into welts, pink and swollen, like a chain of volcanic islands erupting from the sea. They were on his front, on his back, breaking out everywhere. "Oh, dear, I think you've got hives," I said. "Does it itch?"

Max squirmed. "A little," he said. "What's hives?"

How was I supposed to know? It seemed like one of those blanket diagnoses, an all-purpose explanation for just about any rash of indeterminate origin. Maybe he had been exposed to something at the hospital. Maybe he had eaten something next door. But I doubted it. Max had never been that delicate, never allergic or susceptible to anything. In my heart, I knew the answer. His little body had finally sounded the alarm. I stripped him down to his underwear, Power Ranger briefs. I dug around in the medicine cabinet until I found some witch hazel, whatever that was, then wrapped my fingers in toilet paper. I started moistening and dabbing, bathing Max from head to toe, hoping I had found an elixir as versatile as his ailment. He was holding still, studying my face. I had no idea what I was doing, but I felt, with a certainty that I rarely have experienced, that this is what my dad would have done.

Chapter

Ten

I WAS COACHING ONE NIGHT ON THE UPPER FIELD, WATCHING
Max go through his windup, when I heard my name called through
the fence behind me. It was a woman's voice, her distress barely
contained. "Katz," she said. "We need to talk. Now. You have to do
something about this." I was perched on the dugout bench, eating
seeds, making notes, enjoying the sight of my son on the mound.
I gave everything to the park. Why was this lady tampering with
my moment?

"It's going to have to wait," I said, giving my neck half a twist
but not turning to face her.

"What?" she said, disbelieving.

"I'm coaching. Please. This is my team. That's my son out
there."

"You're the commissioner, aren't you?"

"Yes, but I'm off duty at this particular juncture in time," I said. "I will gladly speak to you after the game."

She stormed off, muttering that she was going to complain about me to someone, not realizing, I guess, that nobody else wanted the responsibilities I had assumed, that Carmen and Todd and Chris and Jose and even Gary and Omar and Bob and Lulu all knew what I was about, that respect me or resent me, I was indeed running the league, and that it was in nobody's interest to weaken my standing. Like the folks at the fireworks company, La Loma had found the steward it had been waiting for: dupe, nursemaid, whipping boy, first responder. If nothing else, I was accountable.

It was late, after nine-thirty, by the time Max retired the last batter. I think we won, but the interruption overshadows my memory. She was outside the snack bar, still fuming. I recognized her now, a mom new to the league, with stunning green eyes—rare for a Latina, or was she Armenian, maybe Persian?—and a ten-year-old daughter, with a pink girlie glove, who was playing sports for the first time. I had accepted their application myself, providing the requisite comfort and motivation. *You like baseball,* mija? *That's good. Don't let anything or anyone scare you off. We've got lots of girls in this league, and some of them even beat up on the boys!* Because she was a novice, on the frilly side, I recommended that we place her in Rookies, with the seven- and eight-year-olds. We used a low-density safety ball in that division, somewhere between a rubbery T-Ball and a regulation hardball, and I figured that would go a long way toward allaying her mom's qualms, and mine. I made those kinds of adjustments and exceptions all the time, on the grounds that we were not just administering schedules or anointing victors but selling an experience—that kids were still kids, and because adults sometimes lost sight of that, it was my job to try to right the scales. "I'm sorry if you thought I was being rude tonight, it's just that I get tugged in so many different directions, I don't always get to spend as much time with my son as I'd like," I said. "Come, let's sit down. Tell me what I can do for you."

She did not return my smile. I could tell she already had made a judgment about me, about my leadership and compassion, based on her own sense of injury. Once again, I wondered if I had been too casual in dismissing a constituent—too flippant, too selfish? Maybe I had missed an opportunity to defuse a crisis, or maybe I had provoked one; if only I had taken a minute to hear her out, to allow her to feel attended to. "My daughter . . ." she said, her voice starting to crack. Whatever had happened to rattle this lady, it had struck at her essence, her identity as a parent. "She got . . ."

"Take your time," I said.

"Hit," she said finally.

"Oh, no."

"By a boy!"

"You mean, like, he punched her?"

"No, the boy who was throwing the ball," she said, appalled that I was failing to appreciate the offense that had been inflicted. "The pitcher hit her."

"Ah, she got hit by a pitch. That's too bad. Is she okay?"

"Too bad? It hit her right here, in the back. She's really upset and scared right now. That boy, they say he's only eight, but he throws way too hard. Everyone agrees with that. You *are* the commissioner. I'd like to know what you're going to do about it."

I knew immediately who had beaned her daughter. It could only have been one kid, a little flamethrower named Jacob. He was even newer to our league—I had signed him up just a week or two earlier, midway through the season—and his sudden arrival at La Loma was causing an uproar, mainly among the eight of our nine Rookie coaches being deprived of his services. I was not suspicious of his age. Jacob was a tiny guy, and his dad, a UPS driver, had presented me with a stamped and sealed copy of his birth certificate. But there was no doubt the boy threw serious heat. He was a travel-ball talent preying on rec league marks, and the team I assigned him to—lucky to have had a vacancy on its roster—had just become a cinch to win the championship.

The politics of dropping and adding players was complex and, like other aspects of the draft, prone to manipulation. If a kid was a chronic no-show, his coach might choose to keep it quiet, to cycle the team's top hitters through the lineup more swiftly. On the other hand, if a coach knew that an ace like Jacob was on the waiting list, he might be tempted to shed a player, whether by active discouragement or by simply "forgetting" to update the schedule, to create a well-timed opening. In either case, I was always having to check on missing kids—to determine whether they had, in fact, withdrawn, and if so, voluntarily. Jacob was such a standout, I probably could have insisted on moving him up a division, to face nine- and ten-year-olds, just as I had moved his victim down. But I figured that every child, Jacob included, had a right to play with kids his own age if he wanted to, and if I started tinkering too much, I would risk engineering results that, for everyone's sake, were better off left to chance. Of all the batters for him to get wild on, though, he had chosen a spectacularly vulnerable one—a girl I had tried to coddle, who was now, if her mother was to be believed, very near to hysteria. "It's never fun to get hit by a pitch," I said. "I know, my son's been beaned plenty of times. But it is, for better or worse, sort of an unavoidable part of the game."

This was not what she wanted to hear. I was suggesting acquiescence, and she wanted remedies, guarantees. "It's just . . . just . . . just not *fair,*" she said.

I had been trying to strike a sympathetic tone, to be responsive without validating her alarm. But now I had to shake my head and smile. It was too good of a line to pass up. "Baseball," I said, clearing my throat, "baseball isn't fair."

So much of my commissioner's dealings, the things I sought to accomplish and the ways I was asked to intercede, involved matters of structure. Could I impose a degree of consistency, an element of fairness, on an organization that, by its nature, resisted it? The lights turn off in the middle of a game: Do I reschedule? Do I declare a winner on the spot? Do I recognize the score at the time play was suspended or do I accept it only for the last completed inning? A drizzly afternoon scares away one team but not its opponent: Do I reschedule? Do I declare a forfeit? Do I make my own assessment about the severity of the rain—whether the absent coach was being prissy or just prudent? One year there was a Rookie game in which the home team, by mistake, batted first. They were the feeblest team in the division, something like zero and twelve at that point, and it was not hard to imagine how the strange bedfellows who shared coaching duties—a tatted-down homie and a squeaky-clean IRS drudge—might have accidentally squandered the advantage of batting last. After three innings, they found themselves trailing by just two runs, as close to victory as they had been all season. Time, however, was running out, and the umpire, thinking it unwise to start a new inning, prepared to call it a night. Just then the coaching odd couple, Anthony and Tom, Mexican American and Chinese American, recognized their error and began waving around the schedule, insisting that as the home team, the game could not end until their side took one last trip to the plate. I was responsible for hiring our chief umpire, a prodigiously muscled personal trainer named Cal, the only African American you would see at La Loma most days, who was always making it his business to invite the hottest moms to join him at Bally for a free workout. Cal was good at what he did, a stabilizing presence on the diamond, but his crew was not nearly as reliable. They tended to be on their way up or their way down, creaky old coots in need of a few bucks or community college kids without the juice to manage the designs and anxieties of coaches twice their age. The ump that night fell into the latter camp, which is to say he was no match for Anthony and Tom. More desperate than mere cheaters, they were tired and humiliated, unwilling to concede that their best chance for a win, for giving their team something at long last to cheer about, had just slipped from their grasp.

In an alarming departure from baseball custom, the game was extended by three more outs, and with that extra turn—batting first *and* batting last—Anthony's and Tom's kids somehow managed to rally. When the go-ahead run crossed the plate, their side of the field burst into shrieks, a walk-off victory, improbable, chimerical. I was not there to see it. If I had been, I could have intervened, but I was home, trying to get Max to bed at a decent hour for once. By 10 P.M. my phones were ringing, cell and land, complaints and counterpoints swamping my mailboxes. I spent most of the next day investigating, conducting interviews, piecing together a chronology. I often sank hours, time I did not have, into matters such as these, hoping to arrive at a just resolution. To anyone not caught up in the internal affairs of La Loma, the effort must seem exorbitant, far out of proportion with the child's play that Little League purports to be. I get that. I had no desire to be an "inside baseball" wonk, splitting hairs about rules and dispensing gems about winning methods. But compared to my first years as a coach, I had developed after a few seasons as commissioner a much keener appreciation for the value of guidelines and propriety. As long as I was going to be held responsible for the quality of everyone's experience, there had to be a system that inspired confidence, that was rational and predictable, that redressed grievances, that transcended personalities, that reaffirmed that whatever happened in the park was of consequence—that the whole damn thing *mattered.*

Because even if you had a healthy perspective on competition, even if it was your nature to promote fun, you still had to acknowledge how much was at stake: not so much scores or standings, but time and effort and heart. We asked so much of our kids, reminding them always to do their best. Did we really mean it? We said it benevolently, as if relieving pressure, but doing your best, always, requires uncommon discipline and perseverance. It forces you from the coolness of the sidelines into the heat of the arena. It leaves you vulnerable, exposed to ridicule, injury, manipulation. The last bedtime story I read to Max, before he got too old, was *The Kid from Tomkinsville,* John Tunis's exquisite novel for teens, and there was a line in it that I often found myself quoting: "Courage is all baseball. And baseball is all life; that's why it gets under your skin." The way I saw my job, I had a duty to defend that youthful exertion, to not trifle with anyone's hope or trust. Especially if I wanted people to accept unfavorable rulings from me, I needed to be impeccable in my deliberations—not necessarily perfect, because most disputes offered only imperfect verdicts, but painstaking and unimpeachable. No matter the quarrel, my response could never be just "whatever."

The mom whose daughter took a scalding fastball in the ribs proved to be an easier case than I had thought. I asked if a pinch runner had been used. No, she had managed to trot to first base on her own. What about the next time she was called on to bat: Did she refuse, sticking her team with an automatic out? No, she had taken her turn again at the plate, even drawing a walk. "What?" I asked. "You mean to say she went right back out there?"

"Well, yes," her mom said, "but she was scared."

"I recognize that. But she did it anyway, right?"

"I didn't know she had any other choice."

"Beautiful! Don't you see?"

"She was in tears."

"Even better," I said. "Think about what your daughter just proved to you."

My other dilemma, the double-dipping home team, should have been an easier fix. Nobody gets to bat first and last and walk away the winner. Still, I hated to monkey with the results of a game, to reverse an outcome after it already had been celebrated. I asked the opposing coach why he had agreed to that extra half inning, why he had not just left the field and taken his players with him. He conceded that in hindsight he should have but that Anthony and Tom had been so persistent, so agitated, that he did not want to be cast as the ogre who had thwarted the hopes of their kids. I asked the umpire why he had presided over such an obvious gaffe, and he said much the same, that as long as the opposing coach was going along with it, he felt compelled to be a good sport, too. What the hell was the matter with these people? If any of them had shown a sliver of spine, they could have prevented this inane conclusion. I was almost of a mind to let the results stand—the game had been allowed, after all, to end like this—just to punish all of them for their passivity. As an alternative, I considered ordering both teams to reconvene, on the grounds that instead of ending an inning, they had begun one, and now they just needed to finish it off. I called the losing coach again and asked if he would agree to that, to another trip to the plate, in what would technically be the bottom of the fourth. He said he would, except that the winners never actually finished the top half of the inning; the game ended, with runners still on and outs yet to be recorded, as soon as they went ahead. If we picked up the action where it left off, in other words, Anthony's and Tom's players would still be at bat, trying to extend their lead. I kind of felt like they had already had enough. I called the umpire again and asked if he would have permitted a fourth inning to get under way if he knew he was starting a complete inning, not merely giving the home team a final shot. No, he said, that is why he was trying to end the game in the first place. In fact, he *did* end it—the game was over—but the pressure to resume was overwhelming. "Everyone kept telling me to let them play," the ump said, "to do it for the kids."

My last call was to Tom. He was as by-the-book of a guy as I had ever known, the kind with a voice mail that began, "You've reached the message box of Tom Tang, badge number 9505187." He was reedy and excitable, with a bit of a stutter, but he loved baseball and he loved our park, and I had been trying to recruit him as a coach or board member almost from the minute I took over. In the Asian jargon of Monterey Park, the town was said to be split between ABCs and FOBs—American-born Chinese and those fresh off the boat—and though he was squarely among the former, Tom had the capacity, I thought, to draw both camps in, to make La Loma look more like the community it served. He had resisted, worried that he lacked the cultural and linguistic agility to win over the East Los families, but I persuaded him to volunteer as an assistant, which is how he ended up with Anthony, a comical partnership that they both accepted without complaint. Tom was always telling me how much he admired my leadership, how much more he thought I deserved for my labors. "Nobody here appreciates what you do for us," he would say. "They don't know. They don't understand."

"That's okay, Tom. That's not what I need."

"Have you ever thought of giving yourself a salary?" he once asked. "I mean, holy cow, I don't know how you even have time to do your job."

"You trying to get a cut of it for the IRS?"

"Oh, no, no. C'mon, Jess. I handle bankruptcies, anyway. I'm just saying you work so hard at this. It's not right for you to be taken advantage of."

I was hoping I had accumulated a deep enough reserve of good-will with Tom to weather what I needed to tell him now. I had never voided a win before, and I would never void one again, but my conscience could not abide the fraud his team had perpetrated. Tom was too much of a stickler himself to mount a convincing defense. I assured him that it was not all his fault, that others had been complicit, but instead of standing up for his kids, he had undermined them: Whatever they thought they had won, it could not rightly be called a game of baseball. "You can make me the bad guy if you want," I said. "Go back to your team and tell them you tried, but I wouldn't budge."

"I'm not going to do that to you," Tom said.

"Make sure your kids know they didn't do anything wrong."

"This season," Tom said. "It's been killing me."

"Like I said, use me if you need to."

When I was young, at the cusp of my Little League years, my dad asked me to name the most powerful industry in the world. I was not sure what to make of the question. He still expected an answer. "Someone who sells something that nobody can do without," he said. "A business that has everyone by the short hairs." I had never considered that there might be such an entity, that one indispensable product could leave us all at the mercy of some grim capitalist machine, and I certainly had no inkling as to which hairs could be that short and still be subject to grabbing. I tried to think of every necessity we relied on, every essential in our drab Northwest Portland existence. Finally, I hazarded a guess: "Is it the toilet paper makers?" Dad laughed and said maybe they were second. He must have just written a check for the premium on our Dodge Dart, which he drove without seat belts, relying on a stiff right arm to protect me, because the correct answer, or at least the one he had been fishing for, was the insurance companies. (Dad had already trained me in the indelicacies of another riddle, my childhood favorite: Q. What's the sharpest thing in the world? A. A fart, because it can go right through your pants without making a hole.)

To be the son of Mel Katz meant learning, from a tender age, that popular entertainment was "schlock" and commercial development was "ticky tacky" and people in authority, even the leaders of our nation, could be "yutzes." Bureaucracies maddened him—he was forever railing against rules and regulations—and when I begged for us to join the Multnomah Athletic Club, where all the rich kids hung out after school, where you could watch the Beavers from a private terrace above Civic Stadium's outfield wall, he must have wondered where he had gone wrong. He has been a devout horseplayer since the days of Sword Dancer and Dr. Fager, not so much for the financial stakes but for the mental gymnastics, the challenge of reconciling the impulsiveness of animals with the rationality of odds. He has worn clunky, thick-soled Clarks his entire adult life and the same proletarian blue canvas jacket, which looks like something from Maoist China but is, in fact, even more obscure—the uniform of the French sanitation worker. As far as I am aware, he has never used deodorant, much less cologne, just as he never sweetens his coffee or drinks any beer identified as "lite." He kept a rotary phone in his studio past the millennium and was the only member of Portland State's art faculty to refuse a computer in his office, which caused some trouble when he retired because the university was sure that somewhere he must have had one stashed. Because of his inclinations, his rejection of artifice and pretense, I began referring to him, sometime in my early teens, as "Mellow Mel." Compared to my friends, whose fathers wore ties and carried their work home in briefcases, I had the laid-back dad. It has taken most of my life for me to see that my label for him was not just facile but wrong.

Dad is a product of what was then a working-class Jewish precinct of Brooklyn, raised in a one-bedroom apartment about

three miles from Ebbets Field. If Mom's parents qualified as the
intelligentsia—even in hardship, the Mensheviks could always
drum up some caviar and a bottle of Stoli—Dad's parents belonged to the huddled masses, poorly educated, inclined to super-
stition, their livelihood drawn from the dexterity and inventiveness
of their hands. There was love, but of the sort that tended to
smother: Until he was twenty-two, when he left to marry my
mom, Dad slept in the living room, most of that time on a cot
next to his older sister, who was awarded the couch. Grandpa was
a tailor, and with scraps from the shop, he made clothes for his little
prince, leather caps and wool jackets, far nattier than anything they
could afford. Grandma, the teenage seamstress who had waited five
years to follow him across the Atlantic, used to spit three times
and recite *"keyn aynhoreh,"* lest some celebration or boast draw the
envy of bad spirits. They spoke Yiddish to each other and to their
children, and my dad, just like Max with his mother, answered in
English.

When he first began venturing outside that protective bubble,
it was mainly through sports. On tenement streets jangling with
second-generation kids, Jewish, Irish, Italian, he discovered the camaraderie that can be fomented by a broomstick and a tennis ball.
It was a ritual that shouted Americanness, all the more because nobody's parents had any clue as to what was entailed. By his early
teens Dad had graduated from stickball to softball—he had become
a reliable catcher—and was affiliating with a rogue team called the
Comets. They had no coach and belonged to no league. "We didn't
want to join anything," he would tell me. "The whole thing was
about making it up yourself, about not being directed." With each
Comet throwing in a buck, the team would look for pickup games
with other neighborhoods, the winners getting $10, plus a new
ball. They compiled a good enough record that they were able to
outfit themselves in reversible jackets, blue outside and gold inside,
and because Dad had a knack for drawing, he was entrusted with
designing the embroidered comet that streaked across their backs.

He met my mom at Camp Eden, a refuge, up the Hudson, for

the children of Jewish laborers. She was sixteen and a junior counselor. Dad was a couple of years older, a busboy who was about to head off to Cooper Union. When they found themselves a decade later in Portland, it was with the understanding that after a year, maybe a few, after their adventure had run its course, they would return to New York. If Dad was going to survive as an artist, he could not possibly dream of doing so in the hinterlands, amid the fir and salmon and glaciers, especially if he refused to create anything that might be deemed folksy or decorative.

He rented a studio in Chinatown, halfway between the Bruce Apartments and Portland State. It was up four flights of stairs, cavernous and cluttered and full of dangerous toys, blades, adhesives, matches, thinners. The stereo was stuck on KBOO, the public blues and jazz station, and Marlboro butts swam in the sludge of old coffee cups. On weekends, as a kid, I sometimes joined him, drawing pictures of battleships and ballplayers while he strapped on a double-valve respirator mask and slipped his hands into white cotton gloves. He would sand or spray or patch or laminate, hour after hour, adhering to a sense of integrity, for the materials, for the process, that nobody ever had to demand of him. Sometimes he worked to achieve uniformity, sometimes to muddle it. His sculptures were meticulous configurations, with lines and angles worthy of a NASA engineer. Every cut had to be clean, every corner crisp, yet within that formality he often tampered with the finish, rasping, blending, smudging, so that some juxtaposition was always at play. I learned, in those moments, not to ask what anything was supposed to be; it was whatever it was, whatever you saw.

When I was eight or nine, I got into it with a friend whose dad was a doctor. He was bragging, as boys do, telling me how much money his dad made, how many lives his dad saved, how my dad was obviously not of that caliber. I feared, naturally, that he might be right, that what my dad did was frivolous, or at least inscrutable, but for the sake of family pride, I would have to mount a rebuttal. "Oh, yeah?" I said. "Well, my dad saves lives, too." I did not quite believe what I was serving up, but I liked the sound of it more than I had expected. "His art is his medicine." I was on a roll now. "It heals people's souls."

Right about the time Mom got sick, Dad's shoulder began to break down. He had spent so many years in the studio, bent over sawhorses and manipulating surfaces, elbow pumping, dust swirling, sweat dripping, horns wailing, that he finally wore the cartilage down to the bone. It got to where he could barely raise his right arm—brush his teeth, wipe his ass. Dad was like a washed-up pitcher. He needed rotator cuff surgery. Compared to Mom's cancer, Dad's shoulder was an inconvenience. He was not going to die from the grinding in his joint. But seeing him like that had a similar effect on me. Until then I had been casual about flying up to Portland for his shows—he exhibited new work roughly every other year—skipping as many as I managed to attend. Once the doctors told him that they would have to cut him open, to implant a rod and a ball and a socket, I knew I could never miss another opening. It was not just that Dad was getting older, that his repertory of gallery dates was beginning to look more finite. Dad now made sense to me in a way that he had not before, or that I had only pretended he did. At an age when other dads were puttering around golf courses, mine was still taking monumental chances, testing his ingenuity, pulverizing his bones, inviting criticism, tempting rejection, because he could not *not* do it. Just as I discovered that Mom, the uptight one, the workaholic, was more sentimental than I had realized, Dad, the bohemian one, was more severe, more courageous.

I became fixated on the Monterey Park Sports Club's logo, an inverted triangle with a ribbon draped across its girth. I knew nothing of its origins, how this pointy emblem with its wavy county fair bow came to represent our organization, but the shape was instantly recognizable, the closest thing we had to a brand. During my first season as commissioner, I had been able to obtain a copy on a disc, but it was an all-purpose version, with clip art of a generic basketball player and baseball player together in the triangle, and if it was going to do us any good, I decided it would have to be refashioned, to be specific to the league I was running. I taught myself to negotiate an antiquated edition of The Print Shop, and by the time my second year began, I was rotating and stretching the principal elements, adding color, adjusting outlines, playing with shadows and shading, tweaking fonts, trolling the Web for baseball images—crossed bats, the official MLB silhouette—to drop into the center of my masterpiece. It was an impressive bit of procrastination, taking away not just from my magazine job but also from more urgent matters at La Loma, and yet I could not bring myself to stop. I kept embellishing, refining, as if by perfecting this one small composition I might provide the framework that would restore the well-being of our park. With the logo in JPEG form, it could now be embroidered onto caps and stenciled onto bags and ironed onto banners. I had it die cast onto one-inch pins, which I began handing out every year at our closing ceremony, and I had it woven into a five-foot-five nylon-link welcome mat, which I stationed at the entrance of our snack bar. Our uniform vendor agreed to silk-screen it onto the sleeve of every jersey at $1.25 apiece. I found another company that was able to turn it into a decal, and I ordered $500 worth, which I peeled and applied to the front of hundreds of batting helmets.

Sometime during the 2004 season, the year Carmen joined me as La Commish, I noticed that she was sporting one of those decals on the bumper of her minivan. That was hard-core. I was not inclined to adorn my car with any sort of sticker, even one of my own creation, and I could not think of anyone else who would have announced her devotion to our league so publicly, so permanently. It was an old van—her husband would be replacing it in a season or two—but she had still made a statement that got my heart racing. Without really saying it, maybe without fully realizing it herself, Carmen was letting the world know that she believed in me, too.

Chapter

Eleven

OF ALL THE SUBJECTS I WAS REQUIRED AS COMMISSIONER
to show command of—sociology, politics, engineering, public
health, criminal justice, family counseling—the one that caused me
the most worry was economics. Making money has, thankfully,
never proved too difficult for me, but the managing of it, budgeting,
saving, investing, is not an area in which I have excelled. Money has
always been for spending, often as fast as, if not faster than, it was
earned, and not on material trappings but adventure, experiences. I
could be frugal about cars and clothes, anything designed to trum-
pet one's status, yet when it came to ephemeral pleasures, food,
travel, music, sporting events, I could blow a paycheck without
blinking. To me those were the things that made you what you
were, the things that needed to be lived and felt and drunk in, and
shying from them, because you wanted to build wealth or, at a
minimum, provide for a rainy day, was not a concept I had ever

embraced. I knew I would have to do better with the Monterey Park Sports Club's funds than I did with my own checkbook. It would not matter how creative or committed I was: If money started to come up short, the whole league would go to pieces again.

From the start, even before I got hustled by David Sanchez and bullied by Adrian Magallon, I realized how ridiculously easy it would be to take advantage of the Monterey Park Sports Club myself. Every dollar passed through me—registration money, Dodger money, snack bar money, fireworks money—and no amount of oversight could have kept me from skimming $20 here, $100 there, even a few grand if I was determined. Someone once suggested that all cash should be counted in the presence of at least one other board member, and in the beginning I seem to recall asking for a second pair of eyes whenever I had a wad of bills to deposit, but I soon came to see the folly of pretending this was any sort of promise. What was to keep me from taking a cut before we started counting? Or as soon as we were done? Nobody knew how much was supposed to be coming in on any given day, how much was actually collected, how much made it into the bundle that was to be tabulated, how much was still there by the time I delivered it, to Chris and Valerie, in a brown paper sack. It would have been so easy to rationalize, too, as Tom, the taxman-coach, noted, a small token for all the sacrifices I was making, for all the times I picked up the tab for something without stopping to worry about whether I would get repaid. I am certain that others have done this, that one or more of my predecessors had to have greased himself—and felt no shame—that everyone assumed that this was the way it was done, anyway, or else why would you ever consent to mortgaging so much of your life for a screwy low-stakes baseball league?

I doubt anyone would think less of me if I were to confess that I felt the same temptation. It would make me human, I suppose, nothing worse. The truth, though, is that I was not like that and I refused to be: I was immune to the possibility. I even sort of got off on being so punctilious, on knowing that I could dump $10,000 onto my bed, stack the bills according to denomination, flip them all face up, rotate them all in the same direction, and without any checks or balances, without anyone looking over my shoulder, still be one solid son of a bitch, unshakable, incorruptible, that my integrity was enough to make up for the rest of La Loma's sins. It was my own test, a test I knew I could pass, and I came to look forward to those nights on which I found myself rolling in dough, just to prove it again and again.

Despite my stringency, it was still sometimes hard to keep tabs on all the league's money, especially when I gave struggling families extra time to settle their accounts. Fees were supposed to be paid in full at sign-ups, and failing that, no later than opening day. But I had a soft spot for single moms, for their tales of regret, for their hints of endearment, and every year there were perhaps a dozen women to whom I granted extensions. Commissioner's prerogative. I did it because their predicaments were real, because our organization was grassroots and nonprofit, because it allowed me to play the valiant, understanding male, of which their lives, surely, had been in short supply. Among my board members, I was considered something of a pushover, easy prey for the connivers and hussies. Carmen used to joke—or was she really irked?—that all a woman had to do was bat her eyelashes and I would fall all over myself to be accommodating.

At the start of my third year as commissioner, in 2005, we recruited a new T-Ball coach, a practiced eyelash batter named Marisol. Or, more accurately, I allowed Marisol to finagle her way into La Loma. It was me—shocking, I know—who offered her a seat at my end of the registration table, who took the time to learn her story (half Peruvian, half Cuban), who assured her that female coaches were held in the highest esteem at our park and that if she was willing to manage a team, I would schedule her games at any hour she found convenient. I must have pronounced Mah-ree-SOLE with a nice roll of the *r* and a long, soft tap of the *l,* because she complimented me on my Spanish, and from there, she had to have known, I was not going to sweat her over money.

Marisol had three kids, by two fathers, both of whom she had split from, and she needed a bit more time coming up with the two hundred and change she owed. Normally we withheld the uniforms of nonpayees, but since she was a coach now, a walking advertisement for the Monterey Park Sports Club, I cleared her children to suit up and play. Marisol was relieved. I reported to Carmen, reminding her that a little compassion went a long way. "What-*ever*," Carmen said. The problem turned out not to be with Marisol's team. Her daughter, who was five, enjoyed T-Ball, and the girl's father was a regular at their games. When the phone started to ring, when all my discernment was called into question, it was because of Marisol's two oldest boys. They had been drafted together onto a Single A team, but without the blessing of *their* dad. He was duking it out with Marisol for custody, an ugly fight that, I came to learn, was headed for a courtroom in the middle of the season. She had not consulted him about signing them up for baseball, and he was not about to juggle his schedule to suit her whims, especially since he knew already that she did not have the money to pay their fees. As a consequence, the boys were missing every other weekend at La Loma, half their practices and half their games, and if their team was not on the verge of forfeiting, their coach was having to throw them, unfit for action, onto the field.

The night it all boiled over, I was home again, crossing my fingers that peace would prevail during the hour or two I stepped away. From my back porch I could see the lights glowing above La Loma, a 1,500-watt halo, and even hear the cheers echoing across the ravines—Max and I could be watching the Dodgers stink it up on TV and know that a few blocks away someone had knocked in the winning run—but when things went wrong, and they always did in my absence, there was no signal rising up from the park. It would all go down right under my nose and yet just out of view. One of Marisol's boys had fallen ill that afternoon, with a throat infection, and she had taken him to the hospital. She instructed a baby-sitter to drop off her other son at the park—they had a seven-thirty game—and she asked their coach, a likable, generally placid fellow who worked in the drywall business and happened to be named Steve Martin, if he would be kind enough to bring the kid back to her when they were done. Steve agreed. It was a bit beyond the call of duty, but as coaches we were forever lending our support to families with wobbly foundations, not just reminding their children to keep their eye on the ball, and it was nothing I would not have done myself.

As luck would have it, that turned out to be the night that Marisol's ex decided to stop by La Loma, to see if his kids were indeed being well served by our league. What he found was one son, minus the boy's mother and brother, and a coach he had never met preparing to give that child a ride. He had some angry words for Steve, maybe a few profanities. Steve was at a loss. Even if we had a coach's handbook, which, needless to say, we did not, what chance was there that it would have included contingencies for a flap like this, which parent to appease, whose interests to defend? Steve called Marisol from the park and asked her what she wanted him to do. He had promised to look after her son—it was not an obligation he took lightly—but he had not signed up to fight her battles. Marisol was adamant that Steve keep to their agreement; the kids were hers that week, she had a court order to prove it, and she was counting on Steve to prevent the father from exploiting her emergency. Steve tried to explain to her that the father was just as adamant; the man was berating him, insulting him in front of his own son, and Steve was expected to endure this abuse for—for what, exactly?

Marisol was crying now. She hung up on Steve and called the police. It could be that she was merely enforcing her parental rights. It could be that she also saw an opportunity to stick it to her ex. Before anyone grasped what she was up to, there was a squad car on the lower field, the only time in my tenure the cops were summoned to La Loma. I took that as an affront. The most innocent couple of minutes in all of youth sports, the postgame snack, was being interrupted by men with badges and guns.

When I heard from Steve the next day, he was still bent out of shape. He had been manipulated by Marisol. He had been embarrassed by her ex. The police had told Steve that he would have to let

the boy go home with his father—Steve, by then, was all too happy
to bow out—but that only made the 911 call more of a farce:
Marisol had accomplished nothing by sending the cops, other than
to turn most of the park against her. As much as he hated to take it
out on the kids, Steve wanted Marisol's boys removed from his roster. There was too much drama, too little baseball. If they were not
cut or traded, he insisted, other parents were going to start withdrawing their kids, in which case, Steve added, he might as well
just quit, too. It probably did not help that they were in last place,
winless up to that point in the season. "I'm a pretty easygoing
guy," Steve said, "but this has put a little stain on our team."

"Whoa, whoa, whoa," I said. "I understand why you're upset.
You have every right to be. But this is *your* team. You made a commitment. I expect you to be a man about it and show these families,
all of them, what that really means." I had pushed Steve's buttons, a
gamble, hoping his conscience would exceed his frustration. Guilt
trips did not work on the assholes. He got quiet. "No, it's not like
that," he said finally. "I wouldn't want you to think that I'm somebody who just walks away." Three years into this thing, and I was
getting the hang of it. Mutiny averted. Steve was on board again.
There was one other matter, though, that he wanted to clarify, an ad-
ministrative question that some of the parents on his team had
raised. It was not really his business, he knew that, and it should
probably not make any difference, but as long as they were being
asked to put up with Marisol's BS, Steve just wanted to be sure. "Is
it true," he asked, "that her kids haven't even paid?"

Maybe I still had a bit to learn. "Let's, uh, keep that, uh, separate," I stammered. "You worry about your team, and, uh, you
know, I'll, uh, resolve everything else." Although I had never intended to let Marisol get away with anything, the season was
halfway over already and I had done nothing to force her hand. That
was sloppy, not charitable, as unforgivable as bilking the Monterey
Park Sports Club myself. If I was going to defend her children's
right to play—if I was going to demand that Steve man up—I had
a little business of my own to attend to.

I called Marisol, then her ex. I told them that whatever quarrel they had with each other, it could never spill into La Loma again, and that if it did, I would pull their boys from the league, and moreover, if I did not receive payment in full by the next game, they would be gone, anyway. Why did it take me so long to draw my lines, to hold people accountable? They both thought I was being callous—each had tried to enlist me as an ally—but they accepted my ultimatum and even said they would split the balance. When I mentioned all this to Carmen, she almost spit out her coffee. The father's name was familiar: She had dated the guy long ago. We agreed that I would collect from him, to spare her any fluster, and that she would collect from Marisol, to keep me out of her hooks. There may be no connection whatsoever, but when I found out the following season that Marisol had gotten pregnant by one of the dads on her T-Ball team, I was relieved that my time as her collaborator had been brief.

Most years I gave a similar break to Lulu, sometimes a discount, sometimes an extension, which had its own ramifications, given that we were division rivals. All that jockeying between us, the machinations on draft night, the championships vied for, the shadow of Adrian—if it was not already complicated enough, she usually carried a balance up until the final day. I knew that Lulu would pay it—she always had—and I liked being able to show that I was above vindictiveness, that I could spar with her as a coach and still commiserate with her struggles as a mom. But more often than not I ended up sponsoring my own demise. If anything, Lulu should have been beholden to me, and instead she acted as if I were the one in her pocket. When she drafted Todd's son and held him for ransom, she was already in arrears, yet she was trying to rope me into treating her to a night out. I must have said I would consider it, because she did make the trade, but I just could not bring myself to uphold my end of the bargain. Todd tried to egg me on: "That girl would give you the ride of your life!" Maybe that was the problem. Besides the fact that Lulu did unnerve me—she was both sexy and vicious—anything with her, if the opportunity actually existed, would have been sport, a game of brinksmanship, of bragging rights. What I felt I needed, after Raynelda, after Cuba, after The Lotus Room, was something a little sweeter, less mercenary. If I was going to let a woman back into my life, I wanted her to know me as a writer, to admire me as a father, to be able to celebrate all the imprudent traits that had turned me into the commissioner, and not to be calculating what I could do to improve her prospects. How naive was that? I was holding out for love.

At the end of the 2005 season, Lulu brought me the money she owed, $75, as I recall. When she dropped it off, I was working the fireworks stand, an undertaking that always coincided with the depths of my exhaustion, the week between the championship series and the closing ceremony. Just when you thought you had made it to the end, after tending to hundreds of families and raising tens of thousands of dollars, after two and a half months of prep and another two and a half months of games, you became the recipient of literally a ton of pyrotechnics—2,000 pounds of Quiet Riots and Perfect Storms—and for seven days straight you had to baby-sit them, morning and night, hoping like hell you still had enough brainpower to keep from getting robbed or conned or fined or blown to smithereens.

The stand was metal and rectangular, a glorified shipping container, with a grate across the front, and in the July heat, amid the clutter and chemicals, it felt more like the back of a smuggler's truck. We were assigned a location, in the parking lot of a Mexican grocery store, and after dark, when the market was shut, we supplied our own lights with a gas-fueled generator. It was a boggling commitment of resources for a rather modest payoff. We netted maybe $4,000 our first year, all of which went toward the deficit I inherited. Our second year the generator vanished—a lot of finger-pointing failed to produce a culprit—and with it, half of our profits. Although we created a schedule and board members were expected to volunteer for as many shifts as they could, there were some slots that were impossible to fill. By law you could not leave the stand unattended, even when it was closed, and so I started paying my nephew Christiám for graveyard duty, a hundred bucks a night to camp in his car, with a Maglite for protection. Nobody ever wanted to come at dawn, either, to spell him, so I had to take that upon myself. More than one *Los Angeles* magazine story was written in those wee hours, on my laptop, while I prayed that Max, still asleep at home, would be safe until someone else was available to mind the fireworks after me.

On the afternoon that she swung by, Lulu was wearing a skirt and heels, nothing I had ever seen her in before. I was inside the shed, restocking the shelves. Carmen was there, too, working the counter, and spotted her before I did. "Oh, my," Carmen said. "She's comin' to getcha." I stepped out and gave Lulu a hug. She thanked me for being patient and handed me the cash.

"I'll get you a receipt," I told her.

"Don't bother," Lulu said. "It's for you."

"What—the money?"

"Just keep it for yourself."

"C'mon," I said. "You know I don't play like that."

"You deserve it."

"That's beside the point."

"Nobody needs to know."

I was trying, as fast as I could, to figure out what Lulu was up to, how she expected me to react. My first thought was that she was hoping to curry favor with me, that from her perspective this was the equivalent of breaking bread with La Loma's new godfather. Maybe she also had hopes of resuscitating our bargain: Was I supposed to spend this money on her, use it for our unrealized night out? Or was Lulu testing me in some other way, looking for proof of my avarice, my fallibility? I wondered if she was planning to run back to Adrian and tell him what a phony I was. Maybe it would even bring her satisfaction, to report that after three years on the job I had at last fallen off my high horse. The one thing she was right about was that nobody would ever find out. The season was over; the league's accounts had already been settled. There was money in the bank for next year. There was no spreadsheet, other than my own notes, showing what Lulu had owed and when she had paid. I could slip that cash in my pocket—I *did* slip it in my pocket—and only I would know if it ended up in the right place.

With each season that I survived, I began to see more clearly that I had overestimated the importance of financial acumen. I was hardly a business whiz, much less a tightwad, yet year after year my cash flow exceeded my expenses by thousands and thousands of dollars, which only confirmed my suspicion that somewhere in the Monterey Park Sports Club's not-so-distant past the looting had been rampant. There was money for everything. All you had to do was not steal. Under Christiám's management—I had upped his salary to $300 a week—the snack bar became the hub of La Loma social life. He was young and fly, with his cornrows and pierced nose, wide Sean John jeans and backward Kangol beret, and everyone's kids loved to sit on the countertop and bump to his CDs, the Spanish reggae, the French rap. However awkward it might have been for Max to be the commissioner's son, to suffer all my fastidious hand-wringing and overwrought soul-searching, there was no greater cachet than being Christiám's cousin. I made Max white, but in the snack bar he was the heir to something more exotic, way cooler, a black Central American vibe that not even the Mexicans knew what to make of. Hardly anyone ever saw Raynelda at La Loma, and so Christiám became the most visible symbol of Max's cross-pollination, proof that my son carried in him permeations greater than I alone could have supplied.

Christiám was still sleeping in my garage, which was not exactly habitable—it was neither insulated nor watertight, and lizards scurried in and out of the gaps—but it was free, and with the money he saved, he was able to maintain a long-distance courtship with his girlfriend in Nicaragua. At the end of each day, no matter how exhausted he was from ladling chili and steaming wieners, Christiám stopped by the liquor store and bought one of those prepaid 3 Amigos phone cards, then retreated into the must, through our mounds of soiled clothes and dryer lint, and whispered all night to the sweetheart he had left behind as a teenager. As soon as the season was over, he would fly to Managua to spend a month with her and, after his third year at La Loma, he even used that trip to marry her, and yet for reasons that did not quite add up—legal and financial, I guess—they continued to live worlds apart. Christiám's routine never wavered. While Max and I were still having breakfast, he was out the door with his tools, entrusted with the remodeling of homes more fabulous than I could have ever afforded, then he dusted himself off and raced to the park, where he provided sustenance to a few hundred people, then by 10 or 11 P.M., he staggered back to the garage for his marital conclaves, which in time came to involve headsets and minicams: day job, snack bar, virtual wife. Christiám could have prowled Los Angeles, clubbing, macking, but he was so determined not to be like the rest of his family, so alert to the Gutiérrezes' appetites and impediments, that he denied that part of himself, keeping to his own carefully regulated treadmill. It was like he had settled into middle age already. I could not decide whether it was noble or heartbreaking.

Christiám's probity served my purposes, of course, and because he was in my debt, I was not shy about commandeering him for the park. Knowing he would never undermine me, I gave him license to run the snack bar as his own, to build a business where before there had been only a few desultory boxes of candy. The first year, before either of us fathomed the magnitude of what we were attempting, I started him off with $150 in seed money. By the third year, it took $3,000 just to stock up for opening day. Christiám was getting an education, learning how to conduct inventory, set prices, promote specials, control waste, and the Monterey Park Sports Club was discovering that it had a gold mine atop La Loma, an enterprise that initially earned us five, then ten, and finally fifteen grand in the roughly sixty days it was open each season. I kept looking for ways to reinvest in it, to give folks more reason to visit, to dawdle and mingle. I installed a TV, which we tuned to Laker games during the playoffs, and a DVD player, which was usually showing *The Rookie* or *The Sandlot* or *Field of Dreams* the rest of the time.

I contacted Farmer John, the great porkery on the L.A. riverbanks, and asked for a deal on Dodger Dogs, their signature ten-inch frank.

They agreed to sell them to us at wholesale—twenty-four cents each—and every other week we were at their loading dock, heaving frozen boxes, a thousand dogs at a time, into the back of Carmen's van. She and I found a commercial kitchen supply outlet called Action Sales, which catered to Monterey Park's vast fleet of Chinese restaurants. It was like a Home Depot for chefs, aisle after aisle of stainless-steel industrial-strength cookware: pots, woks, tongs, steam tables, deep fryers, juicers. The first time we wandered in, on one of those mornings the kids were in school and I should have been at work, Carmen gasped and grabbed me by the sleeve.

"Oh . . . my . . . God," she said, tugging me through the cold storage section. It was all so shiny and solid, so rugged and hefty and calibrated, so *substantial*. We had been thinking of selling ice cream at the park, but the snack bar had come with only a city-issued refrigerator. The league had money now. Carmen and I were going to buy La Loma its very first freezer. "Look, look, look, honey," she said, steering me toward a 7.2-cubic-foot model with a sliding glass top. Carmen needed to put her hands on things, to open doors and test hinges and click latches; she was tactile and in-tuitive, as touchy-feely a person as I had ever met. I am pretty sure that I represented some extreme in Carmen's experience as well, because unlike most of the men she had known, I was just as giddy as she was about all this food service gadgetry, the appliances, the utensils, the fantastically specialized accessories. It was a little irreg-ular, I admit, to be that enamored of kitchen gear, especially if you are supposed to be running a baseball program, but I liked how a freezer—or a condiment bar or even just a napkin dispenser—helped restore order and confidence. We were furnishing the park with tangible evidence of our progress, of the community's own re-newal. Each time we returned to Action Sales, Carmen and I went through the same ritual, the pointing, the nudging, the oohing and ahing. I could not think of a time I had ever had that sensation before, of being so in tune with someone so different about some-thing so peculiar. We were a couple of middle-aged Little League

parents—one of whom was still married, with a gazillion kids—
and yet it almost felt as if we were playing house.

I had so much money at my discretion that in time I had to really work to find new and meaningful ways in which to spend it.
We built bullpens and repaired pitcher's mounds and installed bat
racks. I invested in magnetic breakaway bases, which were supposed to prevent injury, and a $200 double-edged Monster Broom,
to spruce up the infield between games. I bought first-aid kits for
every coach and an equipment bag for every kid. Our uniforms were
officially licensed, stamped with the Majestic seal, and our trophies, once barely a foot, were now soaring twenty-inch monuments, too tall for the average bookshelf. The price for all this was
still within just about anyone's reach—I had increased the fee only
once, to $85, and even then rolled it back each year for the first
week of sign-ups—but we were starting to look a bit more like one
of those affluent leagues, in the white-bread suburbs, where everything gleamed and matched and ran on time. La Loma was taking
off, although truthfully there had been nowhere else to go but up,
and people knew it, felt it, gravitated to it, envied it. I had raised
expectations. That came with a downside of its own.

At the start of the 2005 season, we embarked on a plan to erect
canopies throughout La Loma, the most ambitious capital improvement project of my commissionership. It was not actually my
idea—shade struck me as the domain of wimps, a retreat from the
environment in which most of the world labors, including our kids
on the field—but my board of directors convinced me that we
would make a lot of families happy if we could offer them a break
from the sun. Some racial truths, I suspect, were also at play:
White folks, accustomed to privilege, tended to romanticize the
sun's impact on their complexions, equating brownness with health
and beauty. Brown folks, more attuned to the biases that skin tone
can engender, often guilty of it themselves, were forever going out of
their way not to get any darker.

The leader of the canopy movement was a cagey dude named Joe

Rios, who wore a silver necklace and a swinger's mustache and mirrored sunglasses. His son Christian was one of the boys who had defied Omar a couple of seasons earlier—the same Christian who ended up on my Double A team—and as a salute to their valor, as a bridle on Omar's influence, I had invited Joe and his wife, Alma, to join the board. He was a plumber for the county, good with tools, and as happy to end his day at the park as anyone I had encountered. Often still in work clothes, smudged in grease, Joe would show up at La Loma with a pack of menthols and a "Thirsty-two" ounce minimart mug, which nobody ever believed was filled with just soda. He drove an antique Suburban with tinted windows, and on the back he had a series of those stick-figure decals, to represent his family, but instead of putting names under the four children, he had written, "None of your damn business." Alma was built like a Vargas pinup, which is perhaps a crass thing to note, except that Joe liked her to sport her wares, insisted on it, and so Alma wore a lot of tight little V necks that defied you not to stare. A county employee also, in the department that managed disability cases, she was the brains of their marriage, the one who budgeted and scheduled and remained sober enough to drive the Suburban home. Alma coached T-Ball. Joe coached Rookies. Between his willingness to get his hands dirty and her ease with paperwork, I had begun to think that they might just be the best candidates to take over the league from me—maybe not perfect, but how picky could I be?

Even with the park flourishing, this was not a job that anyone in his or her right mind would ever seek. There was no pipeline of contenders and, even if there had been, no procedure for electing one to take my place. Carmen would have been capable, but she doubted herself too much to think about doing it on her own, and after all the work I had put in, I was not about to step down without a successor already named. I had never really stopped to consider how many years I was good for, but if I ever wanted out, I was going to have to orchestrate my own escape.

I had a couple thousand dollars set aside for the canopies, but we needed a design that reflected the league's cyclical relationship with La Loma. During baseball season, the park was ours, and not just because the city issued us permits to play. We made it ours, kicked off our shoes and stretched out our legs, cheered, ate, flirted, cleaned, acted as if we owned the place. If we were going to go through the trouble of providing shade, it might as well be something that could remain out there for months, a semipermanent fixture that would not blow away or be easily carted off. Once we were done, though, La Loma reverted to a more public space—it was invaded by travel teams, seized by tournament organizers—and if we ever wanted to see our canopies again, they would have to be built in a way that allowed us to dismantle and store them, preferably without tearing up the park. I left it to Joe to come up with a blueprint. I already had broached the subject of the league's future with him and Alma. "Don't give me an answer yet," I told them. "Just think about it. Watch. Learn. Let's make sure this is the right fit for all of us." Alma seemed hesitant. Maybe she knew that most of the responsibility would land in her lap. It was clear, though, that Joe had begun to picture himself in my shoes and was liking the way he looked. "You know us, Jess," he said. "As long as it's for the kids."

His sketch turned out to be better than anything I had envisioned. Joe wanted to build a series of A-frame shells out of aluminum piping that could fit right over each set of bleachers. He would stretch netting across the top, battened down with elastic ties. To anchor the feet, Joe was proposing to sink sleeves into the ground, flush with the grass. The poles could be slipped in and locked in place. When it came time to pack up, the moorings would remain, safe and unobtrusive, just below the surface. It met every requirement: sturdy, mobile, perennial, even ingeniously homespun. Maybe I really had found the right guy to carry the torch. I ran the plans by the city's Recreation and Parks staff (it was never the other way, the more common Parks and Rec, because that would leave you with the inelegant Monterey Park Parks pileup), and they granted us approval, on the condition that we start with one field, to give them a preview. We opted for T-Ball. Those games drew the biggest crowds, the fussiest parents.

This was all in early April, a couple of weeks before the first pitch. If we were going through with it, I wanted those canopies up for the ceremony, to signal in yet another way that our league was not just honest and fair but also imaginative, inspirational. I told Joe to forge ahead. I would reimburse him for all the supplies. I had plenty of other things to keep me busy. With a week to go, Joe threw up his arms. He supposedly had tried to assemble a crew of volunteers, to dig holes and pour cement. "I don't know what's the matter with these damn people," he sputtered, "but nobody wants to help." Joe was not the most communicative person at La Loma. His thoughts tended to be rash and his tongue lethargic, even on those occasions when he was not slurping beer through a straw, and what came out of his mouth was often spliced and snarled, like an old stereo gobbling a cassette. I was trying to picture how his entreaties must have come across—did people even grasp what it was he was trying to accomplish?—but I had so many other feats of my own to pull off, I could not possibly make time for the canopies. I had to learn to delegate. "If you need to spread a few dollars around, to get the help you need, I'll sign off on that," I told Joe. "We only have a few days left. Just, please, take care of it."

It would be easy to look back at that as an obvious miscalculation, the verbal equivalent of a blank check. I had been fairly vague in my instructions—no mention of numbers, no need for approval—only that I wanted the job done. On the other hand, the league had money to spare. I was dropping $647.34 on that freezer, $524.50 on that welcome mat, $150 to have the Mark Keppel High School marching band show up on opening day, in full regalia, to play "Take Me Out to the Ball Game." It was my vigilance, my integrity, that had put us in the position to afford such accoutrements, and if I wanted to splurge on something that would enhance the experience of being at La Loma, I saw no reason to hesitate. Whatever Joe needed, truly, it would be fine.

The canopies went up, on schedule and artfully constructed. The T-Ball field was now like a miniature stadium, a tent of cool green mesh shielding the bleachers on either side. Joe even took it upon himself to cover the dugouts on the upper field with more of the same netting, hooking it across the top of each chain-link cage. Everyone was delighted. I gave Joe all the credit, lauding him before the opening day crowd. The city gave me approval to proceed with the next phase of our plans. Then Joe gave me the bill.

It was handwritten on a scrap of yellow legal paper, folded twice. I felt no trepidation opening it up—Joe had delivered, after all, in the clutch—but as I examined it, line by line, the rusty cursive, the manual arithmetic, I found myself blanching, as if I had just spotted a rat in the snack bar. It was not so much the amount: $680 for materials, $355 for labor. I had no idea how much those things should cost, anyway. It was the names that he had identified as his workers, the emergency crew that the extra money was supposed to have drummed up: Joe had promised $7.50 an hour to his son—Christian, my first baseman, who was thirteen—and also to Alma's brother. Between them, forty-seven hours on the Monterey Park Sports Club's payroll. What kind of bull was that? Joe had not gone out and recruited anybody. This was family, his people. Even if they had put in that many hours—and I was plenty skeptical—had they really been unwilling to help prior to the mention of cash? Could he not have cajoled his own kid into lending a hand, just because it was the right thing to do? Or did Joe, perhaps feeling inconvenienced, maybe a little sorry for himself, see my offer as an opportunity to milk from the park whatever he thought he could? To top it off, he was charging me $48.65 for gas. I thought of all the miles I had driven in the course of my duties, all the weekends I had to spend catching up on whatever story I was neglecting, all the years I had to pay my taxes late because, naturally, they were due the week before opening day, and this guy wants me to fill his bloody tank? He had failed a test—my test—one he probably did not even realize he had taken.

I paid Joe for the canopies. I had entitled him to spend the league's money, and as ill as it made me, I felt the need to honor what I had set in motion. The next mistake, my bigger miscalculation, was to say nothing. Rather than chastising Joe or even just

explaining myself, I simply wrote him off. It was not worth my
trouble, I decided, to give him a primer on ethics, or at least my version of them, to get him to see that none of us who volunteered to
safeguard La Loma—commissioners, board members, coaches—
should ever profit from our positions, to make him understand that
journalists for the same reason were forbidden to receive anything of
value, to teach him that it was not so much that money necessarily
corrupted but that the appearance of impropriety called everything else, even your best deeds, into question. I already had fought
those battles, already toppled the old guard. I did not need to take
on Joe. He knew something was wrong—one week he was commissioner in training, the next he was invisible—but he was too proud
to ask. There were canopies to be erected on two other fields: He
should have been working on them already, but he was awaiting my
okay, and I was acting like I was too good for him. I had dangled respect and authority, not just money, then snatched it away.

So Joe stewed. He seethed. Until one weekend, at the end of
May, he took off for Las Vegas. It was Memorial Day weekend, as I
recall, the only weekend all season that La Loma was dark, and I was
taking advantage of the break myself, to host a barbecue on my back
porch. Several board members were there, including Carmen, who
had come with her husband, and even Alma, who seemed relieved to
be getting a break from hers. I was grilling carne asada and pouring
shots of tequila and blasting my Vicente Fernández CDs, a real Mexican party for lapsed Mexican guests at a pretend Mexican's house.

On the pretext of looking for his wife, Joe called. His words were
sloppy, more bloated than ever. "You . . . I . . . God . . . damn," he
said to me. I tried to tell him that this was not the time, that I had
people over, but that was a false stab at etiquette. I had made no
time for him and did not intend to. Joe already knew that and was
seizing his chance. "Who . . . you . . . fuck . . . think . . ." he said.
"Joe, we're really going to have to have this conversation later," I
said. He kept talking right over me. I hung up. He called me back.
"Joe, not now," I said. He was being a pest yet also achingly
human. After weeks of brooding, he had finally reached his limit,

left town, got drunk, and from a safe distance was unburdening himself. "Joe, really, I can't," I said. Carmen had wandered over and was scrunching her nose. "Why are you even talking to him?" she asked. "Here, give me the phone."

I went back to my party and tried to put on a smile. Maybe another belt of Patrón would help. "*¡Qué viva México, cabrones!*" I shouted, raising my glass. A few minutes later, Carmen returned. She looked shaken, worse than I had felt. "What's the matter?" I asked.

"Nothing," she said.

"Tell me."

"It's stupid."

"What's stupid?"

"Joe, his way of arguing a situation."

"Oh, forget Joe," I said. "I don't take it personally."

"Maybe you should."

"Maybe I should what?"

"Take it personally."

"What's that supposed to mean?"

"Never mind," Carmen said. "I probably shouldn't have said anything."

She left that night without elaborating. I tried to imagine what Joe could have said. I knew already that he thought I was a prick. That came with the territory. Was there really some other insult that would have made a big difference? I asked Carmen again the next day. She had stayed up late with her husband and debated it, gone back and forth, to tell me or not. Her husband was apparently of the mind that nothing good could come from this knowledge, that people said stupid things all the time when they were drunk, things they did not mean and later regretted, and that it was unfair to hold Joe accountable for a comment I was never supposed to hear in the first place. Carmen had argued just the opposite, that alcohol was not an obfuscator but a revelator, something akin to over-the-counter truth serum, which was precisely why people tended to regret what they said: All that work to keep your most inopportune feelings bottled up, only to find yourself powerless to stop them from spilling out. "I still don't know if I should tell you," Carmen said.

"I think I have a right to know."

"Maybe."

"It's not like I'm going to go start a war with Joe," I said. "Let's just consider this as more, uh, for my own, you know, edification."

"Okay."

"Really?"

"I'm trying to remember the exact phrasing."

"It was that complicated?"

"He kept saying 'fucking Jew,' that you were running the league like a 'fucking Jew.' "

"The word *Jew* was used?"

"It could have been more like, 'If he wants to be a fucking Jew about it.' "

"Jeez."

"I know."

"I'm not even sure what that means."

I knew, of course, what it was supposed to imply, the stereotypes Joe was trafficking in. He had been expecting a piece of the action; I had cut him off. Ergo, I must be a money-grubber, petty and shifty, wielding inexplicable sway over La Loma's fortunes. But that was not what Joe had said, or rather he could have said all that without punctuating it with *Jew*. As just about everyone at La Loma knew by then, for a Jew I was not very Jewish. I may have been a mystery, some weird cultural amalgam—even a Jewxican, as my friend Abel sometimes called me—but it was hard to imagine that anybody saw me as representative of anything. If Joe's intent was anti-Semitic, if he truly harbored animosity toward Jews as a group, my feelings were not going to be hurt. What bothered me was something else, a line of demarcation that he may not have even been aware of drawing. Forget *my* people: He was separating me from *his* people, disputing my right to belong.

It made me think of another episode, from years before, in the wake of Freddy's accident. We had gone to see a family therapist, a warm, savvy Latina who spoke to us in Spanish and English. I was going nuts. The shooting was nothing like the reprieve I had hoped for. Freddy was out of the hospital within a week, back in school a week after that. He was still blind in the one eye, not that you would know—the only clue was that it tended to wander—but his sight had returned to the other, and all those somber arrangements for life with the visually impaired had fast become a joke. Freddy was fine. Too fine, it pains me to say. The kid had shrugged off death. He was famous now. Bulletproof. "You bad, foo'," I heard one of his friends tell him. "You wuz on the news." More than ever, life's rules, my rules, did not apply. He got suspended. He got arrested. He got expelled. He spent four months in probation camp, then went right back to his antics. He stole my coin collection. He stole my Visa. While we slept, he stole our car. No punishment worked. Freddy would sneak out the window and stay away as long as he wanted. The homies took to calling him Fred-Dogg. Poking himself with a needle and ink, he tattooed a large *F,* Old English style, in the curve between his index finger and his thumb.

My apprehension inspired a colleague, Héctor Tobar, to write a short story called "Once More, Lazarus," which ended up in the anthology *Los Angeles Noir*. It is about a kid in the Central American enclaves of East Hollywood, a child of war and dislocation who stumbles upon a gun and, mesmerized by its authoritativeness, accidentally shoots himself in the face. Surviving what nobody has a right to, he is reborn a minor celebrity, "a wounded warrior, not a boy," only to be shot again, and live to tell about it, and then shot again. Héctor needed fiction to make sense of everything, all that a bullet can destroy and awaken, but in those pages I was seeing Freddy: He was not supposed to be alive, and the realization of that, rather than humbling him, was like a license to cheat. If he had wondered about it before, he could say now, with some validity, he had nothing to lose.

Raynelda was still waiting for me to adopt him. When we first arrived in Houston, I had spoken to his teachers, as I did back in L.A., to see if they would acknowledge Freddy informally as a Katz. But they insisted on going by what was on his birth certificate, which was not the name of Nestor's father, the name he had been using, but that of his biological father, a name he had never used, and so after half a childhood in American schools, Freddy took on his third identity. I promised Raynelda I would fix it. I went to the courthouse in Houston and picked up the forms. I met with a lawyer. We were going to have to place an ad in a Nicaraguan paper, to demonstrate that we had made a reasonable effort to notify the real dad, before that man could be stripped of his parental rights. I was really intending to do it, or at least I told myself I was, but with each disappointment, every crisis, I kept finding another excuse to put it off. Maybe I should have adopted Freddy the minute Raynelda and I married. It would have been simpler, before there was any history to deter me, but the teenage Freddy was not somebody I wanted to bind myself to forever, especially with so few male Katzes in my line. My grandfather had only one son. My dad had only one son. It sounds horrible, but was I really going to risk diluting—or, worse, tainting—the name I was bequeathing to Max? Although Freddy is probably relieved not to be a Katz these days, I am not sure that Raynelda ever forgave me. As much as she loved Max, as gratified as she was that he had a conscientious father, she also resented it: I could give everything to our son, to *my* son, but I was forever sitting in judgment on hers.

When I was done venting, the counselor smiled. "You've covered gangs," she said. "How did you get people from that world to open up, to trust you?"

"Oh, well, that's different," I said.

"Is it?"

"That's out on the streets, doing my job. I get paid to suspend judgment. This is my home we're talking about, my family. We have Max to consider."

"Maybe Freddy is right."

"About what?"

"Maybe he's not the one with the problem."

"How can that be?"

"How different is he, really, from his mother?" the counselor asked. She went on to suggest that whatever reservations had initially clouded my marriage, I had fallen in love with Raynelda. Whatever her background, whatever her limitations, I had accepted her, embraced her as she was, even joined with her to create a child together. Why did Freddy never seem to get the same treatment, the affirmations, the benefit of my empathy? If he had stayed in Nicaragua, grown up just as his mother had, what was the likelihood of his behavior being so scrutinized or condemned?

"But he's here now," I protested. "He didn't grow up that way. He can aim so much higher."

"That's from your point of view," the counselor said. What about Freddy? Was this the life that he asked for? What about Raynelda? Did she expect just as much from Freddy as I did? As the counselor saw it, I was twisting myself into knots to try to get Freddy to conform to my standards, as if he were the odd man out, when the person he was studying, the one he understood the best, the one he felt had wounded him the most, was his mother. My wife and stepson might have both sneaked across the border, but under our roof, in the home I sought to infuse with the drive and exactitude of my parents, I was the alien. "You really are the Jew of the family," the counselor said, eyes twinkling.

Chapter

Twelve

I WAS SUMMONED TO CITY HALL BY MONTEREY PARK'S recreation superintendent. The opening of the 2005 season was still a month away, but already there was rumbling, from neighbors, from the police, even from some of the superintendent's own superiors, that our quaint kiddie league had mushroomed into some kind of baseball Woodstock. I was enrolling 455 players that year, twice the size of the program I had inherited. Noise, lights, parking, trash: The complaints had started to trickle in the previous season, and now with the prospect of even more teams, with more games, there were forces in the community that thought the Monterey Park Sports Club needed to be put in check. I did what I always did in the face of crisis—call Carmen.

"No way!" she shouted.

"I can't tell how serious to take it."

"Who are these people? What's their problem? Can't they see all the great changes we've made at that park? What the hell!"

"Stop screaming at me," I said. "I'm on your side."

"Do I have to go kick some ass for you? 'Cuz you know I will. I can go ghetto."

"Let's not throw down just yet."

"You should really run for city council."

"Will you be my campaign manager?"

"Yeah, right."

"Or maybe I should be your campaign manager?"

"You're crazy."

I took Carmen with me to the meeting. The superintendent, Ralph Aranda, was a bear of a man, with a teenage daughter who played softball, and even though he had to remain impartial in matters such as these, I felt like he had our back. There was a chance that some residents might air their grievances at the next Recreation and Parks Commission meeting, or even the city council meeting, and Ralph wanted to be sure that all of us, both he and the league, could demonstrate that we had been sensitive to their concerns. He had a flyer that he wanted us to make copies of and distribute to every team, urging families not to litter or block driveways. He had a second flyer that he wanted us to deliver to every house within a block or two of the park, about two hundred addresses, thanking our immediate neighbors for their "patience and support of youth sports." Although he saw no cause for alarm just yet, Ralph thought we should also be aware that one of the most vocal neighbors was himself a Rec and Parks commissioner, a critic on the very board that was supposed to oversee us. It sort of made me long for the old days, when we policed ourselves.

"I guess the lights come shining through his window, right into his bedroom every night," Ralph said. "He's not too happy about it."

"There's probably nothing going on in his bedroom," Carmen said. "That's what he's not happy about."

Ralph shook his head, but his smile betrayed him. Carmen was

not exactly diplomatic—more like the bad cop to my good cop—
but she had a frisky wit, a bawdy streak, that made everyone she
dealt with feel as if they had been admitted to her inner circle.
"There's a few other options I think we should discuss," Ralph said,
"just to see if we can find some other ways to relieve the pressure on
La Loma." I sensed that these were not necessarily his ideas, more
that he was obligated to raise them, but I also feared that they might
be a warning—to fix the problem ourselves or have it fixed for us.

"Is there any chance, for instance, that you could reduce the
number of games?" Ralph asked. We had been advertising a sixteen-
game season, plus playoffs, since I had taken over. I liked the symmetry of it, the reliability: Everyone played twice a week, once on
a weeknight and once on Saturday, for eight weeks. It was an easy
way for me to conceive of the schedule, a concise way to break it
down for parents worried about their own schedules.

"Oh, come on, Ralph. Less baseball? That's the solution?"

"I'm just putting it out there."

"What else you got?"

If we were unwilling to shrink the schedule, Ralph said, then
would we be willing to farm out some of the games to another park?
Maybe keep the older kids at La Loma but have T-Ball play elsewhere? Monterey Park was home to half a dozen other baseball
fields, some of them in quite lovely parks, but all I could think of
was that they were normal parks, city parks, horizontal, rectangular,
exposed, not our shrouded little sanctuary, with its invisible diamonds, on the hill. Apart from the logistical headache of supervising
play at multiple locations, apart from the lost business that smaller
crowds would mean for our snack bar, our league would no longer be
synonymous with La Loma—friends would be separated, families
would be divided, everything that I had tried to cultivate would
be scattered.

"With all due respect," I said, "there's no way."

"You wouldn't even consider it?"

"If you split us up, then we'd really be just in the business
of hosting baseball games. I'd be nothing but an administrator,

keeping the trains running on time. The reason I love La Loma is that it's more than that. We're all together, in the same place, doing the same thing, good, bad, ugly, whatever—we're a community. I have a feeling some people liked it more when our league was in trouble, when the park was dying."

Ralph sighed. "It's just that it grew so fast," he said. "If we keep getting complaints, you might have to be willing to compromise."

The truth was that I had maxed out La Loma, stretched it to capacity and even a little beyond. Every available day, every available field, every available time—six games every weeknight, sixteen games every Saturday—it was all booked, with no room for error. I liked it that way, filling the park with kids, with life, maybe because I knew how depleted it had been before, maybe because I thought of us as modern-day homesteaders, staking our claim to land by making it fertile. Or maybe I just liked to show that I could.

Creating a schedule was part art, part science, an exercise in appeasement and computation—extending courtesies to coaches and still getting the numbers to add up. Nearly everyone had a special request, no early games, no Friday games, no games on Cinco de Mayo, and I had to figure out which of those I could grant and which I could afford to ignore, while ensuring that every team played not just the right number of games but also a balanced number of opponents and that upon each of those meetings, they alternated between home and visitor. I am told that there is software especially for amateur schedulers, that you can point and click your way out of these conundrums, but as always seemed to be the case, if I was going to be responsible for the outcome, I felt the need to control the process. So I mapped it all by hand, division by division, half a season at a time, making columns, marking tallies, then double- and triple-checking my math. My methods were not much different from those I had employed as a baseball-mad kid, hunched on the floor, categorizing, systematizing. *If there are five teams in a division and the Dodgers have already played the Yankees and the Angels, then their next two games would have to be against the Giants and the Cardinals— except, whoops, what if the Cardinals still had not played the Giants and the Angels, and thus were not free to face the Dodgers?* That sort of thing. With one flub, if, say, the Dodgers played the Yankees only once but everyone else had to play the Yankees three times, you could undercut the legitimacy of an entire season. Even then, when everything was staunch and airtight, all it took was a hiccup—a rainy day, a coach with a family emergency—and my schedule would fold like a tower of dominoes.

Midway through the 2005 season, as I prepared to sketch out the second half of the schedule, it became clear that there were simply not enough days left at La Loma for every team to get in its sixteen games. If the season ran long, we would be spilling into the Fourth of July—damn that fireworks stand!—not to mention disrupting a slew of family vacations. As much as I had protested to Ralph, he had turned out to be right. I was going to have to scale back, shrinking everybody's season by a game. I started with our oldest division, Triple A. There were four teams, which meant each team had three opponents. If you were to face each opponent five times, you would end up playing fifteen games. An actual improvement: I had freed up space and restored competitive balance. Why had I not thought of this in the first place? Double A proved just as simple. There were six teams, which meant five opponents. Play everyone three times and—voilà—you ended up with a perfect fifteen games again.

I moved on to Single A. There were seven teams, six opponents. If you were to play everyone three times, that would come to eighteen games. Too many. If you were to play everyone twice, twelve games. Too few. Still, not a problem; each team could play all its opponents twice and a few of them a third time. I began diagramming the final weeks of Single A, but to my befuddlement I could not get all seven teams to finish with fifteen games. I was sure I must have overlooked something, so I did it again, and still there was one team that was either a game over or a game short. It made no sense. True, there was an odd number of teams, but my sixteen-game schedule had matched up just fine. If the problem was an odd number of games, why had the older divisions adjusted so easily to a fifteen-game schedule?

It was 1 A.M., and my head had begun to ache. I had been doing La Loma's schedules for three years now—it was always a convoluted business—but I had never been stymied like this, never felt like I was trying to solve some dark cosmic riddle. I reviewed my notes. When our schedule had consisted of an even number of games, every division, both those with an even number of teams and those with an odd number of teams, had balanced out. When I had tried to change the schedule to an odd number of games, only the divisions with an even number of teams had been able to adapt. I found myself saying it out loud: Even could play even. Even could play odd. Odd could play even. But holy mother of crap, that was it—an odd number of teams could not play an odd number of games! I started to laugh. When in life was I supposed to have learned that? I kept laughing, until I had to wipe my eyes.

I had figured that after my first season as commissioner, once Todd and I had stopped the bleeding, my second season would be a triumph of stability and soundness—both mine and the league's— and that by now, my third, with Carmen and I returning as a team, everything should have been on autopilot. Some aspects of the job did become simplified. The league had grown so popular that sign-ups took only four Saturdays, instead of, like, seven, and e-mail finally achieved cultural saturation, even in blue-collar, Spanish-speaking quarters, so I no longer had to call every coach individually to make an announcement. But as with the schedule, just when I thought I had a grip on La Loma's affairs, some new, unforeseen absurdity came along. I learned about a twelve-year-old boy who threatened his teammates with a bat ("He just had this look, like he was in another world," his coach told me), an assistant coach who spit at a mom on the opposing team (but only after she had taunted him with an ungracious "kiss my ass"), a coach's wife who tussled in the parking lot with the team rep she thought he was banging (catfight!), and an L.A. County social worker who, by chance, witnessed one of our players, still in uniform, being haranged by his parents at the local Shakey's (unclear if their putdowns were related to his performance on the field).

I got into a tiff of my own, with a board member named Desiree. She was married to Gary Verdugo, the one who had raised an eyebrow at my Chicano fascinations. It had started brewing during sign-ups. Desiree had volunteered to distribute about a thousand flyers to the parochial schools—her own son went to Our Lady of the Miraculous Medal—but I kept waiting for her to pick them up, and waiting, until I decided I could wait no longer, and I went ahead and dropped off the flyers myself. This was a major faux pas in her book: Because Max went to public school, I could not possibly appreciate the nuances of interacting with the archdiocese.

With Dodger Day came a new glitch, an unbelievably picayune breakdown that spoke volumes about the shape of our league. I had just finished calculating the top five ticket sellers, as I did every year, and posted their names on the door of the snack bar. I had also given each of their parents a call, to review the procedures for checking in at Dodger Stadium for the pregame introductions. Number three on the list was a boy named Eric Marinez, who had sold sixty-one tickets. Besides going down to the field, he would be receiving a mint-condition Eric Gagné baseball card, from the rookie year of the Dodgers' Cy Young Award–winning closer, which I had purchased (for $19.99 on mlb.com) as an incentive. As fate would have it, there was also a boy in our league named Eric Martinez, who had sold forty-some-odd tickets—admirable, to be sure, but not quite top-five caliber. Unbeknownst to me, his parents had spotted my announcement and, perhaps aided by a dash of wishful thinking, deduced that the number three seller, Eric Marinez, must actually be their son, Eric Martinez. Never mind the discrepancy in the spellings or the number of tickets sold or the fact that Marinez, the true number three, was on the T-Ball Mets, a detail noted alongside his name, and that Martinez, the party-crashing number three, was on the T-Ball Cardinals. It was apparently close enough for a Monterey Park Sports Club contest.

Still, just to avoid any misunderstanding, the Martinezes had the good sense to ask their team rep to check with somebody, and Desiree happened to be presiding over a team rep meeting that same week. Desiree was capable of generosity—she sometimes packed home-cooked dinners for Max and me to eat at the park, seeing as how we were single guys—but she also had a prudish, even supercilious manner. Her background was in accounting, and she worked in the business office of a rather tony middle school, in one of the San Gabriel Valley's wealthier communities. She claimed to be grateful for my commitment to La Loma, and I do think she was protective of the park, but if Desiree could have caught me in a mistake—and this Dodger Day question was looking to her like a contender— something tells me she would have been delighted. The team rep had no way of knowing that Desiree was not privy to the Dodger receipts, that only I had the documentation that would have allowed someone to compare the Marinez ticket order with the Martinez ticket order. Desiree knew this, knew that she did not know, but that did not stop her from jumping to the same conclusion and confirming the blunder—that Jesse, our well-meaning but, you know, not-from-around-here commissioner, must have made a typo and dropped that *t* from young Eric's last name.

With that cleared up, the poor Martinez family arrived early at Dodger Stadium and tried to shuttle their Eric onto the field. They were blocked by my girl Carly, the Dodger saleslady. There was no Martinez on the list I had given her, and anyway, the Marinez boy was already in his rightful place. Despite their confusion and disappointment, the Martinezes took consolation in knowing that they were at least entitled to that Eric Gagné card. Eric and Eric—the word in Spanish was *tocayo,* your namesake—and how fortuitous was that, to have had their son qualify for that very prize? It was thus that the whole fuss came to my attention, the Martinezes waiting for me to make good, fearing I had stiffed them, and both their team rep and Desiree sending me e-mails, wondering how I could be so unresponsive. I was puzzled, even a bit testy: I had personally delivered the card to Eric Marinez. Why was everyone on my case? It took me several days to figure out what had happened, to trace the chain of evidence up to Desiree and then back down. The Martinezes had, admittedly, brought some of it upon themselves, but what on earth was Desiree up to? An occasion to celebrate, a fund-raiser I had handled with precision and care, had been twisted into a colossal screwup.

I remembered something about the announcement that I had posted in the snack bar, a red-inked scribble that had caught my eye only after the Dodger game was over and I had gone to peel the paper off the door. The words had barely registered at the time, but now I raced to the park and went digging for it in the trash. Sure enough, "T-Ball Mets" had been crossed out and "T-Ball Cardinals" had been written in its place, as if by moving Eric Marinez to another team you could make Eric Martinez the winner. I assumed that this was the hand of the Martinezes, but their team rep said that no, it was Desiree who had taken the liberty of "correcting" the information. I was beside myself. Had I fought to bring La Loma back from the dead only to see it return as a monster?

I told Desiree we needed to talk. The next time her son had a game, she and Gary met me on the lower field. It was late already, and chilly, the ocean air billowing east. They were good people, original board members, with me from that first tumultuous year, but I had lost confidence in Desiree and she had lost sympathy for me. "You had no business altering that flyer," I said. "It was accurate, and you made it false."

"Who said I did that?"

"Please, Desiree. There were witnesses."

"Well, I don't remember."

"People got hurt."

"I didn't know."

"I know you didn't know. That's the problem. You should have at least checked with me."

"You're always busy."

"That's not it," I said. "I feel like you're trying to undermine me."

"We're just trying to help," she said. "You keep everyone in the dark."

So much of what was still plaguing our league could be ascribed to La Loma's renaissance. Instead of getting easier, everything kept multiplying, magnifying, to the point where our seams were beginning to show. When we were half the size, everyone might have known there was an Eric Marinez *and* an Eric Martinez in the same division, but I was having a hard time keeping up with all the new faces and names. It no longer seemed practical to introduce every player over the PA on opening day, and I sometimes even blanked on the coaches: We had a Javier and a Xavier, a Luis who called himself Lewis, an Ulises who called himself Ulysses, two Sanchezes, two Hernandezes, two Ramirezes, an Alex Poli who was better known in the graffiti art underground as Man One, and a peevish Cubano named Ricardo Cabezas, which could be translated, much to Max's and my amusement, as "Dick Heads." The scale of our Dodger fundraiser was such that I was now meeting Carly at the stadium and picking up $35,000 worth of tickets, enough to make me think I should have had an armed escort or at least a safe; until they could be sorted, I hid them in my closet, then my freezer, then finally settled on a giant bag of Eukanuba dog food.

All our field markings were done in chalk—the foul lines, the batter's boxes, the on-deck circles—and as the schedule escalated, we got to where we were burning through a fifty-pound sack of dolomite every day. Rec and Parks gave it to us free, but we had to pick it up from the city's maintenance yard, a stockpile of junked police cruisers and surplus playground equipment that never seemed to be under any sort of supervision. I had been instructed to drive right through the gates, as if I were on official business, no need to check in or report any quantities. The bags were in the back, stacked on pallets, under tarps, and usually teeming with what looked alarmingly like black widows. I would hold my breath, to keep from inhaling the plumes of powder that escaped from the stitching, then heave about a dozen sacks, six hundred pounds, into my trunk. More than once I had a bag explode on me and left the yard looking like a ghost. Then there was the time I tried to leave, only to find that I was too late. The gates had been swung shut, the last worker had clocked out, and I was locked in, all alone. What did we do before cell phones?

"Carmen."

"What's wrong?"

"You're not going to believe what happened."

"Oh, no, honey. Are you okay?"

"Sort of."

"Spit it out!"

"Promise not to laugh?"

Desiree was, to a degree, right: I had my hands way too full to worry about keeping everyone else in the know. My instincts were telling me that I was near my limit, that to remain on the job much longer was to do so at my own peril. I was getting fat, the buttons on my XL jersey starting to strain, and my blood pressure was creeping into the danger zone. There was no time to run or to cook or to read or to keep a simple houseplant from shriveling on my kitchen sill. I did a story that year on Central Casting, the mythic Hollywood talent agency, and for my reporting I signed up as an extra. I had to note my age and measurements and other distinguishing features. The only hitch was my hair color. I had marked "brown," but the lady who took my application looked up at me, frowned, and changed it to "salt and pepper." When the hell had I started to get old? I saw Carlos Zuñiga's mom, Dorothy, at the park. I must have looked even worse than I felt. She was not in the greatest health herself—and Carlos, by then no longer a minor, had been nudged into retirement—but she wanted me to know that she was available. "If you need help, ask for it," she said. "I don't want to hear that you got sick and that you didn't call." What could I tell her? I knew I was doing it to myself, giving more than I had, tending to everyone's quandaries but my own. I was not good at building organizational structure, at insulating myself from the day-to-day squabbles and pinches. I was a writer, not a jock or a colonel, and after all these years I was still flying by the seat of my pants, running on instinct. I wanted to curse Joe Rios, not for what he had said to me but for sabotaging my exit strategy. It was time to get out, to get back to a normal schedule, to get on with the rest of my life, and yet a fourth season as commissioner was starting to look inevitable.

All around me there were casualties, victims of our success. It seemed like everyone I trusted, who got close to the center of the Monterey Park Sports Club and understood the expectations, who loved La Loma as I did and accepted responsibility for its welfare, had been damaged in some way by the experience. Todd's marriage had sagged under that weight, my constant beckoning of him, to the park, to my kitchen table, having incited more than a few domestic quarrels. Although he spent most of 2004 on the sidelines, he was still feeling the strain, and I was stunned but I guess not surprised when I learned that he had been hospitalized at the end of that year with chest pains. Max and I visited him in the cardiac unit. Todd had been through the wringer, a night of whirring machines and bleating monitors. "Can you not die on me just yet, Doctor Ullah?" I said, leaning across the bed to hug him. Todd was a formidable cat, as educated and insightful as anyone I knew—accountable for so much, to so many—and yet he was still just another guy, with doubts and disappointments, trying to figure out how to live. "I'll do my best to comply, Mister Katz," he said. When I later found out that the episode was being blamed on an unusually piquant Thai curry—burning and numbness, followed by chills and panic—I did not find it quite as hilarious as I thought I might. Whatever the cause, it was hard to say that Todd was at peace.

Over on the basketball side of our organization, my buddy Chris had his own struggles. Although his wife was handling the books for both of our programs and thus was marginally more tolerant of the Monterey Park Sports Club's imperatives than most spouses, Chris was so immoderate—so inclined to turn each season into a sleepless, sodden release—that he still regularly managed to land himself in the doghouse. His finest hour may have been the closing ceremony of the 2003 basketball season, a clear, bright Saturday morning in April, about a month before my first opening day at La Loma. We were a country newly at war, the invasion of Iraq just under way, and Chris, glazed and sweaty, on the tail end of an all-nighter, took the stage of the Barnes Memorial Amphitheater and asked the crowd to honor our troops with a moment of silence. He bowed his head, allowing a hush to fall over the four-hundred-seat arena, in the shadow of city hall. I had never seen him exhibit any sort of reverence, and with each tick of the clock, the more I wondered what had gotten into him. I elbowed Max. He had accompanied me on enough of my sessions with Chris to know the excesses that were usually involved. At last, the desired solemnity achieved, Chris raised his fist and pumped it, "woof-woof," Arsenio-style. "Now let's get this party started!" he bellowed. It almost figured when, a month or two after Todd's scare, Chris was rushed to a cardiac unit himself.

Nobody suffered at home more than Carmen, whose ability to split her time, to compartmentalize her roles, proved less artful than either of us had imagined. Or maybe, by our second season together, she had simply made her choice—baseball over housework—and had grown weary of trying to pretend otherwise. Eddie would call throughout the day to check on her, where was she going, how were the kids, what was for dinner, and then wait for a response, some acknowledgment of their shared commitments, any sign that after a decade of marriage Carmen was still pulling in the same direction. Her eyes would mist over. Her voice would turn flat. "I gotta go," she would say, and hang up. As stung as Eddie was by his wife's indifference, Carmen was even more distraught about being confined and policed. She knew that in Eddie she had security, even a modicum of luxury—Coach purses, weekly manicures, a bottomless ATM card—but she was hungering for something more purposeful, an identity, a validity, that so far she had been able to find only at La Loma. It was as if Eddie had helped her scale the first great hurdle of her adult life, out of poverty and single motherhood, into the routines of suburban comfort, and now that her material needs had been met, Carmen was free to contemplate new frontiers, to consider for once what she longed for—what she wanted to be, as she often put it, when she grew up. The more Eddie tried to keep her in place, sometimes with threats, sometimes with pleas and largesse, the more Carmen recoiled. After every argument, she would call me in sobs, telling me that she was suffocating, that she wanted out, but then she would think of her children, of the price her oldest son had paid for growing up without his dad, and she would sniff back her tears. "I'm stuck," she would say, and from there she would calculate the time until Sebastian, her youngest, reached legal age. "For twelve more years."

It was a good thing, I suppose, that somebody was single. To the extent that I was able to hold myself together, to earn a paycheck and run a league, to be La Loma's custodian and Carmen's confidant and Max's coach, it was largely a function of not having anyone else. There was nobody to help me, but there was also nobody to stand in my way, to divert me or begrudge me or warn me that I was dangerously overbooked. On the occasions when I have been asked how I did it, where I found the time and the stomach to be so embroiled, my short answer, as queer as it sounded, was that the park had become my wife.

There was a longer, more complicated answer, one that I kept secret from almost everyone I knew, from Todd, from Chris, from my parents, from Raynelda, from Christiám, and most of all from Max, even though more than anyone, I think, in his bones, he understood what I was up to. Carmen kept it secret, too, which is to say we conspired together, hesitantly at first and, the longer it went on, with elaborate stealth and gall. I had no idea what I was getting myself into, not that I often have, only that I felt something with Carmen that I had been waiting a very long time to feel. Looking back, I realize I had been taken with her before we had met, before I even knew who she was. I was just a coach still, a year or two away from becoming commissioner, and having spotted her at the park, I found myself riveted by, of all attributes, her skin: the darkest, smoothest, richest, most naturally iridescent brown, like a chestnut fresh out of its burr. If that makes me guilty of some crude fetish, I confess—what stirred in me was primal and irrational, beyond my will to contest. I would come to notice that she had heart-shaped lips and sleepy eyelids and a dimple that cleaved her right cheek, and yet she was not frail or frilly. I liked that, the way Carmen seemed to be both sensual and solid, a beauty and a tomboy. The more our lives overlapped at La Loma, the more I was willing to overlook the hazards that she posed—I did have some experience in the department of chancy relationships, after all—and see what we had in common, devotion to our kids, a sardonic bent, faith in redemption, an unfrugal appetite.

One of my lifelong mentors, a Portland sausage maker named Fred Carlo, once told me that he had three prerequisites for the ideal mate. If she was not passionate about pork, red wine, and baseball, the relationship probably did not stand a chance. It would be easy to dismiss Fred's formula as distinctly male and, perhaps, self-defeating—he is, at thirteen years my elder, a terminal bachelor—but if you really took pleasure in all three, as we both did, you also understood them to be a barometer of dearer traits, of earthiness, of substance. As best as I could tell, Carmen was batting 1.000.

Nothing came of it until the end of her first season as La Commish, the summer of 2004. I had to be at the fireworks stand—the shed had been delivered to the parking lot of the Numero Uno Market, but we were still waiting on our inventory—and Carmen was on her way to the airport, to pick up Eddie from a business trip. She was dolled up for him, in a fuchsia sweater and slit denim skirt, but she had a few minutes to spare, and I scrambled into the passenger seat as soon as she pulled in. We had seen each other almost every day for five months, thrust together, under duress, like costars in some long-running *telenovela,* and even though neither one of us dared to say it, we both knew that with baseball coming to a close, our time was running out. I had just returned from Portland, from seeing my mom in the ICU, and I was about to head up again with Max. I had called Carmen, in tears, the minute I had gotten the news, and although she had told me not to worry about La Loma, that she would care for it in my absence, I understood there was only so much, in the months ahead, I could hope to expect from her. Our lives were going to be pulled back apart.

Carmen reached for my hand. Her fingers were strong and elegant, almost chocolaty at the knuckles and, on the underside, nearly peach. She tugged at the hairs atop my wrist. I leaned across the console—we were in Eddie's Suburban—and with my other hand, I touched her cheek. If there is a place in Monterey Park less discreet to be kissing another man's wife for the first time, someone should point it out to me. We were in front of a busy market, on a major thoroughfare, in broad daylight, next to a Monterey Park Sports Club fireworks stand. It was insane and—oh, what the hell— irresistible. I turned Carmen's mouth toward me. She had on lipstick, the color of brandy, that would have to be redone, and perfume, a scent I could not place, that left my commissioner's jersey with a dusting of pear and musk. It was a simple kiss, quiet and slow, our eyes closed to the traffic rumbling in from East L.A. I was crossing a line that no man was supposed to disrespect, much less a man who purported to be an advocate for youth sports, for families and community, for his own son, but the effect was electric: Carmen was pouring into me, coursing through my veins, overloading my circuits. I was all charged up, and at the same time, powerless.

She had to leave. I sent her a text. "Wow," it said.

"That will never happen again," she responded.

"It was delicious," I wrote back. "You were delicious."

What did it say about me that my texts were always grammatical, without acronyms or abbreviations?

"Dont 4get," Carmen told me. "I am a married woman."

I wish I could say that I was in it just for the thrill, that Carmen, maternal, seductive, expensive, was my forbidden fruit, enticing because she was spoken for. That would have still made me a sneak and a hypocrite—I was holding everyone else to these daunting ethical standards while, behind their backs, I was coveting another coach's wife—but at least it might have kept me on guard, attuned to the traps of falling for someone who was not completely free to reciprocate.

In Carmen I saw more than the prospect of a mere fling, more than a temporary lapse of the commissioner's judgment. She was quintessential Monterey Park, the queen of kingdom La Loma, and her affections, in my addled state, had come to represent the ultimate acceptance. If someone like her might be willing to take a chance on someone like me, to guide me into the sweet, sacred center of it all, then maybe I really had found my home.

I was planning a vacation that summer, at the end of July, my reward to Max, and to myself, for the sacrifices we both had made. I had been working so hard to create an environment that would shelter and sustain him, I sometimes found myself too busy to do the things we used to, even to toss the ball around, the bond that had made La Loma important to us in the first place. I bought Max one of those webbed pitch-back screens, the kind that is springy enough to return your own throw, but it sat, rusting, against the side of our house. Max wanted his dad out in the driveway, giving him a target, calling balls and strikes, providing the play-by-play commentary that would allow him to pretend, as my dad's narration had for me, that an eleven-year-old pitcher might just have a chance against a Hall of Fame lineup. From the moment Max got home from school, though, I was already going at full tilt, scrambling to find him a snack and wash his uniform, to schedule makeup games and program lights, to add someone to the waiting list or to move someone off, to reorder baseballs, to update standings, to calculate umpiring fees; I was saying "I can't" to him, and "not now" and "hurry up" and "sorry," more than I could ever remember. Many nights I would be on the phone so late, ministering to someone else's problems, that Max would end up closing the door on me and putting himself to bed. I would go into his room later and kiss him on the forehead and listen to his breath grow heavy, and I would wonder what was going to come of all this, if I was actually giving him the gift I thought I was or if, unintentionally, without quite knowing what the lesson might be, I was teaching him something else.

One evening, at La Loma, he begged me for a few minutes of catch. I stopped whatever I was doing and said yes, we were due, but we were so out of sync, I was so distracted still, that I managed to throw the ball to him before he was ready and ended up bopping him in the mouth. We had just invested in braces, at Max's insistence. I had told him what my parents had told me when I was his age, that crooked teeth were a mark of character, but he convinced me that orthodontia had become a preteen rite of passage. "Don't you want me to smile with confidence?" he would ask, as if he had memorized every slogan in our dentist's waiting room. The ball smacked his upper lip, pushing it in and grinding it against the metal brackets on his front teeth. Blood leaked through his fingers, dripping onto the mulch. "Oh, jeez, Max," I said, rushing over. "Didn't you see it coming?" He was shaking his head, trying to talk without spitting more blood. "You kept stopping and looking around, like there was something else going on, which made me stop and look around, too," he said. Someone arrived with a damp towel, caked with salt, and told Max to hold it to his mouth. Everyone agreed that no stitches would be necessary, but that one careless toss left him with two diagonal slashes just to the left of the philtrum, scars that have yet to fade.

We needed to get away, and I sold Max on a baseball trip to the East Coast, to catch games at Fenway Park and Yankee Stadium—the Red Sox would even be hosting New York while we were there—with a stopover at Cooperstown. I had never been to any of those shrines, never thought of going, at least not since I was Max's age, never imagined I would spend more on Red Sox tickets, which I scored on eBay, than on plane tickets to Boston. But nothing could have made more sense now: to show Max, to confirm to myself, that baseball was forever, that what we did in La Loma, for all the eccentricities and contradictions of the place we called home, was woven into the fabric of something bigger, a great, enigmatic, bittersweet American story. I was worried about taking such a fanciful journey while my mom's health was still so tenuous. She had started chemo again—in between dialysis, sandwiched by transfusions—but she was back at city hall, refusing to be underestimated, and she urged me to keep my plans. This time I believed she meant it.

Max and I proved to be good teammates on the road, all our years of play, our reservoir of familiarity and admiration, coming back to us, melting away the testiness of my commissioner's life. I let him sleep in every morning while I looked for coffee and a newspaper, and he let me take naps in the afternoon while I pretended to be watching movies with him in our hotel. We carried a deck of cards with us and played gin rummy at every meal—over chowder at the Union Oyster House, over pastrami at Katz's Deli—and I tried to psych him out, as my dad still does to me, making like I was tempted by each of Max's discards, pointing, grimacing, saying something like "ah-ha" or "ho-ho-ho" or "dun-ta-dun-ta-dun," even reaching for the card, maybe caressing it, then at the last instant drawing from the deck. Max was old enough that I could hand him a map and trust his copiloting as I crept through the Central Leatherstocking fog in our rent-a-car but still young enough that he could think I had all the answers, or at least more than I really did.

At Fenway, which felt to me like an antique opera house, so intimate and ceremonious, I took a picture of us in the loge box, my arm outstretched, camera pointing in reverse. It was the year Boston would go on to break the curse, winning its first World Series since 1918, and in my mind we are part of that history, both of us in Red Sox caps and Red Sox sweatshirts, Max's head resting on my shoulder. Wherever we went, including that night in the stands, we met people who wondered about us: How old was the boy, where was his mother, did she not want to come, you mean it was "just" the two of us, a father and son from Los Angeles, making a vacation out of baseball? Sometimes those people were charmed, sometimes mystified, sometimes a bit pitying, but for Max there was nothing exceptional about it: I had been preparing for this most of his life.

On our last day in New York, we took the subway to the Bronx. As someone raised on the folklore of the Dodgers, I could appreciate the angst of the Red Sox nation, but the Yankees were, well, still the evil empire. I cringed when Max said he wanted an A-Rod shirt. "Really?" I asked. I was hoping we could get away with just being students of the game, not buying in to the home team's mythology at every stop.

"C'mon, Pops," Max said

"Are you sure?"

"You know he's a beast."

"I'm not questioning the man's abilities."

"I promise not to wear it back in L.A."

"That's supposed to make me feel better about paying for it— that you're only going to wear it once?"

"You're the one who wanted me to experience all this," Max said. "Remember? 'Ooohhh, Yankee Stadium.' Now you're not going to let me get anything?"

"Golly," I sighed, reaching for my wallet. "I must really love you."

"And a hat, Dad," Max said. "I need a hat, too."

Our seats were cheapies, in the tier reserved section, which, until the stadium was retired five seasons later, stood as the Himalayas of the baseball world. Coming out of the tunnel and looking up, the ascent to row M appeared nearly vertical, so steep that I had to grip the rail and hunch myself over, to keep from tumbling backward. Half a step at a time, one foot to the next, I shuffled up to our perch. Heights have never been good to me, but I was still amazed that a public space, and a venerated one at that, could have been constructed in a way that stirred such premonitions of doom. I was thankful that we had arrived early, and that I was already sipping a beer, to give me a chance to acclimate. Sometime in the early innings, I noticed a commotion at the bottom of our staircase, a guy hugging the banister, battling the same demons. He was young and wearing a suit, the Brooks Brothers look, and I imagined him to have raced over straight from Wall Street, from some feat of high finance, only to find himself paralyzed now, his inability to advance jamming traffic and blocking views.

"The poor dude is really knotted up," I said. Max knew I was a bit squirrelly about heights, even if I had managed to conceal the worst of my fears from him, and I was hoping that if I could strike a sympathetic note for a fellow acrophobic, Max might reflect some of that back on me. "He's thinking too much," Max said. "He needs to just go for it."

Little by little, with nearly everyone in section 10 riveted by the panic below, the guy inched his way up. It must have taken an entire inning, he was that debilitated, but he made it, mercifully, to his row, which was just in front of ours, an achievement that was about to be voided by an even greater humiliation. To get to his seat, to make the transition from stairs to aisle, he would have to let go of the rail, and as best as I could tell, that was proving impossible. Each row was stacked so precipitously upon the last, there was nothing to hold on to, nothing to break his fall, just a slender ledge of concrete across the sheer face of the upper deck. Left with no other options—reversing course and descending would have been just as harrowing—our would-be fan dropped to the ground. I guess you could argue that he was taking control of his destiny, as opposed to, say, waiting for a search and rescue team to arrive with ropes and a harness, but it was one sorry spectacle to see an otherwise competent adult on his hands and knees, crawling to a Yankees game. How do you suppose the New York crowd saluted him? We were less than three years removed from September 11, from the horror of twin 110-story towers being toppled, yet dozens of people were on their feet, cupping their mouths, chanting in unison: "*Aaaass*-hole, *aaaass*-hole." Damn.

Baseball. Life.

Nothing was as simple as it seemed.

I saw Carmen little that summer, with all the kids hovering around, but at the end of August an opportunity came our way. She was headed to her twentieth high school reunion—Keppel, class of 1984—and Max, who would be a freshman there in three years, was spending the week in Portland. More important, Eddie had stayed home with their children, and Carmen thought, just maybe, if I was game, we could meet for a drink on her way home. I had never been out late with Carmen. Ours was strictly a daylight dalliance. If we were going to be keeping company at an unseemly hour and during La Loma's off-season, it would have to be someplace a tad more judicious than we were accustomed to. In Monterey Park at least, we qualified as public figures.

I poked around for a hideout that might serve our purposes, near Carmen's event but outside the Monterey Park Sports Club's orbit, a joint too funky, too ethnic, for any of the families we knew. I settled on a Chinese bar on the other side of the San Bernardino Freeway called Paradise Isle. I got there just before midnight and ordered a beer. The dragon lady hostesses scowled at me, figuring I was either a cop or a perv with yellow fever. I listened to the karaoke machine, a hit parade of Mandarin love songs, and waited for my phone to vibrate. After my third beer, it did. I gave Carmen directions and met her in the rear lot. She was in a satiny black cocktail dress, her cheeks flushed. She told me to get in, and as soon as I did, she squirmed out from behind the wheel and over to my side. There was nothing tentative or gentle this time, all heat and dampness and frustration, then just as suddenly she pushed me away. "I need to tell you something," Carmen said.

It sounded ominous. "Do you?" I was trying to sound ironic.

"I don't know how you're going to take it, but I don't care. I have to say it."

"Alrighty then."

"Okay. Phew. Lemme see. Okay. Here it goes." She touched her neck with her fingertips. I watched her throat contract as she swallowed. "I'm in love with you. That's it. Oh, my God, this is crazy! But I am *soooo* in love with you. If that scares you away, I'll just have to deal with it. Maybe we'd both be better off."

Those were words I had not dared to utter, at least not before she did. Any sort of declaration would have made me mawkish or predatory: Nothing good would come from cornering her. But there, she had gone and said it, said it first, out loud, to me, and even though it came with a caution flag, I allowed myself to believe that it was the invitation I had been wishing for. The sexiest mom in all of La Loma loved me, the commissioner. She loved me for who I was, the way I was, not because she needed money or status. She had it all—as long as she was married, there was nothing she could accept from me, anyway—and by giving herself to me, she had everything to lose. What I felt for Carmen at that moment was, strangely, inappropriately, pure: something truer, more authentic, I thought, than what regular, upright couples got to experience. In the most illicit romance of my life I had discovered the most honest one. How I arrived at that conclusion, and believed it, I am not entirely certain. We were risking not just disgrace, perhaps bodily harm, but everything about La Loma that was precious to me, the stable, protective environment I had sought for Max, the generosity and optimism I was trying to coax out of Monterey Park. If we were to be exposed, good Lord! It would mean chaos for the league, the end of my commissionership. Even if Carmen and I managed to survive, if we emerged from the rubble with our desire intact, how could I possibly think that I would still be welcome in the same circles, that anyone would applaud me for having the deftness and moxie to win over a coach's wife?

If I had stopped to think about it, I might have recognized that I was, indeed, accomplishing just the opposite, that my behavior was confirming all the reasons outsiders tended to be suspect in the first place. Because I was not from here, because I was not constrained by family allegiances or social pressures or a shared history, I was a free agent. For better or worse, I chose to follow my heart.

Chapter

Thirteen

IN MAX'S SECOND YEAR OF DOUBLE A BALL, WE MADE IT TO
the finals again. It was our fifth consecutive trip to the title round,
quite an accomplishment, even in a league as sequestered as ours,
and yet since that triumphant season in Rookies, when my easygoing ways were vindicated, we had been the perpetual runner-up—
knocked out by Omar in 2002, by Lulu in 2003, and, once more, by
Omar in 2004. This being 2005, our showdown was, as expected,
with Lulu, and frankly, it felt like our last, best hope to finish on top.

I still had a roster populated by favorites: Max and Alex, in
their seventh year together; Jonathan, in his fifth with me; Colin
and Natalie, fourth-year teammates; and a slight, quiet lefty
named Justin Lee, who had been on that victorious 2001 squad
but who had eluded me ever since. There were only a couple of
kids I had never coached before and only one who had never played
at La Loma. That boy, Jasper Hernandez, showed up at the start of

the season with a cheapie mitt, so glossy and stiff that I thought he would never be able to catch a ball. When I learned that his dad was in the military, on duty in Iraq, and that his mom just wanted to keep Jasper's mind occupied, I offered him my glove and suggested that he give it a try. At our next practice, I asked him how he liked it, the genuine cowhide, soft and supple, the deep, oil-stained crease down the centerline. Jasper did not seem to know how to answer. The glove was still on his hand. I looked closer. My name, written in permanent ink, had been scratched out of the leather. Jasper's had been scrawled over it. "Oh," I said, "I guess you liked it pretty good."

If we failed this season, Max and I would have to start over the following year in Triple A, La Loma's most lawless division, for kids up to fifteen, and Omar would be there already, waiting for us. Beyond that, who knew? Max would be eligible for a second year of Triple A, even a third, but he would also be a teenager, on his way to high school, and if my own adolescence was any indication, baseball might have ceased by then to be the arena in which he chose to gauge his prowess or build his reputation.

I knew it was silly to be worrying about winning—at Max's age, at my age. No matter how competitive the world might be, no matter what edge in life there was to gain by learning how to impose your will on a foe, this was still just a game. In all my years at La Loma, I never exhorted one of my teams to go out and win, never demanded it of Max. I clipped a cartoon from *The New Yorker* once that showed a father, down on one knee, his hands gripping the shoulders of a little boy with a glove. The caption was so perfect, I ordered the whole thing reprinted on a T-shirt: "Just remember, son, it doesn't matter whether you win or lose—unless you want Daddy's love." I would critique Max, remind him that he needed to keep his chin steady at the plate, to wait on the pitch, to see it deep into the zone, to stop trying to pull every friggin' thing over the left fielder's head, but he knew I would never chastise him about the outcome. By losing, he was not letting me down. Most of my players understood that, too, understood that the swiftest way to my bad side, to the extent that I had one, was to bug me during a game about the score. "Don't know," I would snap. "Doesn't matter." I expected them to play the same, with the same poise and pleasure, whether we were up by ten or down by ten or tied at ten. It was good to care, but not to care too much.

That said, the longer Max's team went without winning a championship, with each season that was ended by Omar or Lulu, the more I began to fret that our lone crown was a fluke. I still lived more richly than the average coach, the coaches unable to lock in a player of, say, Jonathan's caliber, but I should have had a dynasty by now. How do you lose three years in a row with that kid on the mound? What was I failing to teach? Once again, I heard the voice of that nettlesome dad from those dismal early days, telling me to step up, to command my team. The coaches I was losing to were precisely that way, disciplinarians and authoritarians, loud, pushy, coarse, impatient, and, at their worst, churlish and menacing. I did not want to be Omar or Lulu, but I did not want to be their punk, either. Funny how it was becoming a contest between us, the adults, when I, more than anyone, was supposed to know better. Even our lexicon was skewed: Was I going to be playing Lulu? Or Lulu's team? That was easy: *I* was not going to be playing anyone. But was it my team that was in the finals? Max's team? Our team? That was harder to sort out.

There was no Katz system, that much was for sure. I did not produce little Stepford ball players, with identical form or cookie-cutter technique. I had a few gimmicks—cones, buckets, towels, that nutty basketball—that over the years seemed to produce some benefit. But the way I looked at the game, at life, really, was that no method had a monopoly on success. All you had to do was take a glance around the majors, at all the improbable motions and stances: Gary Sheffield's lavish bat waggles, Dontrelle Willis's leg kick to the heavens, Nomar Garciaparra's compulsive toe tapping and glove tightening, Tim Wakefield's sub-speed-limit knucklers. There were a million paths to every destination, an infinite number of ways for a kid to figure it out. That was why I did not yell or punish, why I tried to extol rather than intimidate. I wanted my kids to win—oh, boy, did I ever—but I wanted them to win without really trying to win, if that makes sense. It had to be not just the right way but *their* way, with their touch, their personality, their foibles and pluck. I was in charge only inasmuch as I was needed to preserve the sanctity of that proving ground, to keep grown-up anxieties from intruding. Max and his teammates had to invent the rest.

My parents flew down for the series. It had been a year since Mom had been rushed to the hospital, a year since I slipped two yellow Livestrong bracelets onto my left wrist and swore I would not take them off as long as she was alive, and now, amazingly, she was at La Loma, to see her grandchild play a couple more games of baseball. When she underwent that first hellacious round of chemo, in the recliners of Northwest Cancer Specialists, her sarcoma was so rare, the survival rate so bleak, the medical literature did not even recommend a standard course of treatment. Her oncologist, a spry, sunny, fairy godmother named Rebecca Orwoll, who had a passion for opera and a master's in English, had to make some educated guesses, extrapolating and improvising, knowing there was really only one chance to get it right. I asked Rebecca at the time what she would do if Mom failed to respond, if that tumor kept growing, or spreading, as fast as it had in the previous few weeks. "You really should try to keep your thoughts as positive as possible," Rebecca told me. "That's what your mom needs from you right now."

"Yes, thank you, I understand all that," I said. "But I'm just asking. What would the next step be? If this doesn't work, what's the alternative?"

"We'd be focused at that point on trying to keep her comfortable," Rebecca said. "It would probably just be a matter of months."

Rebecca settled on a cocktail of epirubicin and cisplatin, known by the brand names Ellence and Platinol, which sounded more like hair colorings from L'Oréal. Ellence, which usually is prescribed in advanced stages of breast cancer, and Platinol, which played a prominent role in Lance Armstrong's recovery from testicular cancer, are designed to hunt down and interfere with the body's fastest-multiplying cells—the ones that are so lethal—but the drugs, by their nature, wipe out a whole lot of healthy cells, too. Mom was still trying to keep up with her mayoral duties, wearing a surgical mask at city hall to fend off infection, but when I went back up to Portland later that fall, after Max and I had taken our baseball trip, I could see that her hazel eyes were growing clouded. The lashes and brows were gone. Only a few gray wisps remained on her head. Her arms, even her lips, were covered in bruises. She was losing not just her energy but also her memory, her balance, her taste for food, and, I feared, her will to endure more sickness. As she withered, I thought to myself what brutish medicine we accepted as the state of the art, how centuries from now our best doctors will not look much keener than medieval barbers. Mom was being cured and killed at the same time, and you just had to hope that the one was happening faster than the other.

So maybe I was wrong. Maybe Rebecca was good. Maybe she was lucky. Maybe the folks at Pfizer and Bristol-Myers Squibb made special products. Maybe Mom was resilient. Maybe she was stubborn. Maybe she was blessed, whatever that was supposed to mean.

After a month, her tumor had stopped growing. After another month, the clusters had begun to disintegrate. By the third month, the cancer was gone, or as Rebecca put it, a bit more cautiously, the disease was "currently undetectable." Mom was still on dialysis, three to four hours every Monday, Wednesday, and Friday, and probably would have to remain tethered to that machine for the rest of her life. If she skipped a day, as she would on her visit to our championship series, her face would swell, bloated by the fluids that her kidneys were unable to remove on their own, and with her complexion already a few shades darker from all the toxins she had been forced to ingest, I could not help but think of Violet Beauregarde, from *Charlie and the Chocolate Factory*, the one who gobbles a stick of experimental chewing gum and inflates into a blueberry. She had lost sensation in the soles of her feet, another side effect of her medications, and each step was so tentative, so teetery, it seemed as though she were walking in tide pools. She had a nagging cough and recurring nausea and frightfully low platelets, not to mention an arthritic knee and a bad back, but Mom was not dead: She was not even dying. Nobody knew if or when the cancer would return. It had snuck up on her so ferociously, there was always a chance it was still lurking on some microscopic level, ready to spring back now that the chemo had stopped. Every three months she underwent another CT scan, and each time she braced for the worst. It was not so much that she had turned glum, I would say, but that she did not want to be clobbered by the news, to be seventy-one and not be in control of her final days, and so she prepared herself to die, in September, then in December, then in March, then in June, and somehow kept coming back to life.

She finished out her term, as she had sworn to—thirty-two years in public office. Her staff threw her a retirement party in the city hall atrium. Hundreds of civic leaders and political supporters turned out, friends, lobbyists, artists, educators. My aunt Zena, who had not seen her little sister in a decade, flew up from California's central coast for the occasion. I flew up, too; I had not spent so much time in Portland since I was in high school. My dad was there. My dad's wife, Dianne, was there. "I guess it takes an illness to bring a family together," Mom told me. Her voice betrayed no bitterness. It was just the way life worked, she was saying, one of the treasures to be found in misfortune. She was discovering more of them every day: acts of love, hugs from strangers, entry into what she had begun calling a sisterhood of survivors. From across the country, from around the world, people had been sending her inspirational cards and New Age CDs, homemade sweets and naturopathic remedies, hand-knit caps and scarves and quilts. She had told another audience, the week before, that she had been showered with so many offerings, she had enough inventory to open a Christian bookstore—"and I'm an agnostic," Mom said. After a career in the spotlight, she had a fair sense of comic timing. "For those of you who have more faith than I do," she added, "thank you."

The city hall atrium was four stories tall, all pillars and polished marble. A video montage of Mom's achievements, from those early pickets outside the City Club to the delegation of well-wishers she led to New York in the aftermath of 9/11, was being projected endlessly on the wall. It was announced that the newly unveiled boardwalk on the Willamette River's neglected east side, a project Mom had championed for years, was being renamed the Vera Katz Eastbank Esplanade. There was even beer—"Vera's Audacious Ale"—a gift of the Rogue brewery. Her face, smiling, in a purple business suit, with matching earrings, was etched onto each twenty-two-ounce bottle. "Bold, sophisticated, sometimes sassy, innovative, and delightful," read the label. "An ale that captures the spirit of the mayor who embodies Portland." Maybe I am impressed by the wrong things, but *that* was cool. I stuffed a couple of bottles into my luggage and brought them back to L.A. When the time did come to say goodbye, I wanted to be able to toast Mom with her own vintage.

It said a lot about my parents that they came to see Max play at La Loma together, and not just together but with Dianne, a self-employed property manager and all-around handywoman, whom Dad had wed, in a ceremony at the Laura Russo Gallery, the same year I married Raynelda. Dianne was fifteen years younger than him, with blond bangs and a beatific smile, but far too smart, about stocks and minerals and Greek mythology, to meet the standard of a trophy wife. They watched the Seattle Mariners on TV every night, the adopted home team of baseball-loving Portlanders. They played epic matches of high-stakes Scrabble, and no matter how many bogus words Dad tried to slip past her, hardly a month went by that he did not have to write Dianne a check. She was welcoming to Mom and, more important, gracious about allowing Dad to tend to Mom. There was no need for him to say it—they had been divorced for a quarter century already—but he loved her still. He admired her and he worried about her, counseled her and cheered her. It was almost as if by divorcing, by eliminating their accumulated stresses and disappointments, they were able to rediscover the affection that had united them in the first place. They had taken a chance on Portland together, a crazy leap from the center of the universe to a far-off coast, and even after all these years, even after each of them had left an unmistakable imprint on the city, they were still bound by that shared adventure. Dad liked to refer to Mom and Dianne as his "two wives," and not with quite as much irony as you might think.

Mom had never remarried, never really come close. It was hard with her schedule, with her renown, to find a man secure and accomplished enough to date the mayor yet not so entitled that he would rather be chasing hot little numbers. Just before her hysterectomy, Mom was invited by *Portland Monthly* to appear in a feature on the city's "most eligible singles" and asked to pose, in a black Saks Fifth Avenue suit, with a retired, and apparently well-to-do, sixty-seven-year-old oilman she had never met. She was loath to be trotted out in a magazine as the grand dame of unfulfilled romance, but her staff pestered her to loosen up, to take a chance. During the photo shoot, she found that she shared a love of the symphony with her pretend companion—Mom had season tickets—and they made what sounded like a real date. When the photo was published, their arms were hooked and their heads tilted, their smiles brimming with fondness, but in the accompanying text, her partner was quoted as saying that he hoped to find a lady "in her 50s" and in "good physical shape," someone to join him for a round of golf. Mom knew then they would never be going out. Recognizing just how loyal Dad was to her brought me more relief than I expected. He had become my proxy, there for Mom in every way I could not be. As long as he was alive, she was not alone. "Our family doesn't have such a great track record when it comes to marriage," Mom told me after she got sick. "But I must say, we're very good at divorce."

Perhaps that was not something to aspire to, but it was not a bad quality to fall back on. My breakup with Raynelda had gone about as tranquilly as I could have hoped for, without accusations or lawyers or tugs-of-war over Max. I did not file for divorce, nor did she, and I figured the longer I could put it off, the better chance I would have of preserving our détente. I subsidized Raynelda's rent and kept her on my health plan. She allowed Max to live with me. For a couple of years after she moved out, we actually continued to see each other, with intermittent sleepovers that Max was not too certain what to make of. Even when that ended, I invited her to spend as much time with him as she liked, at her place or ours, although when it came down to it, that proved to be not that much, or rather, I think Raynelda would have been happy to spend more time with him—she was happy when she did—but she was so involved in her own struggles, in Freddy's misadventures, that it was easier to cede Max to me, which, in any case, as she knew, kept him in good hands.

She occasionally would come to La Loma, especially if I told her that Max was going to pitch, and when she showed up, often dressed for a night out, in sheer blouses and leather skirts and knee-high disco boots, I could see the other moms whispering: Was this the elusive lady who had borne me such an assured and mindful son? A few weeks before my parents arrived for that final series, Raynelda had been at a game and found a Monterey Park Sports Club cap in the snack bar. It was the kind I usually wore, with my title and the year stitched on the left side, and thinking it was mine, Raynelda put it on, as if to say, *Watch out, bitches, 'cuz I've had the commissioner, and on paper, he's still mine.* Except that what was embroidered there was not "Commissioner." It was "La Commish." Max noticed it first. He had not yet grasped the transformation between me and Carmen, so what he was pointing out was just a fact. "You're wearing the wrong hat, Mom," he said. "That's not Dad's." Raynelda took it off and studied the writing. "It's not?" she asked, narrowing her eyes. I would have been more than willing to overlook the whole thing, to give Raynelda an easy out, but she was waiting for an answer. "Um, no, it's not," I said.

To this day, I have no idea what Raynelda knew or how she knew it, if she had seen something or, as women can, just sensed it, if she was truly disgusted or merely embarrassed. She flung the cap as if it were teeming with lice. She opened her mouth and thrust out her

tongue. "Bleccchhh," she said, pretending to retch. "Yuccckkkety."
Max was confused. I was turning red. It was the last time, as best as
I recall, Raynelda ever set foot in the park.

I wanted to tell my parents that I had met someone, to let my
mom, especially, know that I was not alone. She worried that I
was becoming a martyr, for my work, for Max, for La Loma, worried
that some of her own patterns had begun to take root in me. "Don't
do what I did," she would say. "Don't grow old by yourself."

"When the time's right," I would say.

"I want you to be happy."

"I am happy."

"Maybe there's a nice Jewish girl out there for you."

"Mom."

"I know, I know, never in a million years."

"Let me get Max through high school and off to college, then
there'll be plenty of time for all that."

"You have such a hard life."

"It's not so hard."

"I don't know how you do it."

"Don't worry about me, Mom."

"I'm your mother, that's what I do."

What exactly could I tell her, at least not without giving her
more to worry about? My parents had met Carmen on previous visits to the park. They had exchanged enough pleasantries to know
that she was married, that she had enough kids to assemble her own
infield, that I would have been out of my mind to be slinking
around with her, and maybe just as deluded, if it ever got that far, to
consider us a genuine couple. From my vantage, Carmen's marriage
was beyond repair—a self-serving analysis, to be sure—and I figured
her feelings for me would only hasten the end. Carmen seemed to
be in agreement, but she wanted to be certain that it was ending, as
she put it, for the right reasons, that she and Eddie had nothing to
salvage, not that she had found someone else. She did not want to
be the kind of woman who swapped her husband for another man—it
was indecorous, trashy even—and to be fair, I was not sure I

wanted that responsibility, either: to be the cause of their breakup, not simply the beneficiary. As if anyone at La Loma would have made that distinction.

So we continued to carry on, in secret, in limbo, Carmen basking in my adoration one day, reverting to good corporate wife the next. We worked hard at avoiding detection, and the longer we succeeded, the more our double life came to be our normal life, a routine that despite its pitfalls and barriers we seemed capable of sustaining almost indefinitely, if needed. We texted like teenagers, bridging our physical distance by cell, even consummating our affair via SMS message, and when we recognized the electronic trail that we were leaving, I bought us a third line, the "bat phone," which Carmen stashed in the bottom of her purse. We concocted a network of make-out and pickup points, expanded our map of incognito taverns and motels and *taquerías,* while for public consumption, at the park, we pretended to be just a pair of unusually dedicated parents. La Loma was swirling with speculation, with sightings, but if anyone implied that they had seen a spark, Carmen would point out, with a tart smack of her lips, that I was merely her "baseball husband" and she was my "baseball wife."

Why I was willing to make these compromises, to settle for Carmen part-time, is something I am still struggling to decipher. Set aside danger or morality: I was sharing the woman I loved, investing in a relationship that was at best incomplete. I had allowed myself to become the Other Man, and even if I had a bit more to fall back on than the typical Other Woman, I was still on some basic level selling myself short. A TV shrink might have said that I liked it that way, that as counterintuitive as it sounds, Carmen was safe— emotionally, at least. I got to have all the benefits of a partner, friendship, understanding, intimacy, without any of the hassle. That was Eddie's department. Perhaps I was not so much stealing his wife as renting her. "If you really had me one hundred percent," Carmen occasionally said, tweaking me, testing me, "I don't think you'd know how to handle it."

I was not willing to concede that point—when we were apart,

I craved her like a junkie, with aches that I would have given anything for her to have salved—but there was one aspect of our subterfuge, I must say, that did prove convenient. As I had been a few years earlier, at the time of my visit to Cuba, I was still all weird about pursuing a relationship in front of Max. It was part of my promise to him, our unspoken covenant, that he would come first, always, and so I passed myself off as this monastic man-mom, with no time or appetite for female shenanigans. How *perfecto* of me! If I did not get to enjoy Carmen as completely as I would have liked, I also did not have to reveal to Max—I *could not* reveal to Max—that he was once more sharing me with a woman. It was, in truth, even more convenient than that: Because we had base-ball as cover, I could still welcome Carmen into the house, bring her around Max without him questioning our intentions. He knew my girlfriend, just not that she was my girlfriend. I was hoping that by the time he figured it out there would be no need to explain.

If my games as a child were easily dismissed, Max's were not. Mom, Dad, Dianne—they had all become devotees of his athletic life, not just because that is what proud grandparents are supposed to do but because they had a newfound appreciation for what they were missing, for the tests and transitions to be navigated on a Little League diamond. They recognized that La Loma was Max's park, his story as much as mine. We had to rush home from the air-port to make the first game, a five-thirty start. I told my folks that what they were about to witness was going to be intense, perhaps the greatest series we had ever been in and ever would be, and that was not even accounting for Lulu's propositions, our clumsy tango. Her team had finished the regular season with the best record in Double A, fourteen and one. We were second, at ten and three with two ties. Two of our losses were to her; her single loss was to us.

At La Loma, I gathered my kids on the grass, in shallow right field, and told them to forget all that, every win, every loss, every tie, that none of it mattered now. The only thing that counted was what happened here tonight, and nobody knew, nobody could know, what that was going to be. "Nothing has been decided," I said. "Nobody's entitled to anything. It's not written anywhere who's supposed to win, who deserves to win. There's no such thing as fate or destiny." By now, they were used to my exalted pep talks, and this one, more than any I had ever delivered, seemed to be holding their attention. "The beautiful thing," I said, "is that you get to decide. *You* get to go out there and write the ending to your own story." This team—the one Max played on, the one I coached—was the culmination of everything I had ever believed in at La Loma, the hours, the weeks, the years we had shared, hoping for another chance to prove that sanity was not a prescription for defeat. I loved these kids, loved them for their earnestness and persistence, for their faith in me, a faith I tried to redirect back into them, and I hoped, I really did, that their families would still love me, that they would remember these times if my secrets were ever spilled. We had created history together, a common past all our own, and now everyone was growing up, preparing to move on.

Just a week earlier Max had said goodbye to the hilltop school he had spent the last seven years at, the school he had entered as a kindergartner upon our arrival in Monterey Park, and he was about to head to a less-than-recommended intermediate school, nearly a thousand seventh- and eighth-graders, puberty flaring, the breeding ground of the Lomas gang. I found my eyes welling with tears at his promotion ceremony—Raynelda, who had left for Nicaragua to celebrate her fortieth birthday, missed it—and I was struck by a premonition of what his high school graduation would be like, how I would surely be reduced to a puddle by the ending of his childhood, by the beginning of our separate lives.

Since we had the weaker record, we were the visitors in that opening game, greeted by Lulu's son, Donnie, on the mound. He was as fast and furious as ever, what baseball people like to call effectively wild. I countered with Jonathan, who was now taller than me and, after a boyhood of Christian teachings, about to enter public school. After all these years, his parents were also about to allow him to join a club team, to get him on the tournament circuit, and it was becoming apparent that this season at La Loma, this series against Lulu, might very well be his last. He gave up a leadoff single to Justin Carleton, the boy I had drafted the year before, the one I had been forced to trade to Lulu in exchange for Alex. I saw her grinning. Poetic justice. I guess I had that one coming. Donnie was up next and drilled a double. And just like that, as Vin Scully might have phrased it, we were down one to nothing. We did nothing in the second. Neither did Lulu's team. Jonathan was settling in, mowing down batters, doing exactly what he was born to. In the bottom of the third, Donnie came up again, with two outs and nobody on. I called for time and summoned Max, from behind the plate, to join me and Jonathan.

Seven years of coaching and I had never ordered an intentional walk. It was bad form, especially for a commissioner, to be robbing a kid, the other coach's son, of his chance to shine in the finals, but it was still part of the game—*hardball, baby*. Maybe I had just been waiting for the right time. I instructed Max to stick his arm into the unoccupied side of the batter's box, reminded Jonathan that he still needed to maintain his mechanics, even though he would be throwing four balls out of the strike zone. The cries were immediate, Lulu's side of the field hooting and hissing, everybody seeming to expect more of me. Oh, well. I was tired of giving in. The next batter was Lulu's daughter. She struck out; end of inning.

In the top of the fourth, we mounted a rally. My newcomer, Jasper, hit a single, knocking in the tying run. Then he stole home on a passed ball, giving us a two to one lead. *Keep that glove, son. Shoot, the bat's yours now, too, if you want it.* In the top of the sixth, we did it again: a double by Max, a double by Jonathan, and a single by Colin. We were up four to one. Three more outs and the game was ours. These kids, wow, they had listened. They had really believed. Three more outs and we were halfway to the championship.

In the bottom of the sixth, we unraveled. My kids played like, well, kids again. Every shortcoming that had ever plagued us— flighty infield, woozy outfield, porous gloves, twitchy arms— conspired to undo our gains. With two outs, Max tried to nail a runner at third, but his throw sailed into left field. That allowed Lulu's team to even the score, four runs apiece. It was atrocious. Jonathan finally whiffed the last batter, giving him fourteen strikeouts for the night. He was better than Donnie, maybe the best twelve-year-old pitcher in all the San Gabriel Valley, and still, again, we had failed to honor his talent.

Now I had a tie game on my hands and in a few minutes a Triple A championship game set to begin on the same field. Ties were not uncommon in the regular season—a necessary evil, just to keep the schedule moving—but this was it, the last week of baseball, and *somebody* had to win. I consulted with Cal, our plate umpire that night, and he agreed to let us continue. In all my La Loma years, I had never been involved in an extra-inning game, never gone off the clock, never felt anything like the agony of knowing that every three outs Lulu's kids would have a chance to end it. Frigid marine air was creeping in from the west, what the L.A. forecasters call June gloom, but I was drenched in a sweat, all hope and nerves. I walked up to the bleachers, where my parents were huddled, and shrugged in disbelief. "Looks like you're going to get your money's worth," I said.

With six innings in the books, Jonathan and Donnie were both done, which left Lulu and me with a pivotal call to make, one that would ultimately tilt the balance of the series. She went with her second-best pitcher, the son of her assistant coach. He was twelve and a lefty, like Donnie, but thicker and moodier, and I was not surprised that he held us scoreless in the top of the seventh. The logical move for me would have been to counter with Max, my own second best, but in the blur of the moment, for reasons that I did not have time to weigh fully, I changed my mind. I told myself that I was saving him for the second game, which was true. I had been. But the more I think about it, the more I suspect I was also sparing him—sparing me, sparing his grandparents—from the possibility that he might falter. I knew he could perform under pressure. He had the year before, against Omar. But lately, Max had been uneven, trying too hard, aiming with his fingers, like the ball was a dart, instead of trusting his entire body to deliver it. In his previous three outings, each just an inning, he had walked eleven batters. I had not lost confidence in him, but I was reluctant to test him under such tenuous circumstances, knowing that in an instant, not even a full inning, it could all slip away, with no chance to recover. I was being a dad, which is usually not a good sign for a coach.

The pitcher I turned to instead was little Justin Lee, the youngster of our squad. The rule that in Single A had required us to get three innings a week from a nine-year-old pitcher applied the same in Double A to eleven-year-olds. It was the weakness in our roster two years before—one that Lulu had been all too happy to exploit—and I had drafted Justin with precisely those three innings in mind. He was not overpowering, but he was consistent, and I hoped, with a veteran infield behind him, that would be enough. I had planned on starting Justin the next day, then finishing up with Max, but here was an unexpected chance to work on our quota tonight. Lulu was going for the kill. I was putting my trust in the kid. Or was I serving him up as a sacrifice?

Justin pitched a scoreless seventh. He got some help from Max, who threw out a runner at second, with Jonathan, now at shortstop, applying the tag. Justin pitched a scoreless eighth. I called for Donnie to be walked again, which, judging by the gasps and growls, seemed to confirm to the entire park that I was no longer myself. Justin pitched a scoreless ninth. It was madness. I was covering my eyes, biting my lip. Nothing like this had ever happened at La Loma. The game was a stalemate. We were on empty, but so were Lulu's kids. The Triple A coaches, the irrepressible duo of Omar and Bob, were shouting at me from behind the backstop, demanding that I clear the field, to let them play. Even Cal had lost patience. He took off his mask. "Jess, I think maybe it's time to pull the plug on this bad boy," he said. Cal had been at La Loma since my first season as commissioner, one of the only good moves I made that year. He had always treated my teams fairly—never once did I have to hear an opponent groan that the umpires were in my pocket—and

I never would have pressured him to fudge a call. But there was too much at stake to walk away now. I had made such a big deal to my kids of viewing the season as a tale, of claiming the final chapter as their own. My parents had traveled a thousand miles to see that happen. I was the commissioner, dammit! What was the point in that if I did not have the authority to allow a game of baseball to end as it should? "I say we play on," I announced.

As we prepared to start the tenth inning, Lulu abruptly changed course. Her second pitcher had flummoxed my kids for three innings, but she was starting to worry about tomorrow's game, about saving the boy's arm for another three innings, and so she yanked him and put in her eleven-year-old, a kid named Mitchell Aguilar. Mitchell was the anti-Justin—in the draft, in fact, Lulu had chosen him over Justin—burly and aggressive, with a football player's build and temperament. He would have crushed Justin on the line of scrimmage, but he did not have Justin's polish on the mound. Mitchell walked the first five batters, and that was it, the start of the meltdown. We went ahead nine to four. I left Justin in to finish off the bottom of the tenth. My motives had been suspect. The kid had been heroic.

By Little League standards, it had been a marathon, nearly two complete games strung together, almost three hours of baseball. I was ecstatic and frazzled. I drove my parents back to their hotel, a DoubleTree that catered to Taiwanese businessmen, and left Max with them until about eleven. I needed to drink some beer and kiss Carmen and call the city, to see if the lights could be kept on after hours for the Triple A game, and then check on Christiám, who was trying to shut down the snack bar and get to the fireworks stand for his overnight shift. It was just another Tuesday in the fusty, somnolent L.A. suburbs, and yet so full, of drama, of promise, of silent craving and extravagant dreams. To think, we were going to do it all again in less than twenty-four hours. Even after I got Max to bed, it seemed impossible that I would ever fall asleep.

He woke up sick. "What is it, champ?" I asked. Max flung himself, in his boxers, onto the sofa. He had crouched behind the plate for all ten innings the night before. His legs, showing the first sprouts of black hair down his shins, around his calves, were like medical illustrations, every muscle taut and striated. That April, a week before opening day, we had run a relay race, a five-mile loop around the L.A. Zoo. Not only was Max's time a minute faster per mile than mine, the official photographs taken along the course made him look to be floating, an ethereal half smile on his lips, while I wheezed, feet mired in some invisible bog. The boy was only twelve. Was he supposed to be beating me already?

"I don't know," Max said. "My head hurts." I rooted around in the bathroom for some children's Tylenol, the liquid formula. "Take this," I said, measuring out a tablespoon. "I'm sure you'll be fine." Max gulped it and handed it back. Then he sneezed. Again and again. "I feel like crap," he said.

I filled a bowl with cereal and set it on the coffee table, in front of the TV. When he was three, my aunt Zena had given him a squat, toddler-size chair for his birthday, with a hand-painted clown on the long wooden back. Max still used it every morning at breakfast even though his knees were now bent almost to his armpits. My parents were waiting for him at the hotel. There was a mall next door, and as was the custom, whether they were down here or we were up there, Mom and Dianne were plotting to outfit Max in new clothes. Before I dropped him off, I put the Tylenol in a plastic baggie. "I don't know if you'll need it," I told my folks, "but Max was feeling a little droopy this morning."

I had stuff to do, preparations to make for that night. Our game was at seven-thirty, and if we won, I needed something memorable for the celebration. I asked Carmen if she knew where to find *cascarones*. They were the pinnacle of down-home Mexican party favors: hollowed eggs, filled with confetti, ideal for cracking over the heads of loved ones. She promised to help me search. I threw Max's uniform in the washer. I mapped out my lineup, moving Jonathan behind the plate, to catch for Max, and I jotted down a few notes for what I hoped would be our final pregame huddle. If we lost, we would still have a third game to play the next day, but

my parents would be gone by then; Mom had to be back in Portland for dialysis. I wanted to win, and I wanted to do it tonight, for
them.

When I called the hotel that afternoon, Dad answered. "Your
son's not doing too well," he said. Max had been dragging at the
mall, feeling cold and achy, until finally he grew so feverish that
they had to turn around and get him into bed. They gave him more
Tylenol and swabbed him with a washcloth. He was sleeping now.
"Oh," I said. Maybe I was one of those psycho dads, after all, conflating my ego and my son. I did not doubt for a second that Max
would suit up. I did not intend to give him the choice to sit out. I
did not go hunting for a thermometer. I did not ask my parents for
their opinion, what they would do, what they would have done.
I knew Max. I knew, already, his answer. I ran my fingers through
his hair and kissed his forehead. "Time to get ourselves ready, son,"
I whispered. He nodded. He understood what was happening, the
weight of the occasion. It was not a question of competition, of the
drive to win, but of fulfillment, of creating his own memories, of
writing his own conclusion. He was a Katz, surrounded by Katzes.
Baseball may have been his thing; my thing, too. But the commitment that gave it meaning—the absolute refusal to shy away—that
came from the old people in the room.

Max was glassy and dazed, but I pumped him with more medicine and laid out his uniform. We got to La Loma early and walked
his grandparents to the bleachers, then headed down the left field line
together, to a blistered log at the edge of the bushes. I asked Max if he
wanted to sit, to take a few minutes, off by ourselves, to meditate on
his performance. We had never done anything like that before.
Without saying a word, Max closed his eyes. He knew that I was
counting on him to keep us in the game, that Jonathan was unavailable and Justin had already walked a tightrope, that it was his turn
now to deliver, to be the pitcher he always knew he could be. "Listen," I said, "very carefully." I reminded Max of his gifts, of his tenacity and his equilibrium, far greater than I had ever possessed. I told
him to visualize himself on the mound, to feel his fingertips on the

seams, to throw a fastball, to experience the sensation of command. I wanted him to savor that moment, to make it his. He did not need to be perfect. He did not need to strike out every batter. He would surrender some hits, some runs even. He just needed to get back to his spot, to see himself in control again, to remember that nobody could take away what he refused to give up.

"If you can do that," I said, "you'll be unstoppable."

I thought it was better to keep Max focused on his role, not on the hole Lulu had dug for herself. By failing to get three innings from her eleven-year-old, she had no choice but to go with Mitchell again, and the poor kid was not much better than he had been the night before. In the second inning, he walked the bases loaded. Jonathan was up. No player in Double A had hit a home run over the fence all season. Jonathan had never hit one out in all his years at La Loma. Physically, he had to be capable of it, more so than most of the adults at the park, but he had never quite had everything aligned, the right pitch, the optimal swing, Mitchell on the mound. Jonathan let one ball go by. Then another. For a moment, I wondered if Lulu was trying to walk him—payback for what we had done to her son—to minimize the damage at one run instead of risking four. But the next pitch was down the middle, and Jonathan was ready. He turned on it with everything he had, with the probability that this game was his swan song, with the understanding that Max needed all the help he could get. I screamed the second it happened—"hoooooly smmmmmokes"—my voice rising as the ball did. It soared out of the park, over the right field fence and halfway up the slope to Chuy's Nursery, a solid 300 feet, the most colossal grand slam that La Loma has ever seen. Even Mitchell, who was trying not to hang his head, seemed to grasp that he had just become part of history, the Monterey Park Sports Club's own priceless folklore.

The game went five innings. Max pitched them all. If he was not quite as sharp as he would have liked—five walks, two hit batters, a wild pitch, an errant pickoff throw—he never faltered. He would take a deep breath and reset and, somewhere within him, find the resolve to strike out the next kid. It is one of the great axioms of baseball that the game starts over with each pitch. When your mistakes are in plain view, dancing on the base paths, behind your back, casting doubt, there is only so much your arm can do; the rest is up to your head. The score was twelve to seven. The last batter hit one back to the mound. Max fielded it, threw to Natalie at first, and we were champions, at last.

I dug out the tray of *cascarones*, which Carmen had delivered, and handed them out as fast as I could—a riot of glitter and shell and polka dots, the remnants sown, maybe forever, in La Loma's earth. As cameras flashed and families poured onto the field, I awarded two game balls. One was for Jonathan. His blast had been retrieved from the bushes by, of all people, Joe Rios, who, even after all the misery we had inflicted on each other, even after his son had endured a stress fracture while running the bases and been forced to withdraw for the season, understood that the ball was a treasure and wanted me to have it, to be the one to present it to Jonathan. The other went to Max. The drugs had worn off, and he was shivering now, burning up, shutting down. When I explained to everyone how poorly he felt, that he had pitched as brave a game as I could have ever dreamed of, Max lost the composure that had sustained him all night, that had defined his entire childhood, and, overcome, buried his face in my jersey.

When I dropped them off at their hotel, my parents were still reeling, from Max's feat, from my compulsions, from the whole fervid theater of La Loma. We could review it later. I needed to get home. I started a bath for Max, as hot as I thought he could stand it, and poured him a thimble of NyQuil. "Let's get you out of these clothes," I said. Only then did I realize that his pants were soaked. So was his underwear, his jockstrap. "Jesus, Max," I said. "What happened?"

"I don't know."

I put my nose to his uniform.

"Did you wet yourself?"

"I don't know."

"When did it happen?"

"I told you, Dad, I don't know."

I left him alone in the bathroom and went to lie down. I took off my glasses and hid my eyes under my forearm. What was I doing to this kid? What thing did I think I was affirming? I had pushed him to some ridiculous limit, drained him of everything he had to give. He was too numb to be elated. I was too stricken. By the next season, if we did this again, he would be thirteen and, from there and beyond, not the same boy he was tonight, the boy who had grown up at La Loma, the boy who had made me what I was. Max bundled himself in sweats and curled up next to me, on the same side his mother once had. I rested my hand on his back. For the first time in years, maybe for the last time, my son fell asleep in my bed.

Chapter

Fourteen

ON A COOL, CLOUDY SPRING MORNING IN 2006, LA LOMA surged with more bodies than I had ever thought possible, a crowd so unwieldy the Monterey Park Police Department had to station officers up and down the hill. Despite the city's warnings, despite my own misgivings, I had allowed the league to expand by another three teams, bringing us to twelve in T-Ball, nine in Rookies, eight in Single A, six in Double A, and five in Triple A—a total of 485 kids.

It was my fourth and final opening ceremony as commissioner, of this I was certain, and by now the first day of the season was like a county fair, all nostalgia and patriotism, as corny as I could possibly make it. To steer our forty teams into orderly queues, I designed each of them a placard, with name, division, coach, and logo printed on cardstock, and with the help of my third baseman's dad, a salty old pipe fitter, we stapled them to wooden stakes, like campaign signs, and fanned them across the edge of the outfield. Every player was promised a free Dodger Dog, a stroke of grillwork that I assigned to Abel, who would be haunted by the scent of porcine brine on his hands for weeks to come. Todd delivered ten gallons of coffee, donated by the Starbucks across the street from East Los Angeles College. An all-Chinese Boy Scout troop, assembled by my auto mechanic, recited the Pledge of Allegiance.

Even though Jonathan was done with us, I unveiled a plaque, with a bull's-eye in the center, marking the exact spot on the outfield fence where he had earned "an unforgettable place in the annals of the Monterey Park Sports Club." It was actually more of a street sign, cut from heavy-gauge, graffiti-retardant aluminum, which I ordered from the same company that supplied the city's department of public works. To counter the self-congratulatory insinuation—I was, after all, using my position to enshrine my own player—I summoned his victim, Mitchell Aguilar, and, through the powers vested in me, thereby designated him the official opening day catcher. When a white limo, courtesy of my basketball counterpart's livery service, pulled up to the edge of the grass and delivered that year's celebrity guest, the dashingly lithe and long-haired Jesse Borrego, it was Mitch who received the ceremonial pitch and scored the first autograph.

Standing in the center of it all, I looked around in amazement at what we had created, how a park that had been given up for dead was now spilling over with life. It was wonderful and messy, a cauldron of grudges and alliances, jealousies and passions, mixed up with all the complications of race and class and geography and culture, somewhere between *Touch of Evil* and *Desperate Housewives*. By signing our kids up for baseball, by paying the fees and abiding by the rules, we had all bought ourselves the latitude of La Loma, the liberty to fuss and dream and flourish on that one magnificent hill. I could not escape the feeling that Little League was like summer camp for adults, a reprieve from whatever drudgery or disorder was besetting our regular lives, a license to care about things, about events and people, that otherwise would have passed us by. For those of us in positions of authority, the experience was even more pronounced, as if we were pioneers, or runaways, or maybe hostages, and had been forced to endure trials, invent routines, that would forever overshadow our former selves. If Little League to me had once been square, it was no longer—or perhaps it was in its very squareness that we found ourselves so free.

All around me I saw families I would never have known if not for baseball, friendships that did not exist until the park brought us together. These were people who had now been in my life for the better part of a decade, not just in season but through birthday parties, back-to-school nights, farmers' markets, and street fairs, folks whose baby showers I attended, whom Max and I went trick or treating with, who kept me up to date on surgeries and layoffs and funerals. I saw their children out on the grass, some I had coached, some perennial rivals, kids whose triumphs and struggles were as familiar to me as my own son's. I knew which ones had stayed innocent, earned merit badges, performed holy communions, and which were in a rush to torment their parents, to be truants and vandals and potheads.

I saw old antagonists, the likes of Omar Robles and Joe Rios, still smarting from my rebuffs. They were hardly the worst of La Loma—they loved their children, wanted for them something very near to what I wanted for Max—but I was done pretending that they represented the best, and I had ousted them from our board. I saw new allies, too, the couple I had chosen as successors, Gilbert and Elizabeth Barajas. He was a periodontist and she was a court reporter, the nouveau riche of Monterey Park, and though I knew that prosperity was no guarantee of virtue, I was willing to bet that Gil and Liz would do nothing to jeopardize the league's welfare. Something about the good doctor's priggishness reassured me: When I took him for a beer at the Venice Room, the seamy cocktail lounge that sooner or later everyone—me, Todd, Carmen, Chris, even Raynelda and her boyfriend—ended up at, he ordered something sweet, with whipped cream on top, and confessed that in his fifty-plus years he had never once thought to peek inside.

Then I turned my eyes to my accomplice, La Commish, the reason I had been able to rouse myself for one last season. We were matching, in white Monterey Park Sports Club jerseys, with navy letters outlined in silver, a new color scheme for our goodbye year. As I addressed the crowd, Carmen played hostess, seating dignitaries, distributing prizes, charming the coaches. She was at her best in the park, a showcase for her magnetism and mischievousness, her aptitude for relishing small joys and fleeting pleasures, all the qualities that she bottled up at home. I used the ceremony to single her out for praise, saying something about how Carmen always went above and beyond the call of duty, words that I realized, as soon as they left my mouth, were destined to come back to haunt me. She seemed closer than ever to breaking free, to escaping the atrophy of her gilded cage, and the longer we trusted each other, the more she led me to believe that I was the key to that, to adventure, to intellectuality, to art, to her own culture, to maybe, in time, solving herself. She talked about getting a tattoo after she was divorced, a symbol of her rebirth. The leading idea was a vine, with five blossoms and a single hummingbird. If I had been patient at first, out of respect, out of fear, waiting for Carmen's marriage to expire on its own, I had found myself becoming increasingly restless, worried about our ability to continue without baseball as a smoke screen.

One day I needed to drag the fields—we had a giant crimped-steel mat that could be hooked to a car bumper—and I asked Carmen to ride with me. I drove onto the lower diamond and began orbiting the bases, from first to second to third to home, in concentric circles, each loop smaller than the last. The dust rose, engulfing us in a shroud of clay and brick, and as I kept the wheel cranked to the left, I reached for her knee with my free hand and looked in her eyes, just the two of us, spinning, invisible, sending plumes into the sky. If this was going to be our final season together, I wanted it to be the beginning of something, not the end.

At every opening and closing day, from my first year to my last, I invited the members of Monterey Park's city council to be our

VIP guests. There were always a couple of them who could be counted on to deliver a grandiose speech, about staying in school and saying no to drugs. I liked how they added fanfare to our ceremonies, the way their presence signaled to our kids that what we did at La Loma was important, but I was also being shrewd, trying to buy us a measure of civic protection. The complaints about our program had not ceased—that unneighborly Rec and Parks commissioner was actually trolling La Loma, cornering families, asking where they were from—and I wanted to be sure that our council members, whom I always presented with a Monterey Park Sports Club cap or pin, would feel compelled to side with us, if they were ever called on to intervene.

Like so many of the other battles I had fought, I was learning that our access to La Loma, the right of any league to operate in a city park, was also a financial equation. We got everything for free—the fields, the lights, the chalk, the snack bar—but it was all predicated on at least 51 percent of our participants being Monterey Park residents. Every municipality, I suppose, is entitled to regulate its resources as it sees fit, but our enrollment was so moribund when I took over, the urgency so great, it was ridiculous to think we might turn people away solely on the basis of their address. As the league thrived, I probably could have afforded to be more discriminating, but I hardly thought of that as my mission. A healthy La Loma, as I saw it, benefited all of Monterey Park. We were a small town, far from self-contained—folks traversed the city limits all day, to go to work, to school, to the supermarket—and I, of all people, was not about to police who belonged and who did not.

Nobody asked me to in the beginning, but by my third year, even more in my fourth, the city had begun invoking the 51 percent rule. It became a tool, for reining us in, or if not that, squeezing us for money. I never did learn what the fee schedule would have been if we had come up short—prohibitive is my guess—because I kept pledging to the city that we were in compliance and the city had no way of proving that we were not. I knew that whatever our numbers were, we were still ahead of the other programs that used the fields in our absence. I was hesitant to stir up a heap of trouble, but it had become clear that some local sharks were securing permits for La Loma—any Monterey Park resident could claim to be running a club team—then subleasing their access to out-of-town squads. You could go up there and discover a tournament going on, ostensibly hosted by a Monterey Park–based organization, even find the snack bar open and bustling, and not see a single Monterey Park kid on the field. It was hard to say how much cash was changing hands or going to whom, but there was no doubt that La Loma had become a commodity: Whenever we packed up for the winter, someone else was pimping it out. If we ever had to defend our claim to the park, to prove that our league, regardless of percentages, provided the greatest good for the greatest number, I was prepared to lead the charge, to rally a few hundred Monterey Park Sports Club families and march on city hall. Some of La Loma's most loyal and generous volunteers, Jonathan's family, Colin's family, lived in neighboring communities, and frankly, Monterey Park was lucky to have them.

One day Jonathan's mom pulled me aside. "I'm not sure we share the same politics," she began, a polite bit of understatement. Her values were strictly biblical, and my life, by comparison, was unorthodox and profane—and those were just the parts she knew about—and yet Mrs. Muñoz was offering me her endorsement, attesting to the fact that, at La Loma, we shared the same faith. "But if you ever run for office," she continued, "I'll vote for you."

I gave her a hug and shook my head. I had spent my life creating distance from Portland, from my mother's legacy, from anyone who might know me as Vera's son, and somehow, without quite realizing it, I had become the mayor of La Loma. Baseball was enough to sate my ambitions, but I was tickled when people saw themselves reflected in what I was doing, when my regard for the park reinforced their identity. One day I spotted my mailman wearing a Monterey Park Sports Club cap. That was strange. It looked just like some I had left, in a pile of baseball equipment, outside my front door. I was prepared to believe that his had come from some other source, maybe a board member, perhaps a niece or nephew in the league, but I had never even seen him at La Loma. I let it go the first time. A few days later he was wearing it again. I swung open the front door. "Nice hat," I said.

"It was sitting right there," he confessed.

"I see," I said. I wondered if he always helped himself to goodies on his appointed rounds. "I'm the baseball commissioner."

"I know."

"Really?"

"I thought, 'Maybe he won't mind me taking it,' " the mailman said. "I thought, 'Maybe he'll actually like me walking around with it on.' "

My mom's love of baseball, her appreciation for how a franchise can boost a community's fortunes, actually led to one of her sorest political disappointments. During her final term as mayor, she threw her support behind a bid to lure a Major League team to Portland, something that would have been unthinkable, for both Mom and the city, back when I was a boy wishing for more than the Beavers. With the Montreal Expos up for grabs, Mom helped stitch together a $350 million financing plan, then led a delegation to New York, to make her case before Commissioner Bud Selig's relocation committee. The city looked to have a fair shot—it was the largest market in the nation without an MLB franchise—and Mom even drummed up average rainfall statistics, which showed that during baseball season Portland was dryer than half the league's venues. A bumper sticker campaign was launched: BRING BIG LEAGUE BASEBALL TO PORTLAND.

If any mayor ever had the capital to make something like that happen, it should have been Mom. After her retirement, she would be getting a life-size bronze statue on the banks of the Willamette, and when I flew up for the unveiling, all three of us, Mom, me, and statue, landed on the front page of *The Oregonian*. But the reaction to her boosterism was merciless. Sportswriters accused her of naïveté and desperation, of allowing Selig's office to play Portland against other cities and sweeten the pot for the Expos. Teachers, fearing that resources might be diverted from public schools, printed their own bumper stickers: BRING MAJOR LEAGUE EDUCATION TO OREGON. One editorial compared Mom to Charlie Brown. In the end, as the baseball faithful know, the Expos became the Washington Nationals. Portland was not even among the finalists. The irony of all this is that Mom was undermined by the very city she helped to shape, by Portland's independence and liberalism, by its view of itself as the exception, not the rule. She insisted over and over that she was not blinded by sentiment, that a franchise would generate jobs and tourism, that the numbers made sense, but Portland had become such a baroque city, precious, green, European, that angling for a cut of the national pastime was thought to be on the verge of socially irresponsible. Baseball was the mainstream, and that was the last thing Portland wanted to be.

It was funny that Monterey Park was just the opposite, a city bypassed by corporate America and anxious to prove itself worthy of another chance. The Chinese metamorphosis that I had witnessed two decades earlier was complete: The Asian councilwoman I had met as a cub reporter now represented Monterey Park in the state assembly; her husband, an Asian immigration attorney, had just completed a term as Monterey Park's mayor; the Asian gang detective I had once interviewed had become Monterey Park's police chief; even the 7-Elevens sold the *Chinese Daily News*. Monterey Park had settled into a kind of Asian-American middle age, no longer quite a phenomenon, not even the front lines of new immigration and investment, which was spilling east, out Valley Boulevard and through the Puente Hills, into spiffier, more enterprising suburbs. The city had turned Chinese yet somehow remained as mom-and-pop as it had always been, lots of noodle houses and herb shops, still virtually no major retail or entertainment centers. It was killing the tax base and giving politicians, even those of Chinese descent, a bit of a hang-up: Where was our Olive Garden, our Gap? Many of them felt cheated, as if Monterey Park had finally learned to embrace its Asian identity only to be branded as too ethnic for the commercial mainstream.

Using words like *balance* and *choices,* the city began drafting a new set of guidelines, mandating that redevelopment projects reserve at least 51 percent of their square footage for nationally recognized chains. Baseball we wanted to keep homegrown, you might say, but our shopping—that we hoped to coax in from the outside. Council candidates would knock on my door, campaigning on the promise of a Target or a Krispy Kreme. It was so petty and parochial. I understood the economics, and admittedly, a decent bookstore would have been nice, but I had chosen Monterey Park precisely because it was not that kind of place. Maybe it was the Portlander in me: Why would I want my home to look like everywhere else?

Every Saturday afternoon, either before or after my team played, I would leave Max at La Loma and drive out to the Heman G. Stark Youth Correctional Facility, the largest juvenile prison in California. It was in Chino, about thirty miles to the east, on the frontier of the exurbs, where Mediterranean-style town houses abutted dairy farms and strawberry fields. A few hundred yards before I had to turn off the highway and check in at the guard shack, the city fathers had erected a sign: CHINO—100 BEST COMMUNITIES FOR YOUNG PEOPLE. I had to assume they meant the young people of free Chino, not the eight hundred or so killers and thieves and druggies who lived behind the rolls of razor wire on Euclid Avenue. Under the auspices of a nonprofit called InsideOUT Writers, I had started teaching, along with Abel, just about the time I became commissioner, first in Central Juvenile Hall, later at Heman G. Stark, a state institution for what might be described as criminal 'tweeners—teenage boys who had committed serious offenses but had been convicted as minors, not adults. The staff tended to eye volunteers like us with suspicion, do-gooders who were sure to be manipulated by the lies and laments of the wards. It was easy, I admit, to be cynical about what I was doing there, to ask why a bunch of adolescent knuckleheads were entitled to the guidance of a professional writer. Nobody was offering to help the guards unlock their creative potential, to see if the victims might benefit from putting their feelings down on paper. Did you have to do something really bad to qualify for my attention?

Freddy might have asked the same thing. He was on my mind every time I made the trip: our oddly parallel forays into the gang world, his recklessness, my blind spots, all that had been lost to the chasms between us. Every felon I mentored at Stark could have been him, just as every child I watched over at La Loma was one I hoped to keep out of this place. It was all part of the same reclamation project, the need to mend, to heal, to repay. I could not predict whether it was too late for Freddy—I hoped not—but I had to keep proving at least one thing, that it was not too late for me.

It was strange making the transition from park to jail, baseball to lockdown. One minute I would be surrounded by kids in Dodger uniforms, the next by kids in government-issue Dickies. Once, while I was still at juvenile hall, I found myself trying to explain metaphors to a sixteen-year-old space case, and when he mentioned his last name, I nearly choked. There were two boys in our league, a T-Baller and a Rookie, with that very name, an uncommon one, and I was beginning to suspect that I was not just their commissioner but a literary coach to their older brother. "Where are you from?" I asked. That was a loaded question in L.A. street culture, often the precursor to a fight or a shoot-out, and I should have known better.

"What do you mean?" he asked warily.

"Sorry," I said. "I mean, you're from Monterey Park, aren't you?"

"You know Monterey Park?"

"Dude, I'm the baseball commissioner."

"La Loma?"

"I think I know your family," I said. His mom scared me a little, a haggard lady with purple bags under her eyes and a mouth of missing teeth. She always seemed to have a gaggle of kids clinging to her, whether at the park, where I often saw her volunteering in the snack bar, or at Max's elementary school, where she served as membership coordinator for the PTA. "Man, that's such a trip," my student said. He had a brown scar across the base of his throat, the remnant of a tracheotomy tube. Paramedics had apparently found him shot in the belly, choking on his own blood and bile. "If you see my mom," he added, "will you tell her I said hi?"

I said I would, but I never got around to it. I was reluctant to embarrass her. Not too many people at La Loma knew I had a foot in both worlds, youth sports and youth crime, and I thought maybe I would be doing her a favor if I tried to keep them separate.

At the front gates of Stark, I had to empty my pockets and pass through a metal detector, then slide my driver's license through a slot in the bulletproof glass. A scrolling message board offered digital greetings from the Department of Corrections and *Rehabilitation,* which did not bode well for anyone who still held out hope that some rehabilitation might be going on within these walls. I was issued a PAD, a personal alarm device—basically, a panic button on a rope—which I could trigger on my own or which, if I were to ever become horizontal, would automatically do it for me. On my first visit, I tried to explain to the guards that I would not be needing one, that it seemed like a poor way to start off, to signal to my students that I feared them. "It's not optional," the supervisor said.

Stark had a medieval reputation, with order maintained by a regimen of isolation cages and pepper spray and antipsychotic drugs, but I was allowed to teach in the Catholic chapel, away from the daily mayhem, even to fire up the Mr. Coffee and share the candy I brought in from the 99¢ Only Store. Most of my students, among them Tripper and Angel and Bad Cat and Risk-e, were uncomfortable with the protocols of proper English, but they had stories to tell: They had suffered and plundered and sabotaged themselves and still, with all their scars, remained alive, resolute. We would sit around a long wooden table, like at some graduate seminar, and I would slip off my PAD, wedge it upright between a stack of books, and urge them to write honestly instead of *correctly,* to teach me, in whatever words spilled forth, about their capacity for regret and compassion. "We're all gangsters, like fuck the stuff and hope to die and all that kind of shit," Risk-e told me one day.

An accessory to a gang hit, he had perpetual Fred Flintstone stubble and black hair slicked into a ponytail and an unnerving certainty that bad karma awaited him on the outs. "But you come in here," he said, "and you see something in us, something that no one else does, not even our own parents."

For Christmas, I hired the Monterey Park Sports Club's trophy company to make them T-shirts, which featured a pen crossed over a sword. For the Fourth of July, my students made me a batch of pruno—prison moonshine—fueled by ketchup, sugar, and rotten fruit. It was big-time contraband, but, hell, I had not smuggled it in. The crud was brewed on Heman G. Stark's watch. "If I go blind," I told the boys, "you're going to hear from my lawyer." They laughed and called me a lightweight. The first sip was sweet and syrupy, like unset Jell-O, but I swallowed it and kept on drinking, my pledge to them and theirs to me that there was no divide that could not be bridged. "Just be careful driving home," each of them said.

The year that I added Stark to my rounds was also the year that Carmen started making jailhouse pilgrimages of her own. For as long as I had known her, she had pleaded with Christopher to stay off the streets, to think of his future, to consider the harm he might bring to his half brothers and half sisters, but her son was twenty by then, an adult, and determined, it seemed, to squander every chance. On the surface there was no rationale for it, no deprivation or abuse even close to that weathered by my Chino boys, and yet I am sure that Carmen was right, that it all came down to his father, the missing link of his childhood, the stranger who had run off with Christopher's past and swindled his future, just as Freddy's dad had with his.

On a Sunday night that August, some time around 2 A.M., a pair of East L.A. sheriff's deputies pulled into an alley just beyond the Monterey Park city limits. They saw two men spray-painting graffiti on a garage door and, standing next to them, Christopher, as if he were the lookout. The officers shined their lights. Before Christopher took off running, the cops saw him toss away a gun, a

loaded .22. At the preliminary hearing, a sheriff's investigator tes-
tified that Christopher was a member of the Lott Stoners gang—
"Lott," the name of a hilltop party spot in East L.A., was tattooed on
the back of his neck—and that he was known as Villain. "Villain
from the Lott," the investigator told the court. Christopher was
being held on $50,000 bail, which Carmen was unable to come up
with. She was almost relieved, truthfully, to have him in jail, to
know where he was, to be able to sleep at night without worrying
about getting that call, the one she dreaded. She was also not going
to ask Eddie to pay for a lawyer again, not the way their marriage
was going. So she resigned herself to a long autumn, then winter,
of visits, driving up the Golden State Freeway on weekends to the
Wayside detention center, out near Magic Mountain. She asked
me to recommend books for Christopher (my first choice: Luis J.
Rodriguez's *Always Running*), and I said, with a hint of jest, that it
was too bad that he was not a few years younger, so that he might
have ended up in my writing class. Somehow that was not what Carmen wanted to hear. She was a full-time stay-at-home mom—
Eddie's salary afforded her that option—and raising kids was
supposed to be her forte, the one thing she had always known she
was good at. How had it slipped away? How had Christopher become Villain? How had she allowed herself to drift so far from her
husband, from the relationship that was intended to fix everything?

Carmen and I had been together for a long time by that point,
longer than either of us would have ever thought feasible, and never
once had she appeared to wrestle with her conscience. To the contrary, she had felt guilty about not feeling guilty and wondered what
that said about her. Now with Christopher locked up—he had
pleaded no contest to carrying a concealed weapon, a sixteen-month
term—Carmen was starting to doubt it all: baseball, me, herself,
everything she had done to gratify her longings. While she was busy
playing La Commish, the Lott had been looking after her son.

"I'm just so weak," she told me. "You've been taking advantage
of a weak lady."

That stung. I thought I had been endorsing Carmen, exhorting her to stretch her wings and soar, not scheming to have my way with her. I wanted her to see that I could be counted on, that if she could get herself unstuck, I would be there for her, waiting, prepared to help with anything. "I want to be a good person in your life," I said. "I want to be someone who lifts you up, not drags you down."

Carmen was pushing back. She knew my patterns and predilections, the leaps I had made for my marriage, the chances I had taken for my stories, all that I had put up with in the name of La Loma— and she did not want to be added to the list, another challenge, a new test. "I don't want to be rescued," Carmen said, exasperated. "I don't want you to be with me just because you're trying to prove something to yourself." Could it have been that simple? That I was still that boy being pulled away from the piñata, forsaking the candy, wondering what it was about me, my family, that kept us outside the circle? Was I still so worried about being a fake, that milksop in San Miguel, that sightseer in The Lotus Room, that buccaneer in Cuba, that I would do anything to convince Carmen of my trueness, my mettle? She may have been a citizen, every bit as Americanized as I was, but she did come with a lot of baggage, if you wanted to be blunt about it: Why was that not scaring me off?

What should have alarmed me more than anything was the tumult I was poised to visit upon Max. My connection to him was supposed to be inviolate, nonnegotiable. One squint, a cough, a nod, a grumble, and we could read each other's thoughts, crack each other up. We spoke to each other in Rasta patois and Deep South ebonics, Nicaraguan pidgin and Renaissance Faire English. Every morning I woke Max up by tugging his toes and singing him "Home on the Range." He mimicked the basso profundo of the afternoon deejay on the smooth jazz station, inviting me to join him on the "no stress express," and he quoted me lines from *The Shining*, about Jack, the mad writer, needing to "correct" his troublesome son. Even with Christiám in the garage, we had a small and quiet house, our bedrooms side by side, and with Freddy gone, I had been able to turn the third bedroom into an office. Our life together was just how I

wanted it, how I had fought for it to be, and now I seemed to be prepared to dynamite the whole thing. Was I really going to drag Max
into a lopsided Brady Bunch, Carmen's five to my one, or expose
him to the capers of yet another gun-toting stepson? Max was the
center of my universe, except for when Carmen was. I was not even
sure I was making sense to myself. I was swearing my love to her without alerting him, imagining a future before I could even admit to the
present. Something about that picture was warped, and yet I was so
caught up in it—in exiting La Loma with Carmen as my award—that
I ignored the peril, my own contradictions.

Max surely picked up some hints along the way. Whenever he
needed to transport a group of friends, more than I could fit in my
car, I borrowed Carmen's minivan, and whenever we went on vacation, I hired one of her daughters to care for Sheba, the jealous
Korean guard dog we had adopted after the guinea pigs disappeared. Still, we never discussed what I was up to, why there
seemed to be no other females in my life, until one night in 2007
when a pair of headlights flashed in the driveway and I found Carmen outside, in her pajamas, trembling and barefoot. It was after
ten—Max had school the next morning—and I tried to slip her
past his bedroom, into my office. "I'm so done, so done," she kept
saying between sobs. There had been an ugly fight at home, about
where she had been and what she had been doing, and to escape the
questions, her husband's rising mistrust, Carmen had simply run
for the door. I wrapped her in a blanket, as if she had stumbled in
from a storm, and held her as tight as I could. I had heard her say
those words before, but now I believed them to be true, and I realized how much I had been waiting for this to happen, for Carmen
to come to me in her darkest hour, to let me show her that I was not
a threat to her freedom but her ticket to it, for her to show me
how much I was needed. Once she had stopped shaking, I dried her
eyes with my fingertips. She wanted to call a girlfriend, to find a safe
place to sleep. I left her alone in the office and went to check on Max.

He was lying on his back, in the dark, wide awake. I sat down on the edge of his bed. "How you doin', champ?" I asked. We had been through so much together, my boy and I, so many changes, so many seasons. He had known me as a father, a coach, a commissioner, a writer, a teacher, even a homemaker, but he had little experience with me as a man in need of a woman. "Dad," Max said, "do you mind telling me what the hell's going on?"

Chapter

Fifteen

FOR MOST OF HIS LIFE MAX HAS HAD A SKATEBOARD TO play with—a *squirt*board, he called it at first—but from one day to the next it ceased being a toy and reentered his life as a tool. It happened in eighth grade, the same age I was when I walked away from baseball, and just as suddenly every teenager in Southern California seemed to be ollying over something, a pop culture outbreak of athleticism and rebellion. Skating was the one sport, as best as I could figure, that existed primarily because parents feared it. You could say that about music, about dance, about pink Mohawks and pierced lips, but I could not think of another game or contest that offered middle-class kids such subversive delights. It had more in common with my father's stickball days in Brooklyn than with what we did at La Loma: no schedule, no rule book, no umpires, no designated playing area. No coaches.

Max started in the driveway, practicing tricks off the curb. He scavenged cinder blocks and plywood from around the house, assembling makeshift ramps that teetered and bowed. He spent hours on the computer, glued to YouTube videos, dissecting the styles of skating's new pioneers, the vocabulary and brands, the pain tolerances. He hung a poster above his bed, with a caption intended to make even the most liberal parent queasy: "Because bones heal and chicks dig scars." The winter after I became commissioner, Max had written half a dozen New Year's resolutions—get straight As, walk the dog farther than ever, encourage friends to be better people—that were so sweet, I stuck them to the refrigerator door; now he had amended, well, to my eye, *defaced* them, to include the battle cry "SKATE IT UP!"

As he got better, he got bolder, stretching the boundaries of skatable terrain from out of the cul-de-sac to the end of the block, then around the corner, then up to the parking lot of his old elementary school. I gulped the first time Max skated off like that—he had been right in front of the house, suddenly he was gone—and I marched out the door like a bounty hunter, cracking my knuckles and clenching my jaw. I caught up to him on the next street over.

"Where the hell do you think you're going?" I barked.

Max had found a curb he liked more than the curb on our street. "Sorry, Dad," he mumbled. "I'll tell you next time."

"No, you'll ask me next time," I said.

I was playing the heavy, a role I knew already I could not possibly sustain. It was my responsibility to keep tabs on Max, to know where he was at all times, but it seemed futile, even counterproductive, to think I could keep him tethered to a dead end. Max's passion was shared by Alex—this was the juncture at which they became Blackness and Cream—and together they continued to push the limits, physical and geographical and parental, of where their boards could take them. They scoured the neighborhood, and then beyond, for stairs and banisters, ledges and breaches, assigning names to their favorite obstacles: the Montebello Ten, the DMV Nine, the Hazard Rail, the Library Gap. It was almost as if they were seeing the place we lived for the very first time, inventing functions for what would otherwise be mundane features of the paved universe, reimagining public space and claiming it for themselves.

Maybe I am phrasing that a little too fancily. I was worried sick. It seemed almost inevitable that Max was going to break his neck or get ticketed or stumble upon some homies with their own ideas about turf. I tried to get him to wear safety equipment, a helmet if nothing else, but that was antithetical to the street skater's ethos, which was to feel every scrape and bruise in the depths of your being, to wear your misfires as your trophies. We talked about respecting the job that security guards were hired to do, about what constitutes trespassing and vandalism. I pointed out certain neighborhoods, certain parks, that I expected him to avoid, and set curfews, usually dusk, that were not open to compromise.

"Dad, I know what's up," Max would tell me. "I know how to handle myself."

I would chuckle and snort and fold my arms across my chest. "That's true," I would say. "Generally speaking. But things have a way of creeping up on you before you know it, before you even have a chance to get yourself out of it."

Max was sure that he had a fuddy-duddy for a dad, that I was in the grip of some alarmist hangover from my gang days—and the fact was, he had begun to skate all across East L.A., through communities whose tribulations I had written about before he was born. With his mophead (the Jew-fro, he called it) tucked under a Yankees beanie (he lied about wearing that crap only in New York), my son appeared to fit right in, or at least he did not seem conflicted about whether he did or not. He had his own reference points, a skater's map of the city, and little by little he convinced me that his board granted him something akin to free passage, even in the barrio—that it announced him as neutral and transient, concerned only with topography, not with the rivalries and transactions of whatever fiefdoms he happened to be traversing.

While working on a school project about Ruben Salazar, the *Los Angeles Times* columnist slain in East L.A. by sheriff's deputies, Max happened upon a 1971 account by Hunter S. Thompson—"Strange

Rumblings in Aztlan"—and when I gave him a brief primer on gonzo journalism, his mind leaped directly to skating. There were three or four boys, including Alex, who were his regular partners, and Max decided from that point on they would be Team Gonzo.

For Christmas, he asked for a video camera, which his grandparents helped me finance, and with it, skating was transformed from mere adventure into material, the stuff of highlight reels and demo tapes. Max's existence revolved around capturing Team Gonzo's most harrowing stunts on film, both the triumphs and the wipeouts that made the triumphs even grander. It was how you got noticed by a skate shop or a board maker or a fashion house, the path to sponsorship, his ticket to the X Games. He would come home from a day in the trenches, from loading docks and schoolyards, office parks and rooftops, and start editing his footage, then posting it online. "Check it out, Dad, this is sick," he would say. There were clips of Max leaping staircases, flying over nine, ten, eleven steps, hitting the ground on his back, skidding over the concrete, wincing and moaning, then springing to his feet and doing it all over again. "This is where I beefed it," he would tell me. "This is where I gooched it. This is where I pop-shoved it and got mad air."

If I found it hard to share in Max's enthusiasm, or even to understand what he was saying at times, I was just as reluctant to discourage him. Given a choice, I would not have picked skateboarding to be the first great obsession of his adolescence, but I was not given a choice—I did not *get* a choice—and I made the calculation that reining him in, even if it spared him from serious injury, would do more harm than good. Skating was his love, an expression of his courage and creativity, and as much as I fretted that I might be wrong, I refused to be in the role of teaching him to doubt himself.

The first casualty of skating was, not surprisingly, baseball. Once it became apparent that I was stuck with a fourth year as commissioner, Max had agreed to play that season, but after 2006, it was understood, he intended to quit—or, from my perspective, to terminate his Little League dad. It did not help that we had made the move up to Triple A and that without Jonathan, who was committed to travel ball, and without Colin or Natalie or Justin, who had all stayed behind in Double A, the season had gone even worse than predicted. We had devolved into the flunkies of the division, winners of just a single game. Max was going through the motions, as if he had left everything he had out on the field in that preposterous title series the year before and now had nothing more to give.

I had tried to cater to him at the closing ceremony, to recognize his life beyond baseball, by inviting him to perform the national anthem. He had started a thrash metal band called Confucius Say—or at least until the other guitarist's mother, a longtime associate of the Asian Pacific American Legal Center, vetoed the name—and I thought he would get a kick out of plugging in his golden Stratocaster knockoff at home plate and doing a Jimi Hendrix impersonation. Max humored me. He cranked it up and rocked La Loma, the last hurrah of his farewell tour. I took one final bow myself: "I love this park, this league, and to see it grow, as if it were my own child, has made me immensely proud." A friend of the Muñozes draped a lei of purple orchids around my neck. I gave my keys to Gil and Liz.

I felt relieved but also strangely unsettled, about what I was going to do with myself, about what was going to come of Max. I hated to think that baseball was so expendable, that my son could turn thirteen and all our years of practice, of play, could simply grind to a halt. I wondered if maybe, had I been a better coach, more demanding, more sure of my own ability to perform what I was teaching, I could have kept him motivated, engaged by the game. I wondered if maybe, had I not been so distracted by my duties as commissioner, by my pursuit of Carmen, I could have kept La Loma simpler for him, less fraught with adult predicaments. It was too late to change any of that. Max was all about finding his own footing now, about trying to extract himself from my shadow.

Every morning in the kitchen, as I made coffee, he would greet me, toe to toe, in his boxers. He would puff his chest and cock his chin, taking his measure of me, of himself. "How tall are you, again?" he would ask.

"Taller than you," I would say.

"I'm not so sure about that."

"In your dreams, son."

"No, in *yo'* dreams, son."

"Huh?"

"Oh, you heard. I think I done passed you by."

He would flex his biceps for me, then his abs, and dare me to punch him as hard as I could. I noticed that he had begun to pluck his eyebrows and that he was dousing himself in some drugstore body spray that smelled of citrus and leather. His showers were getting longer, the bathroom door consistently locked. He was spending a lot of time on MySpace, IM-ing with an enticing Vietnamese girl from school, but as best as I could tell, skating also came before romance, and for that I was grateful. The U.S. Army had somehow flagged Max, and recruiters were leaving messages on his cell, trying to woo him into becoming a soldier. Having just spent half a year on a story about the life of a new enlistee, I knew how the spiel went. Someone had to serve, but my son was not fair game. "The next time those fuckers call," I told him, "you're putting me on the phone." If I did something that Max approved of, say, spiff myself up in a creased Pendleton or do an interview with Ice Cube, he would tell me that I was gangster. Not *a* gangster; it was an adjective, spoken with varying degrees of irony, to indicate fortitude and panache. If I did something that Max associated with weakness, say, listen to the Dixie Chicks or wear my Crocs out in public, he would call me a fruit. As for himself, he had concocted another alias, a stage name that sounded half porn star, half pro wrestler: M. Fury. It was written on his social studies notebook. We were as close as ever, but the balance of power was shifting. My influence was eroding, and his invincibility was off the charts.

Max had agreed to one more season of basketball, the winter of eighth grade, which would take us into early 2007, then I would officially exit the Monterey Park Sports Club—return to what I had remembered as "civilian life"—and he would head off to high school. It would be the end, too, of my partnership with Todd, who had found that our league, for all its aggravations, was still more of a balm and had continued, in one form or another, to function as my adviser and ally. Our boys had given us a lifetime of memories, and now Max and Alex were doing exactly what teenagers have been doing for eternity, which is to separate themselves from the tribe, to know it all, to make it up. Every couple of weeks, the four of us went out for wet burritos, always at the same cheesy combo-plate joint, and while the kids turned the silverware into a terrain park for their Tech Decks, Todd and I would slurp margaritas and try not to be morose.

During that final basketball season, my dad and Dianne made arrangements to fly down, to see Max play. It was just a regular game, no title at stake, no scores to settle, but it was going to be their last chance to catch us in action, father and son, coach and pro-tégé. Their flight was due on a Friday afternoon. I was tied up that day, teaching a journalism class at the University of California, Irvine, but I told Max that we would head to the airport as soon as I got home. He would have to wait for me there, alone, for an hour or two after school, which was not a big deal. He had a key and he had Sheba, and as a backup, I let Christiám know that Max would be by himself, if he had a chance to slip out of work early and check on his little cousin. I left the campus about 3 P.M. and headed up the 405, no place to be with a weekend on the horizon. My folks were already in the air, and I would have to ride the brakes for at least an hour just to get to Max. I called his cell. I heard laughter before he answered. "Where are you?" I asked. There were more voices, more giggles. "Home," Max said.

"Why am I hearing other people?"

"Um, just a couple friends."

"Nobody should be there without my permission." The voices turned to whispers and shushes, then another burst of giggles. "Max?"

"Yeah, Dad. It's cool. They were just leaving."

"Not cool. I want everyone gone. Now."

I hung up. Max knew better. He was taking advantage of my schedule, of my inattention. We would have a talk when I got there. A few minutes later, my cell rang. It was Christiám. He was twenty-six already, a grown man, but he had become part of our family, at once a companion to Max and a defender of my interests as a dad. He was not going to let either of us lose sight of what we had. "Hey, *tío,*" Christiám said. "I think we have a problem."

"I know," I said. "I already told Max they had to leave."

"That's not, uh, really the problem," Christiám said.

"What are you talking about?"

"Well, Max told me not to say anything to you."

"And?"

"But I don't think that's right."

"What's not right?"

"I got home early, because you told me that he would be there, and I've just sort of had a feeling about him lately, about what he's been up to, and when I opened the door, they were in the bathroom, and I could smell it. They were, you know, *fumando —fumando marijuana.*"

"Smoking pot?"

"I told Max I wasn't in favor of that."

"Put him on the phone right now."

There was rustling, a hand over the mouthpiece, then Max, quieter this time, unsure of what I had been told.

"This is bullshit, Max," I said.

"They're gone," Max said.

"I'm talking about you. I don't know what the hell you're thinking."

"I'm sorry."

"That's not what I'm fishing for."

"I promise it won't happen again."

"We'll talk about that part later. What I'm concerned with right now is that we're headed to the airport in a few minutes, to pick up your grandparents. Did that even cross your mind? They're flying down here to see you. Not just because you have a basketball game tomorrow but because they love you. They want to spend time with you. They want Max. They're not coming to see some smoked-out zombie."

"Please, Dad, don't tell them. *Please.* They don't have to know."

"No, they probably don't. If I can help it, I'll try not to ruin everyone's weekend. But don't think for a second that this is the end of it."

"I know."

I put down the phone. "Fuck!" I shouted. I slammed the steering wheel with the heel of my hand. I was stuck in traffic, and my son was getting high. I was angry at Max, at myself, at Team Gonzo, at puberty, at middle school, at Dave Chappelle and Harold & Kumar and Seth Rogen, at Freddy, whose left shoulder bore a tattoo of a skull puffing on a joint, at the DEA, at NORML, at the Mexican cartels, at the great American ritual of self-medication. I knew that weed was not the end of the world; actually, I knew that too well. I was exactly Max's age the first time someone handed me a pipe, just finishing eighth grade the moment I realized that smoking dope, for a supposedly bad thing, had the power to make you feel pretty damn good. I smoked it a lot for about a year, even fancied myself something of a connoisseur. I bought *High Times* at the neighborhood record store, which also sold me roach clips and rolling papers, and I moved my bedroom into the basement, which was ancient and mossy but two stories away from my parents, and I covered the rafters in Kiss posters and zoned out to Rush, *2112,* on eight-track. As a freshman—as the freshman class president—I got stoned on my way to school in the morning and got stoned on my way home in the afternoon. Sometimes I ditched lunch and walked across Eighteenth Avenue to Civic Stadium, home of the Beavers, where I sneaked through a fence and crouched under the bleachers and got stoned in the very arena that had introduced me to grown-up baseball. My folks, as I remember, never policed me, in part because of the era we were in and in part because they were not by nature forbidders. I was expected to think for myself, to reject absolutes, to make my own mistakes, and if I could do all that without feeling guilty—this was one of my dad's maxims—I could finally consider myself mature.

I had never talked about any of this with Max, and I was not sure that I was ready to share it just yet, but I had time in the car, as I smoldered on the freeway, to think about what I did want to say. Like so many parents of my generation, I agonized over being exposed as a hypocrite about drugs, feared that if my own experiences were to come up in conversation, my ability to set boundaries and enforce rules would be compromised. Everyone I knew in high school and college smoked pot—something like a hundred million Americans have partaken at least once—and most of us turned out reasonably well. But you go and have children, and then what? Do you strap on that death mask, the one that adults wear to pretend they know more than they actually do? Do you lie? Omit? Avoid? Do you fess up but trot out the lame argument that things were somehow different back then? If I was really honest with myself, I did not want to raise a child so incurious about the world that he would never think of taking a puff. It was inevitable that Max would do so—and probably, dare I say, a positive indicator—and yet I certainly did not want to be in the position of encouraging it or suggesting that it was inconsequential. Even if most pot smokers never became druggies, I knew enough who were. I had to ensure that Max did not get derailed like Freddy. Or like Christopher. Or like any of my boys in the juvenile pen.

Sometimes I confused myself with all these competing plots, all my conflicting inclinations. I seemed to be unusually permissive about certain matters and unusually directive about others, indulgent and diligent, a risk taker and a control freak, at once impetuously following my heart and steadfastly keeping my word. How could I possibly make sense of all that for Max, convey to him that what he had done was okay but not okay, that his little afternoon smoke session belonged to a narrative I had been grappling with most of my life? He was waiting for me when I got home. Before I could say anything, he hugged me, his arms strong, like fireplace tongs, and I knew at that moment that Max would be the one to show me, just as I had with my parents, the way out of our discontent.

On Saturday we took Dad and Dianne to the gym. They were delighted, as always, to get reacquainted with Max—I had kept them in the dark about the flare-up that had preceded their arrival, and he had comported himself well—but there was a part of me that just wanted to get it over with, the game, the season, the whole illusion that my son and I were still invested in the same thing. As we walked toward the doors, I noticed the old folding table out front, the same old chairs and flyers, and I realized that baseball registration was already under way and, for the first time in four years, without me running the show. I had reconciled myself to that, knew it was for the best, but to stumble upon sign-ups, to be reminded that I was done not just as commissioner but as a coach and a parent, was the most tangible indication yet of everything that had changed. La Loma was gearing up, another year, a new chapter. Max and I were limping to the end. "Looks like a pretty good turnout," I said.

"Yep," Max said. "Why don't we sign up?"

"What?"

"One more season."

"Are you serious?"

"Let's just do it."

"What happened to the boy who wasn't 'feelin' it' anymore?"

"Well, yeah, I know," Max said, "but I need to earn your trust back. I thought this would be a good way to start."

My son was about to turn fourteen, and he was offering me an extension on his childhood. He was doing it as penance, under stress, maybe even to distract and placate me. Bless his guilty little heart. I was taking it. I waved to Liz, the female half of my replacement team, who gave me a sigh and a sneer, as if to ask what the hell I had roped her into. "Hello, Madam Commissioner," I said. "Would you happen to have room for another Triple A coach?"

"I thought we had gotten rid of you," she said.

"Slight change of plans," I said.

"Let me see what I can do," she said, "but I'll probably have to check with Gilbert." Her husband performed dental surgeries on Saturdays, made more money that one day of the week than most Monterey Park families made in a month, which meant he was missing sign-ups and, in fact, would be ceding a good chunk of his baseball duties to Liz. She did not seem too thrilled about holding down the fort while he got to play figurehead—the pope of La Loma, Gil drolly had begun to call himself—but that was for them to work out. I just wanted back in for another season, a chance to make up for all the years I was forced to put the league before Max. I have no memory of the basketball game that afternoon. I was already thinking ahead to baseball, to rosters and practices and equipment, to oiling the gloves and loosening our arms. Todd was there, at the gym, and I tried to explain to him, as discreetly as possible, what had happened, that I had just signed up Max for a ninth season of baseball, our eighteenth in the Monterey Park Sports Club if you counted both programs. "I'll have to fill you in later," I said. "But we're back in business, baby!"

"That's unbelievable," Todd said.

"My head is spinning."

"I don't know about Alex."

"Just give Max a chance to work on him," I said. "I think peer pressure will be in our favor."

I was on the phone that evening to Jose Muñoz. I had to have Jonathan back, no matter what. He could be a prima donna, skip every practice, show up with his private batting instructor, roll a Barcalounger into the dugout for all I cared, but our lone Triple A season without him had been a catastrophe. "Take pity on us," I pleaded. There was really nothing at La Loma for Jonathan any-more, nothing to gain, nothing to prove, but he had been aware of our struggles, even witnessed a drubbing or two, and for old times' sake, Jose thought the whole family would favor an encore. "Every-one felt bad about last year," he said. "If Jonathan can help Max, I'm pretty sure he will."

Then I put in calls to Colin and Natalie. Each of them should have moved up to Triple A the previous season with Max, but because Natalie was a girl and Colin was, well, a lot frailer than Natalie, I had granted them waivers to spend a third year in Double A. That probably would have been the end of their La Loma careers, too: Triple A was so rough-and-tumble, neither family was intending to risk it, not if I was in retirement and unavailable to usher them through. "We heard you weren't coming back," Natalie's mom said. There was no need to go into details. "I was as surprised as anybody," I said. "Tell me you'll sign her up."

"Oh, gosh, Jess. I don't know. Do you really think she can handle it?"

"I don't have the slightest doubt. She might be the only girl in Triple A, but she'll still be better than a lot of these boys."

For everything to fall into place, I had one more piece of business, a somewhat rotten card to play. As a returning Triple A coach, I was supposed to inherit my team from the previous season, an advantage under almost any circumstances. Our two championships were both won that way, by keeping the roster intact and coming back for a second year in the same division. If I were to have done that in Triple A, though, I would not have had a shot at Jonathan, probably not even Colin or Natalie. My returning players would have locked me out of the first seven or eight rounds of the draft, leaving my ace to fall into enemy hands. Besides, some of those kids were so ungainly, I was ready to be free of them, anyway. I had done enough nurturing over the years. I wanted to spend my final season, Max's final season, surrounded by a team that could really play.

I called Gil and explained that he should not consider me a returning coach, that I had elected to dissolve my Triple A squad and start over from scratch. There was no rule prohibiting it, not that there was ever a hefty rule book to refer to, but it smelled of chicanery: I was shedding the weak to clear space for the strong. In theory, some kid I had coached the year before could have signed up, certain that he was guaranteed a spot on my team, only to be told that I was no longer coaching *that* team, that my team was actually a new team, and while, yes, a few players from the old team would still be on the new team, he was not among them. Gil deferred to me. Fortunately for both of us, the gawkiest of my former players never bothered to return, and with Triple A rules allowing for six freezes instead of the usual two, I was able to secure Jonathan and still reserve places for almost everyone else.

If you thought about the team I ended up with as the cast of a sitcom, the 2007 season would have been our reunion show, lots of hugs and tears, polished performances and sentimental flashbacks, and yet like every reunion show, I think we all knew that we had long ago jumped the shark, that we were clinging to memories, milking the laughs. It was sweet but familiar, which is not such a bad thing, just not the same thing as being at the start of your run, or in your prime, when it is all new and splendid and the end is still too far away to think about.

I loved having Natalie back in the infield, hair moussed and lips glossed, with a glove that could scoop anything out of the dirt. She had grown curvier, to the point of distraction, and it was not unusual to overhear middle-aged men slyly taking note, muttering about how it was just not right for a fourteen-year-old to be in such, um, good shape. I felt protective of Natalie—in my dugout, it was understood, nobody was to hound her—but I did get a charge out of watching her effect on the competition. I even put her in to pitch a few times, to let her shred some boyish egos. It was not a stunt: She had a crisp fastball and a deceptive sidearm, and those who underestimated her did so at their own risk. The first time it happened, on a June night, we had been thumping our opponents into a torpor, but when I sent Natalie out to start the fourth inning, the other team suddenly snapped out of it and began whooping as if a Hooters girl had just taken the mound. "H-O! H-O-M! H-O-M-E-R!" they chanted, rattling the fence and stomping their cleats. The whole park, in fact, seemed to come to life, a mix of curiosity and admiration and prurience. A chick was pitching in Triple A—unheard of—and if you checked out her MySpace page, you would know her as "MiiS.BooTY," the notorious "Natz," whose occupation was "Hottest Girl Alive." I looked over at Natalie's grandpa, a classic from the zoot suit era who had lost a couple of fingers long ago in a sheet metal accident, and we shared a smile. He had grown up on the Eastside when it still had a Jewish presence, when a Mexican boy could earn a quarter lighting the candles at the Breed Street Shul, and to have his granddaughter coached by a Jew, he once confided to me, was oddly consoling.

Natalie struck out the first batter she faced, and over the next three innings she struck out three more. It was a joyous spectacle— her victims did not know whether to fume or to blush—but one also tinged with melancholy. Natalie had bloomed so fast, her parents were already preparing to put an end to her coed days. In the fall, she would be headed to an all-girls high school, operated by the Sisters of the Holy Names.

As I had predicted, persuading Alex to return had not been difficult, even though his heart was less into baseball than Max's. They were inseparable—"homies for life," they both insisted—and if Max had stuck himself with another season, Alex was going to join him, if only out of solidarity. Besides, they had taken a new-found interest in La Loma's infrastructure, its steps and ledges and picnic tables, which seemed to invite kickflips and tailslides. They wore their skate shoes to the park and carried their boards with their equipment bags. To the league's younger kids—Carmen's middle son, Gil and Liz's two boys—Alex and Max were like Pied Pipers, heralds of a sport cooler than the one their parents coached, and soon La Loma was full of little skateboarding baseball players. When they freestyled, Alex may have been a hair better than Max, nimbler on his feet and jazzier in his execution. Max probably qualified as the leader, a bit worldlier in his knowledge and humor, but Alex was the actor, kinetic, giggly, malleable, often one step ahead of himself. For as long as we had been playing at La Loma, it had been Alex's job to get on base and Max's to knock him in.

I was sure that one last season of collaboration would do us all good, but before we could get started Todd once again called with bad news: He was suspending Alex, indefinitely, from all sports.

"He's in a world of trouble," Todd said. "I think you have some idea. But there's a lot more."

"Oh, man," I said. "I'm really sorry, Todd."

"No, we owe you an apology. Alex really needs to make some changes in his life."

"Max is going to be so bummed."

"Maybe you can get him to talk some sense into Alex. Max is the one friend who I think can lead him in the right direction."

Max knew most of the story already, a dispiriting tale that involved one of Alex's older brothers and featured many of the setbacks I had endured with Freddy, minus the bullet. Whereas Max was ten years younger than Freddy, Alex was just three years behind his brother, old enough to be lured out of the house in the middle of the night with him, to joyride and party until it was time for school, while Todd slept and his wife nursed newborns on the rich side of town. "Honestly," Max told me, "I don't know what he's thinking." I could tell it was weighing on him, not just the disappointment of losing Alex as a teammate and a skate buddy but the fear of losing Alex altogether, of having the greatest friend he had ever known stray into the mire, beyond Max's reach. He felt obligated but also powerless; our homes were separated by only a dozen blocks, but Max and I, for all the gambles I was taking, had achieved our own brand of stability, and Alex was caught in the middle of a whole bunch of unknowns. It was about that time, I noticed, that Max started giving hugs to Todd, too. A month into the season, after missing the first eight games, Alex was allowed back on the team. He had salvaged his grades—the school year would be over in a couple of weeks—and whatever else was still amiss, Todd figured that Alex could do a lot worse than spend time at La Loma.

"I was sort of hoping you would come to that conclusion," I told Todd. "He belongs out there with us."

"Whatever Max has been saying to him," Todd told me, "it's had a real impact."

We even started making plans to send Alex up to Portland

with Max that summer, to bask in the restorative glow of the grand-parents. The boys would spend a week getting spoiled by Mom, Dad, and Dianne, capped by a train ride to Seattle, to catch a Mariners game. I was so proud of Max's example, of the duty he felt to straighten himself out, if only to shore up a friend. In another year, though, Alex would begin to slip again, and this time Todd would not hesitate, vowing to save his son with the toughest love he could muster. It killed Max to have to say goodbye. He never imag-ined Alex as a cadet, shipped off to an all-boys military school.

I spent a lot more time playing catch with Max that season, out in the same cul-de-sac that had been our training camp for nearly a decade. Across the street lived the world's crankiest Hawaiian, with a pristine lawn and a forest of white plumerias. Ever since we had moved in, he had eyed us with irritation, complaining loudly about every loose ball that happened to roll onto his property. "Can't you do that in the park?" he would growl. We had learned over time to adjust our angles, to avoid putting his house on the receiving end, but even after all these years of practice, it was futile. The ball seemed to delight in stirring up trouble, invariably getting away from one of us and caroming into his garden.

"Go get it, Max."

"You go get it."

"I told you first."

"Maybe if you had thrown it halfway decent I could have caught it."

"Quickly, before he comes out."

"You need to man up, Dad. Grow a pair."

"You need to go get that ball if you ever want to see your fif-teenth birthday."

Max wanted to concentrate on his pitching, to see if he could rival Jonathan, if not in velocity then in the junk department. Breaking balls—curves, sliders, splitters, slurves—were the one aspect of the game that mirrored the inventiveness and variations of skating, the only occasion on which a player was said to have *stuff*, a repertoire of feints and frills. I had little time for that his first

Triple A season, my last as commissioner, but now that I was just a coach, I was still not much help, and it had nothing to do with being cautious, with labrums or ligaments. I quit playing the year I turned thirteen, the age at which curveballs traditionally were introduced, before I was allowed to throw one, before I was forced to hit one. I hated to admit it, but I had never learned.

"C'mon, Dad," Max insisted. "Just show me."

"You know, kiddo, pitching is all about location," I told him. "Hitting your spots, painting the corners. You don't need all that fancy stuff."

"Is this how you grip a curve?" he asked, stretching his thumb and forefinger around the seams.

"Um, well, if I were you, I would really be working on a change-up," I said. "That's all you need at this age. Fastball and change. Keep the hitters off balance."

"Tell me if this breaks," Max said, rearing back and flinging one over my head.

"It could use a little fine-tuning."

"Teach me, then. You must have *some* idea."

What I never learned in the 1970s, I was shamed into tackling the twenty-first-century way. I went to YouTube, just as Max had done for his introduction to skating tricks, and in the search field I typed, "How to throw . . ." A menu of options instantly dropped down, from a sinker to a screwball to a cutter (not to mention a knife and a boomerang), and I began clicking through instructional videos, looking for someone marginally authoritative and not just a kid in his bedroom talking smack. I took notes on grips and arm slots, release points and rotations—"turn this hand in, cock that wrist, and pull straight down," one coach advised—and after I deemed myself reasonably certain of what needed to be done, at least in theory, I summoned Max to the cul-de-sac again, and we began to experiment. Balls were flying everywhere, skidding across the asphalt, pinging off the back of my car, hurtling through rose-bushes and lava rocks. I chased them all down and lobbed them back to Max, who wiped his brow and doused the pavement with spittle. He needed less speed, more follow-through, better spin off his fingertips—I thought—or maybe it was more pressure on his middle finger, less flicking of his wrist.

"Okay, Dad, this one's for you," Max said.

The ball started high and inside, another duff toss, and I instinctively reached to the left, extending my glove out past my shoulder, but about three-quarters of the way through its trajectory, the pitch lurched and plummeted—my kid was defying physics, bending a straight line—and I had to backhand it near my right knee.

"Nice," I said.

"Filthy," Max said.

"Whatever you just did, do more of that."

We continued to work at it, gradually expanding his arsenal, tinkering with a knuckleball, toying with a sidewinder. Max would cycle through five, six, seven pitches—way more than was necessary or even advisable—mastering none but reveling in all the options, the embellishments he had previously been denied. He was using the cracks in the street as a rubber, and I was trying to save my knees by crouching on a Costco stepladder, wedged against the curb.

"Okay, Dad, this one's for you," Max said.

I must have been expecting another curveball. Either that or Max dug down and reached for something I had never known him to have, a heater that seemed to gain steam as it approached, because I was caught napping, defenseless. He was supposed to be fifty-four feet away, to mimic the Triple A distance at La Loma. If he threw his hardest, I would guess he topped out at seventy miles per hour, which meant I had about half a second to react. Under normal circumstances, that should have been sufficient, but this time, for whatever reason, that ball exploded, leaving me no chance. I got nailed on the inside half of my thigh. The impact knocked me off the stool and into the gutter and left me writhing, like a cockroach, on my back. My shorts had somehow come undone as I tumbled, and as I tried to lift myself up and dust myself off and hold on to my pants at the same time, I was reminded of the shot that Max had drilled into Abel's throat as a toddler and how enthralled he had seemed by the powers that baseball afforded him. He was standing over me, eyebrows at attention, mouth twisted into a corkscrew. The ball was already in his mitt. "Leakage problem?" he asked.

In the middle of June, with only the playoffs remaining, Max spent his last day at Garvey Intermediate School. His hair was longer than ever, spiraling over his ears and spilling down his collar, as woolly as the pelt of some Ice Age mammoth. The chief La Loma umpire, Cal, would tease him on the mound: "Oh, look, we got Goldilocks pitching!" Max had tried to tame it for the promotion ceremony, combing it and slicking it and tamping it down with a beanie, but as soon he removed the cap, his hair sprang back into action, which all the girls likened to the curliest-headed of that Disney band the Jonas Brothers. His feet were ten and a half, bigger than mine already, and laced into his first pair of dress shoes. He was decked out in a white button-down Ralph Lauren shirt and a silk tie, with glints of copper and pewter, that Carmen had once helped choose for me. We had Christiám with us, and on the way to the auditorium, we picked up Raynelda, too. I was relieved to have my nephew, her nephew, there to entertain her, to chatter in Spanish about duplicitous siblings and raucous parties and journeys north. It allowed my mind to wander, to reflect on all the graduations we were in the middle of, not just Max's but mine, not just school but baseball and boyhood and the mysterious tentacles of male authority, my standing as Max's coach, Max's dad. As we waited for the procession to begin, I must have appeared unusually sullen, remote enough that Raynelda at last turned to me and snapped, "What's your problem?"

With the end of eighth grade, Southern California high schools were free to begin recruiting for their summer leagues, and I was flabbergasted to learn that Max was intending to try out for the basketball team at Mark Keppel. We were still eking out this last year at La Loma—all sports continued to pale against the supremacy of skating—and I had not even dared to entertain the hope that Max might go on to play anything as a freshman. He was about to post Team Gonzo's first video on YouTube, one minute and eighteen seconds of spills and chills, all set to Mötley Crüe's "Too Young to Fall in Love." It was hard to imagine the same kid buying into the hallowedness of the California Interscholastic Federation, the demands and threats and rebukes of a professional coach, but maybe that was part of the allure. He would be reporting to someone who was not me. Tryouts were the very next week, in the middle of La Loma's playoff schedule, and these were real tryouts, not the Monterey Park Sports Club version. For the first time in his life, Max had to earn his spot, to battle roughly forty kids for one of the fifteen openings on the freshman roster.

The head of Keppel's basketball program was a biology teacher named Hung Duong, a child of the Vietnamese boat exodus, who would probably not take exception if I described him as one intense motherfucker. Because he coached at a high school that was more than 70 percent Asian, Duong rarely had much height to work with—the varsity squad usually topped out at five foot ten or five foot eleven—and to compensate, he had become a zealot about fitness and loyalty. Keppel's only hope was to press, trap, fast-break, hustle, dive, scrape, scrap, and never, ever, let up. Duong himself was just five foot eight, but seventeen years earlier, as a senior at neighboring Alhambra High, he had led the entire San Gabriel Valley in scoring: smallest guy on the court, twenty-six points a game. Pacing the sidelines in his flip-flops, twirling his whistle like a circular saw, he screamed and cursed and challenged his players to be tougher, quicker, *manlier* than their opponents. Water was for pussies. Stretching was for pussies. Fouls were for pussies. Nobody was sacred, no position safe. "Just because you make the team doesn't mean you're going to stay on the team," he warned at tryouts. "Every day is an audition."

Under his command, Keppel had blossomed into a legit basketball school—three league titles in the previous five seasons, including a trip to the regional quarterfinals that earned him a coach of the year award. It was not my style. Frankly, it was everything I had tried to guard against as a coach, the imperiousness, the head games, the whole objectification of kids as fresh meat, would-be soldiers. But Max did not flinch. He ran and ran, back and forth, 50, 100, 150 court lengths, and dropped for push-ups, 50, 100, 150 reps, and wrestled for loose balls until his neck was scratched raw and his nose streamed blood. He made the team—the only non-Asian on the freshman roster—and I was left to sort through my pride and dismay, to wonder what part of me, of our years playing ball, had prepared him for this test.

We still had baseball to wrap up and a valid shot, I thought, at winning one last championship. Our nemeses, Omar and Lulu, had both moved on, and Jonathan, who was ranked fourteenth among all of California's incoming freshmen, according to the Perfect Game amateur scouting service, was back on the mound. The only hurdle for us was a PONY League team from across the freeway, in Montebello, that I had allowed to merge with the Monterey Park Sports Club my last year as commissioner. They were a slick group of kids, more disciplined than any of our previous rivals, and even though they were ideal guests, respectful of La Loma's charms and traditions, I could not shake the feeling that my hospitality was about to do us in. Max was practicing at the Keppel gym six days a week, furious two-hour sessions that left every square inch of fabric on him drenched. By the time they finished, it was almost 4 P.M., and I had to get Max showered, fed, and dressed for baseball by 7 P.M. for the start of the championship series. I wanted him to pitch on the first night, to put his new bag of tricks to use, but I could see that he was spent already, and I did not intend to push him. What had worked in 2005 was not going to fly in 2007: He was no longer that boy.

I had been banking on Max in part because Jonathan, who normally would have started for us, was not ready to go, either. He had pitched the maximum number of innings in the semifinals, which had ended only forty-eight hours earlier, and I owed his arm another day of rest. Our big moment, my final series, the conclusion to La Loma, and the team that was commemorating it with me, my son's team, was running on fumes. I tried to camouflage our deficiencies, even sent Natalie out to give us a boost, but we were never ourselves. Max did nothing, popping up twice. The score was a miserable eleven to three. Our only hope was the second game—our last game if we failed to win—the following night. We needed it to force that third game, the tiebreaker, to keep this farewell alive. I prepared as I always had, reviewing the score book that Colin's dad maintained for us, crunching numbers, assembling a cheat sheet of which batters to challenge and which to avoid. None of that would make any difference if Max continued to flounder, to be worn down and wound up and checked out all at once.

He had basketball practice that morning, a little earlier than usual. I was relieved—more time for him to recover. That was, indeed, the plan, except I was not the intended beneficiary. The freshman boys had been entered in their first basketball tournament of the summer, an annual showcase known as Best in the West, which opened that same night and ran through the weekend. Max handed me the schedule with a gruff wave. "You do know I have to be there, don't you?" he said.

"I don't see how you can," I said. "We got a championship on the line."

"Dude. If I don't show up, I'm off the team."

"Don't be silly."

"They'll say I'm not committed."

"I can't believe this is even open for debate. Our entire season is at stake. Maybe your last game at La Loma, ever. Nine years of history, and it's all coming down to tonight. Anybody would understand that."

"You don't know how it is."

"Well, I'm telling you how it is. If those coaches really care about commitment, if they want you committed to basketball, then they should understand what it means for you to honor your commitment to your baseball team. Commitment is commitment."

"This is high school, Dad. They don't care about no rec league."

Okay, so maybe I was not entirely done pressuring Max into fulfilling my expectations. There was no way I could allow him to miss our finale at La Loma. Best in the West might technically be more important—NBA stars, guys like Paul Pierce and Tayshaun Prince, had played in it as kids—but the results would soon be forgotten, lost to the tide of more tournaments, more seasons. These last moments in the park would stay with us forever. "There's nothing to discuss," I told Max. He glared at me. "I'm not going to apologize for this," I added. "La Loma comes first."

If not for Jonathan, we might have been blown out again, but that second night he turned in a typical performance: fourteen strikeouts and a monster home run. I almost felt like we did not deserve him. He kept us in the game, but as had become our habit, we frittered away his gifts, entering our final at-bat in a heartbreakingly familiar place, down three to one.

"Listen, guys," I said, calling a huddle. "We're the home team. We get the last say. We've kept it close. Now your fate is in your own hands. That's exactly how we want it." How many times had I made that speech? How much longer was I going to insist that I still bought it?

Two quick outs later, Max was up. I put my hands on my cheeks and silently groaned, feeling the silvery stubble as I slid my fingers toward my mouth. Max had not gotten a hit the entire series. For all intents, he was playing this game under protest. *Oh, please, don't make the final out. Don't give up. Don't sabotage it. Whatever happens here tonight, my son, don't be the one who ends it.* Max dug his back foot in, measured the plate with the tip of his bat. He stroked the air a few times, flapped his right elbow, cocked his left knee. *Bam!* A single up the middle. I took off my cap and fanned my face like a church lady. Maybe the boy still cared, after all. Jonathan was next. He had delivered our lone run. This time, he got the Donnie Magallon treatment, an intentional walk. So be it—the tying runs were on base—and as if to reward my faith, the next two batters knocked them in. My dugout erupted, big kids bouncing up and down like little kids, their howls of jubilation mixed with fatigue and disbelief. We stranded the winning run, but it was still three to three. "No way!" I cried. We were headed, incredibly, to extra innings.

Jonathan had pitched seven, the Triple A limit, and just like the Double A finals, I was going to have to make a switch. I had managed to pick up Justin Lee again, the hero of that endless game, and I thought of sending him out under what were nearly identical conditions. Instead I turned to Max. Two years earlier I had not dared to risk it. One night earlier I had not dared to push him. But now I was calling on him, putting him on the spot. There was nothing left to save him for or from: If this was our last inning of baseball, I wanted my son on the mound. "Are you sure?" Max asked. He was creaky, from basketball, from catching, probably from some skateboard mishap I had not been apprised of. "Yes," I said. "I'm sure." It was getting late, close to ten already, but he headed for the rubber and took his warm-ups, working out the kinks, casting off the nerves. A puff of the pipe four months earlier, and it had led to this, the ball in his hand, the game on the line, another fantastical, overwrought night at La Loma at the end of a very long road of them.

Max fanned the first batter on three straight pitches. *That's right, kiddo. Just like the cul-de-sac. I know it, I've seen it. You've been showing it to me your whole life.* But then there was trouble, an error, a fielder's choice, a double, and even though Max had looked reasonably sharp, we had, in a heartbeat, squandered our comeback. It had slipped through his fingers, on his watch. I had no regrets, but I knew—he knew I knew—La Loma was not where he thought he should be.

Again we were down by two runs, in need of one more implausible finish. One more huddle, one more appeal to perseverance and spunk. Did I dare let myself believe we could really pull this off? Somehow we loaded the bases. Bottom of the eighth, nobody out. I was clutching my chest like Redd Foxx, wondering if this nonsense was at last going to kill me or if it was even better than I could have wished for. If we could just get to Max, to give him another crack, to give *me* one last chance, I knew for sure, as surely as I had ever known anything, that he would drive in the winning runs. Natalie was up. She struck out. Alex was up. He struck out. Justin was up. He worked it to a full count, but then he, too, struck out. End of game, end of series, end of season, end of park—and on deck, the next hitter, left waiting, was Max.

I was in a stupor. Disappointed, I guess. But mostly beat and confused and a little sick. My feelings did not have much to do with the score. I thanked everybody for once again entrusting their kids to me. The center fielder from the winning team came over and shook my hand and told me that he had been rooting for us, to force that third game, anything to keep on playing. The lights went out, and we were still standing around, marveling, saying our goodbyes, holding on. Colin's dad handed me the score book. He kept rubbing his forehead, swallowing hard. "It's like we didn't know what to do with ourselves," he said the next time I saw him. "Nobody wanted it to end."

Best in the West was in full swing already. In Max's absence, Keppel had lost its first game, but there were still a few more to be played. I sat in the bleachers, like any other parent. Max sat on the bench. He was not scolded. He did not get cut. But his status on the team had sunk, nosedived to where he was the last kid to see any action. He stayed that way all summer, playing so infrequently that he began to lose heart, wondering if it was even worth the trouble to suit up. It would be easy to suggest that his skills were lacking, that he had failed to impress in some more substantive way. But we knew. Everybody knew. It was whispered, understood. Max had chosen unwisely—the wrong sport, the wrong coach. That was unfair. It was not like I had allowed him to choose.

Chapter

Sixteen

WITH AUTUMN CAME THE WINDS, AS DREAD AND PRICKLY AS advertised, the siren of fire season, a bad one. They roared across the desert and barreled down the canyons, whipping through drought-stricken chaparral and beetle-ravaged conifers, exploiting accidents, inciting arsonists. By October the Santa Anas had swept flames across half a million acres, a state of emergency from Santa Barbara to the Mexican border. The fires never got close to Monterey Park, just the smoke and ash and malevolent itch, but they were burning the morning Carmen pulled into my driveway, in sweats and no makeup, her hair tucked under an "Evil Queen" cap from Disney's Snow White collection. I had been waiting all summer for the fall, to recover from the enforced separation that always came with vacation, to see where we might be headed after our first season apart. I was pouring her a cup before she could take a seat, black for me, hers cut with the fat-free French vanilla Coffee-mate that she kept in my fridge.

"No toast?" she asked. She liked it extra dark, with butter and orange marmalade.

"Coming right up, dear."

No matter what admonitions she had delivered about playing the rescuer, I had continued to do what I always had for her, to advise and nudge, to coach her through every dilemma and crisis. Over breakfast once I had pulled out a legal pad and drawn a triangle, each corner representing a different aspect of Carmen's well-being, and we would review it from time to time, checking off goals and adding new ones: counselor, résumé, mammogram, Spanish lessons. I had found it hard not to keep offering myself to her, my empathy and my expertise, and she, understandably, had found it hard to keep refusing. If she had once struck me as a woman without canniness or desperation, who at least, as she liked to joke, had all her "papers and shots," the closer Carmen came to independence, the more she seemed to be lost at sea, in need of a hand whether she wanted one or not.

"We have to stop," Carmen said.

"I'm sorry?" I said, baffled.

"We need to stay away from each other. I can't do this any-more."

"What are you saying? Like temporarily? Or like your feelings for me have changed?"

"Nothing's changed about how I feel. I just need to focus on my marriage. Eddie wants to work at it. He wants his wife back."

Somewhere in a psychology textbook, or maybe a daytime soap, this scene could have been easily predicted, long ago foretold. I was a cliché, only worse: I never saw it coming. I had known, obviously, that I was engaged in a risky affair, but I had always thought that the danger was in getting caught, in having an aggrieved husband wish me harm, not in loving Carmen too blindly. All my experience, as a journalist, as a teacher, as a commissioner, as an ex-husband—and I was back to being a novice, no wiser, no less susceptible, than a starry-eyed teenager.

"But . . . but . . ." My chest was tightening, my nose was dripping. I raised my shoulders, to get air, and instead a horrible sound came out of my throat. Whatever mystique Carmen had once been drawn to, whatever she had found admirable or assuring, there were no more illusions. My heart was breaking in front of her, and it was falling apart in the most regular, unbecoming sort of way. "But . . . but . . . I love you."

"Stop," Carmen said. "You don't know how hard this is for me."

"I just . . . I can't . . ."

I was leaning against the sink, trying to steady myself. Carmen got up from the table and walked over and, without saying a word, put me in her arms. I wanted to fight it, to start being smarter and more scrupulous right away, but I was crying too hard already, and I surrendered to her mothering, sobbing against her neck until her sweatshirt was stained with tears. "No matter what happens," she whispered, "I'll always love you."

"Oh, God," I moaned. "How did I get myself into this mess?"

It was not hard to see that Carmen had done me a favor, that she was trying to save us both before it was too late. Three of the most intoxicating years, three seasons of love and Little League—and I was being offered a dignified exit, the opportunity to walk away, to count my blessings, to get out alive. If I cared about what was best for her, it was time to let go, to let Carmen figure out some things that only she could solve for herself.

It was probably a good time for me to start trying to figure out a few things of my own, to come to terms, finally, with this rescuing gene that keeps steering me onto precarious ground. I was the son of an extraordinarily proficient and assertive woman—Mom always seemed to have one of those pins or stickers that insisted, "A woman's place is in the house . . . *and* the senate!"—and yet I was forever seeking out damsels in distress, women who were in some ways earlier versions of my mom, the foreign girl who was rescued

by America. The problem with that brand of romantic adventure
was not in getting dragged down by the damsel. If nothing else,
I had demonstrated that little could deter me, that whatever the
challenge or encumbrance I would somehow muster the reserves to
hold on. The flaw was something else, an imbalance of power that
sooner or later left the rescuee feeling inadequate, trapped anew by
her rescuer, no matter how well intended his efforts. It was the reason Raynelda had grown resentful of *el perfecto,* why Carmen was
freer to love me before she started worrying about how she was going
to escape her marriage. I knew all this, or at least I knew I was supposed to be arriving at these conclusions, but I was too far gone, too
stubborn, too exposed, to pay it any heed. Rather than take a step
back, I did precisely the opposite—upped the stakes, put even
more of myself on the line. It took me a month or two to find the
words.

"This may not be what you want to hear right now," I said one
morning to Carmen. We were still so habituated to one another, our
lives so enmeshed and our routines so ingrained, that we had continued to do everything as we had before—the coffee, the texting, the
mutual soothing—only now without removing our clothes. "But I
have to say it, to satisfy myself, to make sure you know what kind of
man I am."

"You don't need to convince me," Carmen said. "I know already."

"Well, I don't want to live with the regret of having not said it
and then later wished I had," I said. My words were getting un-
comfortably close to Hallmark territory, but that was the state I
was in.

"Just say what you gotta say."

"Okay, the bottom line, Carmen, is that I'm proposing to you.
I'll say it better to you later, I promise. I'll do it the right way when
it's a more appropriate time. But as you make your decisions about
what you're going to do, I just need you to know that you can count
on me for everything, not just the frills and pleasures, but real security, a future together. I want to look into your eyes for the rest
of my life."

"You're talking like a desperate man."

"It's hard not to feel like a desperate man these days."

"I told you already," Carmen said, "this isn't about you."

Something was seriously wrong with me: to ask a married woman to marry me, to do it knowing I was technically still married myself, to even think such a sorry proposal might somehow be the lifeline that would embolden Carmen to leave her husband. It was at once too much and too little, both drastic and unconvincing. There was something perverse, too, about contemplating marriage under incautious circumstances for a second time in my life, eighteen years after I rushed to the courthouse with Raynelda. (Well, a fourth time, actually, if you counted the hopes of my other green-card suitors, Lee and Yannarys.) This time the haste was all my own, but I was still going about it backward, treating marriage once again as a last resort, an emotional Hail Mary. I cringe to think that I had become one of those goobers who pop the question without knowing what the answer will be, but in fact I had to have known that Carmen was going to shoot me down. Is that why I proposed— because there was no chance she would say yes? That was what Carmen believed. All I can say is that I asked, and had she accepted, I would not have wriggled out.

The fall was a milestone for Max, the true start of high school. Because of basketball, it should have been an uncomplicated transition—he had spent much of the summer in a Keppel uniform—but in the last week of July, with just two days to go before vacation, Max had quit. Maybe that suggests too much deliberation. He had simply failed to appear, forfeited his position. If I had been available, I would have given him a ride to the gym, as I had been doing all along, but I was tied up at the magazine and I told Max he would need to arrange his own transportation. We lived only a couple of miles from Keppel—he could have walked, even skateboarded—but Max used my absence to kiss off the season. I was furious, especially since he had made such a fuss about this rigorous new commitment, so much graver than our flights of fancy at La Loma. He had believed that, tried to live up to what the program expected of him, but he had grown weary of busting his hump at practice, only to be reduced to a spectator at the games. As soon as I got home, we had it out. "Look, Max," I said. "You don't have to play basketball. It's your choice. I'm not making you do it. But you can't just quit like that."

"Well, I did," he said.

"You were so close. All you had to do was finish up the summer, wait till school starts in the fall, then make a decision. Now it's been decided for you. You've confirmed to these coaches exactly what they were testing to see about you—that you're a quitter."

"Maybe if you hadn't made me miss Best in the West, I'd be the starting point guard by now."

"Don't give me that shit," I snapped. I was madder about this, I think, than about the pot, than about anything Max had ever done. "You better take a hard look at yourself. This is not how we handle our business."

With classes under way, Max learned the cost of his desertion. When the bell rang for sixth period, the final fifty-six minutes of the day, all his former teammates gathered for basketball workouts. The season did not officially begin for several months, but they were allowed to use school time for learning plays and lifting weights and building camaraderie. Max was stuck with fourth-period PE, which meant PE for nonathletes, the geeks and slackers who had neither the capacity nor the inclination to qualify for a sport. He was dejected and bored, a seasoned competitor relegated to the social wilderness of plebeian gym class, and he was recognizing that if he could just finagle his way back on a team, any team, he would get to train during sixth period like the rest of Keppel's jocks. I could see the gears turning, my son plotting his escape.

"You know, I've been thinking, Dad," he said one day after school. "I might go out for baseball."

You had to hand it to the boy: He had a flair for winning me over. "That's quite a change of heart," I said.

"That's just how I roll. Keepin' it real. Old school status."

"I see. You realize, this is still a big commitment. If you start this, you cannot quit, under any circumstances."

"Fo' shizzle."

"I'll take that as an affirmative."

"What do you say we bust out the gloves, loosen up the ol' arm?"

"Oh, Max, I don't have time."

"C'mon, Pops. I know you wanna."

It was toward the end of September, at back-to-school night, that I bumped into Colin's dad, Bill Yee. We reminisced about that momentous last game, how close we had come to extending the series, what a difference there was between the Monterey Park Sports Club and my brief encounter with Keppel basketball. "It's a whole other world," said Bill, who, in addition to his teaching duties, was the freshman basketball coach at Alhambra High, Hung Duong's alma mater. Few families in the Monterey Park Sports Club were as mannered and thoughtful as the Yees; I could not imagine that Bill was anything but that on the court. "So tell me," I asked, "is it a requirement that all high school coaches be certifiably insane? Or from time to time, does an exception get made?" Bill looked down at his shoes. He was not one to speak ill of anybody. Colin had wanted to play basketball at Keppel—he tried out in the summer, with Max—but had failed to make Duong's cut. That must have been especially tough on Bill, to be a high school coach and not have his own son qualify for the sport, but Colin was undeterred. He was planning to go out for baseball in the spring. "Hey, believe it or not, so is Max," I said. "What's the coach like? As crazy as Duong?"

"From what I understand," Bill said, "there are no coaches right now."

"How can there not be a coach?"

"No *coaches*. Not at any level, varsity, JV, frosh. Keppel's not exactly a baseball school."

"Really? That's disconcerting. They'll have somebody by the

time the season starts, though, won't they? I'd hate for Max to lose out."

Bill cleared his throat and raised his eyebrows. I frowned and squinted.

"Oh, no," I said. "No, no, no, no, no."

"It would be pretty special," Bill said. "Colin would be thrilled to play for you again."

"That's nuts. I'm not a high school coach."

"In these situations, it's usually a kid they end up hiring, a recent alum, just to have a warm body out there. If nothing else, you're an adult. That alone would be a big improvement."

"I . . . uh . . . jeez . . . can't believe we're even having this conversation."

A part of me knew that, as with romance, the time had come to let go of coaching, of Max's sporting life. I should have been heartened that baseball still meant something to him, that he still believed in the splendor and subtlety of the game, without having to feel like I needed to continue orchestrating that experience. I had shepherded him from kindergarten, through elementary school, to the end of middle school—nine of his fourteen years spent as the coach's son—and now that he was in high school, the arena in which winning and losing were finally said to count, I had to think that we would both be better off if I was not responsible for the outcome. So what if basketball, his first taste of prep sports, had ended disastrously? I had still managed to back off, to let Max navigate it on his own. Why did baseball have to be so different?

I mentioned the situation to my boys at Heman G. Stark one afternoon. They always asked about Max, about his athleticism in particular, which from their vantage seemed to be his most accessible feature. I would regale them with the latest highlights, and they would tell me to wish him luck, his very own prison fan club. I was sometimes hesitant to say too much else about our bond—I hated to think I might be making them feel lousy about their own dads—but that was my hang-up, not theirs. Most of the guys had a pretty realistic understanding of what gets bequeathed, intentionally or not, from fathers to sons. The smartest of them, a fidgety dude we called Chucky, suggested that I read the chapter on children in *The Prophet*, Kahlil Gibran's pseudo-mystical book of paradoxes. Chucky had a Hispanic last name to go with "White Pride" tattooed across his knuckles, so it was easy to be skeptical of him, but when I picked up *The Prophet,* a title I had not looked at since I was Max's age, I had to marvel at his perceptiveness.

"Your children are not your children," Gibran's narrator, the oblique Almustafa, proclaims right off the bat. Instead, our sons and daughters are "living arrows," with their own speed and angle, their own infinite flight, while us parents are merely the bows that launch them. "You may strive to be like them," Almustafa advises, "but seek not to make them like you."

It was a philosophy that appealed to me, one that sounded a lot like my own, except that I had been juicing that arrow with just a little more marksmanship than was necessary. As much freedom as I allowed Max, as much as I sought to grant him the same latitude my parents had extended me, I had still treated his coaching as my exclusive domain, and I was finding it harder to relinquish than I would have ever thought. I was out of my depth at Keppel—these were real jobs, paid, requiring district approval—but would one more season be so wrong? There was a need, my son's, the school's, a breakdown that I had the capacity to fix. On my deathbed was I really going to look back at Max's freshman year and wish that I had spent less time with him on a baseball field? Without even asking Max for his thoughts, I sent an e-mail to Keppel's athletic director: "I had assumed I was done with sports, but given your circumstances, I do think I could possibly be helpful—maybe not as the long-term solution you would no doubt prefer, but perhaps, for the present, to keep the ship from sinking." Funny how it was all about them needing me, not me holding on to my son.

The athletic director wrote back to say that, in fact, he had just hired a varsity coach—it turned out to be a name from La Loma, Ricardo Cabezas—but there were still openings on the JV and freshman teams, and as long as Coach Heads had no objections, I could be considered for either one. There was no great love between us: Rick was a grouser, forever disenchanted with the output of his players, and I suspect he viewed me, his commissioner and occasional rival, as some kind of simpering egghead, but he needed help and he knew, if nothing else, I would not be a flake.

The obvious choice was to apply for the freshman job—to be paired with my son—but given his experience and the school's reputation, I was willing to bet that Max would be at the top of his class. What if the JV coach, whoever that might turn out to be, decided to promote Max, to put him in with the sophomores and juniors? That would defeat my whole purpose. Better, I thought, for me to be the JV coach, to do the promoting myself. It was rather presumptuous, I had to admit, to be months away from tryouts and practices and to be already predicting Max's ascension. The advantage, though, was that if I was wrong, if he proved not to be the standout that I imagined, I could still move him up. I might be working for Mark Keppel High School, but I was not going to stop being a dad.

The district required no particular evidence of my expertise, just the standard clearances that at La Loma we had never gotten around to enforcing: fingerprint scan, tuberculosis test, CPR certification. The job came with a stipend of about two grand, which I initially planned to donate back to the school, but then I thought about all the years I had done this for free—gladly, to be sure—and started to relish the idea of earning a paycheck: My love of baseball had, astonishingly, endowed me with a marketable skill. When I mentioned it to Max, informed him that starting in 2008, I would be showing up at school every day, that I would be coaching a twenty-game schedule that would keep us together until May, he seemed neither enthused nor imposed upon. It was familiar behavior on the part of his dad.

As it turned out, Max did not need me, or baseball, to remedy his PE dilemma. His basketball friends had begun urging him to stage a comeback, to join them in sixth period, and Max resolved to give it one more try. "You realize, you can't just show up," I told him. "You're going to have to apologize first, ask for the opportunity to earn back your spot." To Max's credit, he did that, looked Coach Duong in the eye and said he was sorry for letting him down. "These kids are young, they make mistakes," Duong told me in the gym parking lot after I thanked him for giving Max another shot. "But if it ever happens again, that'll be it. This is his last chance."

"I'm sure he understands that," I said. What I did not say was that Max had been given a bad rap, that while I was as disappointed as anyone in him quitting, we all damn well knew why he had quit.

"I hear you'll be joining us for baseball," Duong said.

"You know, just seeing what I can do to help out," I said.

Duong grinned at me, the grin of a fanatic, a basketball legend who turned little bitches into men. It was hard to say who was more discomfited, him or me, to have the other as a colleague. "Well," he said, "good luck, then."

The Keppel gym was a throwback, a stifling, rustic Works Progress Administration vault, caked in grime and stained by leaks. As in most high schools, its rafters served as the shrine for decades of heroics, the place where every athletic program on campus hung its championship banners. All that fall and winter, whenever I picked up Max from basketball, I always took a moment to review the history, to make note of which sports were on the rise and which were in decline. Keppel had posted five league titles in baseball, but they were all from the 1950s and 1970s, when it was still a predominantly white school; former San Francisco Giants pitcher Mike McCormick, winner of the 1967 Cy Young Award, was Keppel's ace in three of those seasons. As the school first adapted to Latino immigration, then to the influx of Asians, baseball died out at Keppel. It had been thirty-one years since the last league title— and that in a league with only five other schools. It had been years since Keppel's varsity squad had even won a league game, an almost unthinkable schneid. How could the school not get lucky at least once, or at least not draw an opponent that was a hair unluckier?

The explanation was not that Asian kids somehow lacked the

ability to play baseball. The few who did play were among the program's best athletes. It was that most Asian kids, for whatever social or cultural reason, stayed away from baseball at Keppel, just as they had at La Loma. Basketball at Keppel, by contrast, was a virtually all-Asian activity, fed by CYC, the year-round Japanese-American clubs that Max had missed out on. There was no Asian equivalent in baseball, which in the San Gabriel Valley was ruled by Latinos. Keppel's baseball roster was mostly Latino, too, but there were so few Latinos at Keppel to begin with, it meant the program was drawing from a much smaller pool of prospects. If there was any question about the confluence of demographics and sports, I was staggered to discover that Keppel's greatest success ever had come in, of all things, badminton: beginning in the 1990s, eight state championships.

Baseball started in February, on a spectacular Southern California morning. The temperature was in the eighties, and the San Gabriel Mountains were capped in snow, and even though the grass was splotchy and the fences were frayed and the roar of the freeway running past the outfield nearly drowned out our words, it was glorious weather for shaking off the rust and daring to dream that, just maybe, Keppel might be poised for a turnaround. I arrived with a notebook, prepared to help assess talent and draw up rosters, whittling the program to about forty-five players—roughly fifteen on each squad. That would have been the process in any other sport, except that only twenty kids showed up on that first day of the season, and it was fast becoming apparent why nobody else had wanted these jobs.

During warm-ups, before we had launched into a single drill, one boy got dizzy and had to sit himself, head down, on the bench. Another puked up his breakfast somewhere between second base and the pitcher's mound. Several were complete novices, teenagers with not one game of organized baseball under their belts. A few, with skills, belonged to a vaguely metrosexual party crew known as Pretty Squad Productions, whose members shaved their legs and worried that Keppel's maroon caps would clash with their everyday wardrobes. A couple of the top prospects were on the school's ineligible list, meaning their GPAs had dipped below 2.0 for two consecutive grading periods, and I had to send them home. A couple more were on academic probation and would be lost to us as soon as midterm report cards were issued. A solidly built junior, a lock to make the varsity roster, was about to attract the nose of the campus narc dog and earn himself an expulsion. One boy would end up breaking his wrist, another would shred the ligaments in his knee, and a third would chip his front tooth while learning to bunt. As delicate as he was, Colin still looked better than half the kids trying out, and Max, even more than I had predicted, moved like an old pro. "Dude," he told me as we headed home together after our first day. "It feels like we have a Monterey Park Sports Club team."

Max had started going in for buzz cuts, clean and tight, asking the barbers at Eli's Trim N Style to etch his hairline with a razor— a lineup, it was called. He was looking shipshape, almost severe, and with his braces off and a date with the DMV on the horizon, little seemed to be left of the shaggy renegade of eighth grade. Max had even lost interest in skating, not so much because it failed to satisfy him but because it required so much effort to carve out time and find companions with the same leeway. Organized sports, Max was learning, had the advantage of being *organized;* it was part of school, built into his daily routine, and because it was sanctioned by adults, it was always important. He had heard that you could even get into college that way, for playing a game.

"Will they really give you everything for free?" Max asked.

"Well, yeah," I said. "But it's a long shot."

"I don't care," Max said. "I'm going to get scouted."

"You know," I said, "they do give scholarships for academics, based on your intellectual talents."

"Maybe if I learn to switch-hit," Max said, swinging his right arm as a lefty would, "that'll give me a better chance."

That February turned out to be not just the start of baseball but a month of change, a season of renewal, all around us. I got word from my mom that she had cleared another CT scan, a result that had been repeated so often—forty-four months without cancer—that she was no longer being treated as a patient but a survivor. "It's time," her oncologist told her, "for you to live your life as if you were cured." There had been so little data to suggest that a recovery was possible, there was now even talk of writing her up in the medical literature. Mom had become a test case, a pioneer in yet another realm.

The Oregonian was preparing a story and called me for comment. I was still wearing those same two Livestrong bracelets, which over the years had turned grungy and passé. It was hard to convey exactly how I felt: relieved and thankful, of course, just as Mom was, but also a little bewildered, caught by surprise, by the incongruities. People who lived through what she had, it seemed to me, were usually the sort who claimed a miracle. They were relentlessly faithful, sometimes to the point of denial, Pollyannas, dogmatists, Jesoids, certain that angels watched over the afflicted. I knew that Mom had grown more spiritual, that she had taught herself to pray, even if those prayers were not necessarily addressed to a divine Creator. I knew that she had exhibited astounding strength, that it had taken everything she had to get through the chemo, to not give up before she was granted an extension. What struck me as so remarkable, though, was that Mom had never denied or discounted her illness, never swore like John Wayne that she was going to lick the Big C. She took it on, but she always acknowledged its power. She recognized that it could kill her, that she could wage a courageous battle and still lose, and from what I saw, she had figured out how to be at peace with that.

It was almost as if by letting go, by accepting that life was finite, she was able to defy its limits. I could not think of a lesson that I had ever needed more.

With Max in high school, Raynelda had also begun to look ahead, which in her case involved a certain amount of looking back. She had been traveling to Nicaragua with greater frequency, staying for weeks, even months, at a stretch. In February she returned to L.A. after spending Christmas and New Year's there, and for the first time I grasped that she was considering a permanent move, probably after Max's graduation. She had a place of her own in Managua, a two-story spread that a Scottish *internacionalista* boyfriend had bought her in the early 1980s, before she headed north, and she was trying to fix it up, to assure herself a measure of security. She still had three sisters who had never left and her mother, Doña Thelma, who had moved back a few years earlier. "I'm tired of all the pressure and uptight people," Raynelda told me. "I'm ready to be back in my own country and just, you know, live tranquilly, without so much bullshit."

She was clearly free to do whatever she wanted—it was not as if she were seeking my blessing, anyway—but I was surprised by my reaction, by how disheartened I was to learn of her plans. Even though Raynelda was waiting until Max left for college, I hated to think that his relationship with her would become more distant, more fractured, in the years to come. As it was, she could go several weeks without seeing him, intervals that were growing longer the older he grew. There was no impediment still, but between school and sports Max was booked solid, and Raynelda had become so estranged from those aspects of his life that she often felt herself at a loss, unsure of how to gain his attention and uncertain about what to do once she had it. She would call him on his cell and grow weepy. "Yes, Mom, I miss you, too," Max would tell her. "Yes, really, I'm sure. I promise. I do." In her guilt and frustration, Raynelda often blamed me, implying that I had launched Max on a trajectory that, by design, excluded her. I was not about to apologize for the kind of dad I had been, but it was true, baseball, La Loma, my imprint as a coach, my sway as a commissioner: None of it had done her any favors.

By plotting her future in Nicaragua, she almost seemed to be giving up, on him, on me, on L.A., on the hope that had brought her here in the first place. I wondered what that spelled for Freddy. From what I could see, he had been staying out of trouble, even finding a bit of nourishment in the Chicano art underground, but he was twenty-five already and the prospects for a one-eyed high school dropout with a criminal record were less than encouraging. Whatever Raynelda's plans were, something told me they would hinge on Freddy, that mother and son would ride this out together, in the land of their birth if she could persuade him, in this unquiet haven if he refused.

All the women in my life had news to share, I guess, because Carmen, that same February, announced that she had at last reached the limits of her unhappiness and was filing for divorce. It was an audacious move—the path of least resistance, I had feared, would forever hold her in place—but Carmen was determined to fulfill the promise of what she had discovered at La Loma, to find purpose beyond the confines of suburban domesticity, and, to her own surprise, had marshaled the strength to fight her way out. I was proud of her, not that it was for me to say, and as unseemly as it may have been, elated for myself. I had continued to hold out hope for us, to think of her as the fulfillment of *my* investment in La Loma, and maybe now, the obstacles cleared, we could stop the lying, give ourselves the chance we deserved. If Carmen was making no promises, she did welcome me back as her most trusted ally—"my second brain," she would call me—and together we spent hours assembling declarations for her lawyer, preparing her, emotionally, financially, for the trials ahead. Rather than feel put upon, I was delighted to be of use, practically begging for it, to be the man I had pledged to her I would be. Even when her husband began to zero in on me, when he found the Valentine's Day card I had given her that month and paraded it around as Exhibit A, vowing to kick my ass, it was almost a relief. The drama was better than the wishing and waiting. Whatever I had done wrong, I was prepared to take the fall, to stand up for La Commish.

Those were some fairly madcap days, months actually, of chaos and theatrics. A friend of mine at the magazine, one of the few who knew the whole story, kept urging me to snap out of it. The sea was full of women, far less complicated, far more accommodating and available. I did not think Mike was the best font of advice: He was about to take an absurdly romantic plunge of his own. A product of

the Baptist heartland, a bona fide Oklahoma cracker, Michael
Mullen had undergone a bohemian epiphany after college, swapping
a life of restraint for the license of a cultural vagabond. With his bald
head and terra-cotta goatee, he had set off for South America, and
there, on the beaches of Cartagena, the same ones that had inspired me
and Raynelda an eternity ago, he had fallen for an enchantingly wry,
educated Colombian beauty named Susie. Because of borders and
politics, there could be no casual dating, no gradual escalation of
their feelings. If he wanted to be with her, at least in this country,
without employing a smuggler, it would have to be as husband and
wife. Mike applied for a visa, and after a year of long-distance pin-
ing, Susie arrived at LAX. They had ninety days to marry—and Mike
wanted me, of all people, to officiate the wedding. As a lapsed Jew,
a philanderer, the (sort of) ex-husband of an ex-illegal alien, I had no
business sanctifying much of anything. But Miguelito (he had
taught himself Spanish) was hoping for a service that was bilingual
and ecumenical, and he was counting on the writer in me to come
up with some pretty words about new beginnings.

So it was that as I helped to end one marriage, I prepared to
bless another. I applied to the Universal Life Church for a minister's
credential, and with the click of a mouse and a charge of $12.99, I
received an ID card designating me the Reverend Jesse Katz. Coming from a fiercely Catholic nation, Susie was understandably dubious, but under California statute I was now authorized to perform
a legally binding ceremony, and, indeed, it would be my signature
on their wedding license that would compel the INS, or whatever
it was called these days, to issue her a green card. Even Carmen got
excited by the romance of it all—she thought my backyard would
be perfect for the reception—and if the bride and groom wanted to
consider it, she would help me clean and decorate. Mike accepted
warily, grateful for the offer but fretful about anything that might
steal the spotlight from Susie. "Just be a good rabbi," he pleaded,
"and keep your tawdry shit under wraps until after the ceremony."

As it turned out, all that was settled rather abruptly, my years
of self-delusion, every bit of futile longing. With the wedding just

a few weeks away, we had gathered at my house for a walk-through. Mike and Susie and Carmen were there. So was another Monterey Park Sports Club friend, Aurora, the mom of the girl who had been poached upon by our grifter coach, the fake uncle, way back when. We were finishing dinner and drinking more wine, and while I cleared the dishes, I happened to overhear Carmen gossiping about the special man in her life, how he was so good and so fine, and the closer I listened, the more it became apparent that the special man was not me. Poor Aurora was the only one in the room who did not know about the extent of our relationship, so instead of shushing Carmen, she was egging her on, and it suddenly dawned on me that I had reaped the worst of both worlds: I was the culprit and I was still not getting the girl.

I never did see Carmen again. All that time we spent nursing La Loma back to health, day after day, season after season, and just when I thought, maybe, that my story really was our story, she vanished, as we both knew she had to. Not that he would ever wish for my sympathy, but I felt a lot like her husband at that point, the coach I betrayed. For longer than I cared to admit, I had been groping in the dark, reaching for shadows, willfully ignoring my own intuition, just so that I could hold on longer, to something that was never mine to possess. Carmen was out of the wedding—Mike insisted on it, lest I go chasing after her—but I was still expected to be front and center, in a brown satin *guayabera,* to swallow my disillusionment and, for the sake of the newlyweds, act like I knew something about the mysteries of the heart. Me, the love doctor. Before I could pretend to do that, I needed to fix something else.

I went to him at night. It was late, and he was under the covers. I tried to scoot him over, a fifteen-year-old kid on a twin mattress. There was not enough room for us both. "I know you have a pretty good idea of what's been going on," I told Max, "but I think I owe you a bit more of an explanation." It was harder than I thought, to try to sound reliable after all I had done, all the scandal I was subjecting him to. I had taken a beautiful thing, this game we loved, the park we cherished, our town, his home, and I had mucked it up, not because I was careless or corrupt but because I thought I had found it, what we look for, all of us, and for one fleeting moment, I had. We were silent for a while, listening to each other's breathing. "The only thing that really matters is that you know where you stand with me," I said. "My love for you is unconditional and forever. I hope I've never given you a reason to doubt that."

I stayed there, scrunched at his side, for a long time, until I felt myself drifting off.

Epilogue

I WAS GETTING TO KEPPEL EVERY DAY AT SIXTH PERIOD,
which started at one forty-one, and working out with the JV squad
until five or six. Once our games began, I would be required by
state athletic rules to wear a full uniform on the field, jersey *and*
pants, the tight polyester calf-high kind, which was sort of embar-
rassing, but in my woeful state I had started practicing yoga and
was feeling trimmer than I had in years. I was even introducing my
players to the stretches and poses I was learning, and the other
coaches on Keppel's faculty, including the fearsome Duong, would
look at us going through the *vinyasas* on the outfield grass and wonder what sort of freak was on the baseball staff these days. When I
was first hired, Max had taken some flack, mostly from the basketball folks, about his dad choosing the JV job. In basketball he was
still only on the freshman roster, and though there were grudging
signs that his talent was being recognized, he had continued to ride

the bench. Now here I was, the new guy in the athletic department, and merely by virtue of the job I had applied for, I was already plucking him out of the frosh ranks, punching his ticket for JV, without requiring him to earn a thing. He heard the snickers: Max was going to be on Daddy's team.

It was a gamble, but alas, not the gamble I thought I was taking. Max was easily good enough to make JV. I had not been wrong about that. He was so good—and Keppel's baseball program so rickety—that after we had sized up all the kids, the varsity coach claimed Max for himself. How could it be that I had never seen *that* coming? I was trying to preserve something, to maintain our proximity, and Max had leapfrogged right over me. A freshman on varsity. All those years together, all my fumbling and fealty, on the front lawn, in the driveway, atop our magical little hill, had actually sunk in. My son was a baseball player. It would not have been right of me to hold Max back, not for him or for the school. I thought getting myself hired would give me leverage, but my job, in fact, demanded that I let him go. I was still obligated to my JV boys, which was fine. They cracked me up. Just like a La Loma team, what they lacked in prowess they made up for with wit and style. The disappointing thing was our schedule. My games were on the same day as Max's games, at the same time, but on opposite fields. When I was home, Max was away, and when I was away, Max was home. My grand scheme was to keep us together, and in the end, because of my scheming, I did not even get to see him play.

I wondered if that was a glimpse of what awaited us, if I had any chance of keeping Max in my life, under my gaze, in the years ahead, or if he was destined, like me, to search for himself elsewhere, to find his own arena, a new La Loma. I missed that old park already, the slopes, the nooks, the dust, the moon, the skunks darting across the diamonds on damp summer nights, but we each, in our own way, outgrew it. Wherever his path leads, whatever patterns he repeats and whichever cautions he rejects, it was time for me to step aside, to let the choice be his, to be there for him, always, in the stands.

ACKNOWLEDGMENTS

Although books of this nature are said to be acts of memory, not history, subject to the fuzziness of the author, this story is nonetheless a work of nonfiction. Everything is true, maybe to a fault. Not a single name has been changed or a character stitched together or a scene ginned up. Put another way: No performances have been enhanced. Because of that, my first debt is to the people who inhabit these pages, real people who are my friends and neighbors and, in some cases, antagonists. Most of them are members of the Monterey Park Sports Club, an organization that continues to be essential to the community I call home, and I extend to them and their families my deepest appreciation. My story would not exist without theirs.

My thanks to Joe McGinniss, the author and teacher who gave me permission, a lifetime ago, to call myself a journalist, and to the many editors along the way who have kept me from losing sight of what that can mean, including Don Hunt, Steve Chawkins, Mary Heffron Arno, Pete King, Joel Sappell, Leo Wolinsky, Mike Miller, Scott Kraft, Roger Smith, Mary Ann Meek, Karen Wada, and my original *Los Angeles Times* mentor, the writer who is still my compass and inspiration, Mark Arax. For almost nine years, I was fortunate enough to work at a remarkable magazine, *Los Angeles,* and for a remarkable boss, Kit Rachlis, who knows things that nobody else knows about the mystery of writing, about the music and meaning of words, about the architecture of stories, and about the fragile psychology of the people who put them together. Not only was this book assembled on his watch, and with his help, but he—and the magazine's parent company, Emmis Communications—provided me with a job that allowed me to *live* what is written here; for that I will always be grateful.

I owe much to Bonnie Nadell, the first agent to see the shape of a book in my Little League commissionership, and to Jay Mandel, of William Morris Endeavor Entertainment, whose sure hand shepherded me through the process of finding it. My sense of possibility was stoked by three smart and funny TV minds, Maher Jafari, Michael Edelstein, and Warren Bell, and by the two William Morris agents, Alicia Gordon and Lauren Heller Whitney, who led me to them. With an editor like Rick Horgan, at Crown, I can do away with therapists and shamans. In ways that were occasionally painful but always enlightening, he taught me to pry deeper into myself and to also stand back, to be in the moment and, at the same time, outside of it. His keen eye was complemented by that of his colleagues Nathan Roberson and Julian Pavia, whose insights proved equally trenchant. I consider myself lucky to have been under their care.

In the course of my research, I was the beneficiary of many generous and patient guides, among them Daniel Sabadin, Jack Jacobs, Francisco J. de Lys, Catherine Aubert, Michel Berta, and the dear, late Dina Vierny. I would be remiss if I did not also acknowledge a few of the texts that have informed my thinking, starting with Timothy P. Fong's *The First Suburban Chinatown: The Remaking of Monterey Park, California,* and including André Liebich's *From the Other Shore: Russian Social Democracy after 1921,* Bertrand Lorquin's *Maillol,* Joan Kruckewitt's *The Death of Ben Linder: The Story of a North American in Sandinista Nicaragua,* and "Once More, Lazarus" by Héctor Tobar, which appears in *Los Angeles Noir,* edited by my friend Denise Hamilton. I am especially thankful for Gloria Russakov's and David Kelly's 1977 profile of my mother, "The Ways and Means of Citizen Katz," in the bygone *Oregon Times* magazine, and for Erin Hoover Barnett's thoughtful coverage of Mom in *The Oregonian.*

I enlisted several people to read my early drafts, to save me from myself, and Michael Mullen and Cara Van Le were the first. To employ another baseball metaphor, they took one for the team. An eternity later, Mike stepped up to the plate and did it again. During my recurring bouts of doubt and despond, I was goaded on (and intermittently cautioned) by friends old and new: Lianne Hart, Fred Carlo, Aurora Ontiveros, Frank Magaña, Jennifer Nhan and family, Eric Nazarian, Dick Shoemaker, Michael Montgomery, David Bangsberg, Steve Oney, Rick Meyer, Barry Siegel, Robert Lopez, Paul Dounian, Jeff Baskin, Fergus Reid, Evan McGlinn, Sandy Gibson, Forest Casey, CC Stark, April Yamashiro, Chris Contreras, Julia Steele, Todd Ullah, and my *camarada* Abel Salas, who has been showing me how to cross borders from the day we met. Just when I fooled myself into thinking I had reached the end, I was rescued yet again, first by a very pregnant Jiyeon Yoo, the nitpicker extraordinaire I needed her to be, and then by Matt Segal, the most careful reader I know.

I would be nowhere without the love of my parents, who have managed the rare feat of supporting my every decision without dictating a single one. They are living practitioners of Almustafa's wisdom. In whatever I have done, their gift is present. I reserve a special affection for *la familia* Gutiérrez, all of them: *Gracias por haberme aceptado como su propia sangre.* Without Raynelda, there would be no Max, and without Max there would be nothing. He is the best idea I ever had.

1. In the prologue, Jesse Katz describes La Loma as being "on the wrong side" of Los Angeles, "beyond the margins of the tourist maps" [p. 2]. Later he calls Los Angeles "the capital of artifice and celebrity and unsteady earth" [p. 10]. To what degree is Katz trafficking in stereotypes about L.A., and to what degree is he puncturing them? How does his depiction of the city's social geography jibe with your own perceptions, whether from firsthand experience or through the lens of film and TV?

2. As a newcomer to Los Angeles in the 1980s, Katz goes looking for love in a seedy, working-class cantina: "Whatever I was up to, it was complicated—risky, humbling, generous, conniving— a paradoxical, politically incorrect hunt for affection" [p. 23]. What draws him to the immigrant experience, especially to the Nicaraguan barmaid he later marries? In what ways is she his entry into "the real L.A." [p. 26]?

3. In his early years at the *Los Angeles Times,* Katz finds himself assigned to the gang beat: "As with so many of my leaps, the whole idea was almost comical, folly bordering on arrogance" [p. 43]. How does Katz compensate for the ways in which he is ill-suited for the streets? In what ways would these experiences relate to his future adventures at La Loma?

4. After the birth of Max, Katz rediscovers his own childhood obsession with baseball, only to find that his nostalgia for the game is entangled with the chaos of his personal life. Instead of "warm, fuzzy memory making," baseball has become "a tool" [p. 49], one that is "too precious, too useful" [p. 50] to entrust

to someone else's dad. To what extent is Katz's decision to become a coach—and, later, commissioner—honorable? To what extent is it calculating? Is it common for well-intentioned goals to be driven by selfish motives?

5. Presiding over his first opening day, Katz is surprised to find himself celebrating "the middle-classness" of organized sports [p. 100]. Four seasons later, at his final opening day, he elaborates on that notion, marveling at how Little League no longer strikes him as square—"or perhaps it was in its very squareness that we found ourselves so free" [p. 273]. In what other ways does that tension—between structure and latitude, diligence and indulgence—shape *The Opposite Field*?

6. As he immerses himself in La Loma's customs and rules, Katz grows dismayed by the lengths to which parents try to manipulate the process. What is it about the mantra It's for the kids [p. 114] that he takes issue with? Are there times he is guilty of such scheming himself?

7. After a humiliating experience in Mexico as a college student, Katz vows to learn Spanish—a language that makes him "privy to a secret code" [p. 144] and grants him "the keys to a parallel world" [p. 145]. How does being a writer shape his feelings about the power and poetry of a new language? Why does he appear so consumed by borders and boundaries, by gaining access to cultures not his own?

8. When he learns of his mother's illness, Katz travels to Europe and retraces her escape, as a little girl, from Nazi-occupied France. The Pyrenees are a long way from La Loma. Why does Katz feel compelled to include this scene, to ruminate on "the enormity of her journey . . . the impulses she has handed down to me" [p. 159]?

9. In Chapter 9 [pp. 179–188] and Chapter 11 [pp. 223–225], Katz writes of the horrific accident that partially blinds his stepson, Freddy. To what extent does this episode validate Katz's

early frustrations as a stepfather? In what ways might Katz's reluctance to adopt Freddy have contributed to the tragedy? If he were the narrator, how might Freddy have portrayed these events differently?

10. A disagreement over the construction of canopies at La Loma—and how that work should be compensated—triggers a bitter dispute between Katz and the board member he has picked to succeed him: "He had failed a test—my test—one he probably did not even realize he had taken" [p. 210]. Is Katz being meticulous or self-righteous? How might the incident have been avoided? To what degree is race or culture at issue in the final showdown?

11. When he confesses his infatuation with Carmen, Katz pays special attention to her skin: "the darkest, smoothest, richest, most naturally iridescent brown, like a chestnut fresh out of its burr" [pp. 240–241]. Do you consider that description generous or gratuitous, an affirmation of a woman of color or the kind of detail that fetishizes her? To what extent do you find yourself frowning on their illicit relationship and to what extent do you find yourself rooting for them? Do you buy Katz's rationalization that Carmen represented "the ultimate acceptance" [p. 242]?

12. In his seventh La Loma season, Max makes it to the championship series, only to wake up sick on the day he is supposed to pitch. It does not even occur to Katz to let him sit out: "Maybe I was one of those psycho dads, after all, conflating my ego and my son" [p. 267]. Was he? Did he push Max too far? Or do you agree with his assessment that father and son were of the same mind, that Max understood "the weight of the occasion"?

13. As a volunteer in California's juvenile prison system, Katz ponders the intersection of youth sports and youth crime, the connection between his experiences as a baseball commissioner and a gang reporter and a father to two vastly different boys: "It

was all part of the same reclamation project, the need to mend, to heal, to repay" [p. 280]. What do you make of that conclusion? Where do the similarities between La Loma and the Heman G. Stark Youth Correctional Facility begin and where do they end?

14. As he struggles to accept Max's foray into adolescence, Katz turns to a passage about children in Kahlil Gibran's *The Prophet:* "You may strive to be like them, but seek not to make them like you" [p. 321]. To what degree does that quote reflect your own philosophy or upbringing? How hard of a maxim is it to live by?

15. What does Katz learn about himself in the process of writing this memoir? Do you think he discovers what he expected, or might some of his insights have come as a surprise? How can Katz, as a character, be so bumbling, and at the same time, as the narrator of his story, so self-aware?

16. In the Acknowledgments, Katz emphasizes that he took no creative liberties with *The Opposite Field,* that he chose not to change even a single name: "Everything is true, maybe to a fault" [p. 335]. What are the pros and cons of writing so frankly about "real people," especially in one's own community? How might you have felt if you had found yourself depicted in the book?